T0319974

Academic Entrepreneurship in Europe

Academic Entrepreneurship in Europe

Mike Wright

Professor of Financial Studies and Director, Centre for Management Buy-out Research, Nottingham University Business School, UK, Visiting Professor, Erasmus University, The Netherlands and Editor, Journal of Management Studies

Bart Clarysse

Professor of Innovation and Entrepreneurship, Vlerick Leuven Gent Management School, Gent University, Belgium and Professor of Innovation, Institute for Enterprise and Innovation, Nottingham University Business School, UK

Philippe Mustar

Professor of Innovation, Entrepreneurship and Public Policy, Centre de Sociologie de l'Innovation, École Nationale Supérieure des Mines de Paris, France

Andy Lockett

Professor of Strategy and Entrepreneurship, Centre for Buy-out Research, Nottingham University Business School, UK

Edward Elgar

Cheltenham, UK • Northampton, MA, USA

© Mike Wright, Bart Clarysse, Philippe Mustar and Andy Lockett, 2007

All rights reserved. No part of this publication may be reproduced, stored in a retrieval system or transmitted in any form or by any means, electronic, mechanical or photocopying, recording, or otherwise without the prior permission of the publisher.

Published by
Edward Elgar Publishing Limited
Glensanda House
Montpellier Parade
Cheltenham
Glos GL50 1UA
UK

Edward Elgar Publishing, Inc.
William Pratt House
9 Dewey Court
Northampton
Massachusetts 01060
USA

A catalogue record for this book
is available from the British Library

Library of Congress Cataloguing in Publication Data

Academic entrepreneurship in Europe/Mike Wright . . . [et. al.]
      p.   cm.
   Includes bibliographical references and index.
   1. Education, Higher—Economic aspects—Europe. 2. Universities and colleges—Research—Europe. 3. Universities and colleges—Europe—Finance. 4. Academic–industrial collaboration—Europe. 5. Business and education—Europe. I. Wright, Mike, 1952–   .
   LC67.68.E85A23   2007
   338.4'73784—dc22   2006024415

ISBN 978 1 84542 648 4 (cased)

Printed and bound in Great Britain by MPG Books Ltd, Bodmin, Cornwall

Contents

Preface

The nature of universities is changing as reduced public funding reflects a public debate about their role in society. An important aspect of this international phenomenon is increased emphasis on the commercialization of university research. Of particular interest is academic entrepreneurship, which relates to the development of commercialization beyond the traditional focus upon the licensing of innovations to the creation of new ventures that involve the spinning-off of technology and knowledge generated by universities.

While there has been substantial university spin-off activity internationally in recent years, a number of major aspects are little understood. First, considerable debate surrounds the ability of spin-offs to generate the wealth benefits expected by universities. Second, much research focuses on the US context, and especially on high-technology (high-tech) clusters of academic entrepreneurship within that country. This institutional environment contrasts markedly with that prevailing elsewhere. Universities in different environments may face varying challenges in the development of successful spin-off companies involving the transfer of technology and knowledge from universities.

This book aims to go some way to filling the gap in our understanding of the process of spin-off creation and development in environments outside the high-tech clusters of the US. First, we focus on the process of spin-off creation and development in several European countries, selected to reflect the diversity of the institutional environment. Second, we adopt a multi-level approach to examine the process of spin-off creation and development. In particular, we consider units of analysis involving the university, technology transfer office, spin-off firm, individual entrepreneurs and teams, and finance providers. Third, we utilize extensive quantitative and qualitative studies to examine these different levels of the process. Fourth, we identify policy implications for the future successful development of spin-offs.

The research reported in this book was funded by a number of agencies, notably the UK ESRC (grant # RES-334-25-0009), the EU PRIME network of excellence, the EU INDICOM project and the Bank of England. We are grateful for their support.

This book reflects the efforts of a number of colleagues who have collaborated with us on the projects that form the basis for the results reported here. In particular we acknowledge the inputs of Massimo Colombo, Margarida Fontes, Mirjam Knockaert, Nathalie Moray, Simon Mosey Evila Piva, Marie Renault, Iris Vanaelst and A. Vohora. We are also grateful to the various technology transfer officers, founders, chief executive officers (CEOs) and team members of spin-offs and venture capital executives who contributed their experiences to the study. Thanks to Louise Scholes for commenting on the text. We also thank Francine O'Sullivan for her encouragement and forbearance.

Acknowledgements

The publishers wish to thank the following who have kindly given permission for the use of copyright material.

Elsevier Ltd for articles:

Clarysse, B., Wright, M., Lockett, A., van de Velde, E. and Vohora, A. (2005), 'Spinning out new ventures: a typology of incubation strategies from European research institutions', *Journal of Business Venturing*, **20** (2), 183–216.

Mustar, P., Renault, M., Colombo, M., Piva, E., Fontes, M., Lockett, A., Wright, M., Clarysse, B. and Moray, N. (2006), 'Conceptualising the heterogeneity of research-based spin-offs: a multi-dimensional taxonomy', *Research Policy*, **35** (2), 289–308.

Vohora, A., Wright, M. and Lockett, A. (2004), 'Critical junctures in the growth in university high-tech spinout companies', *Research Policy*, **33**, 147–75.

Wright, M., Clarysse, B., Lockett, A. and Binks, M. (2006), 'University spin-out companies and venture capital', *Research Policy*, **35** (4), 481–501.

Every effort has been made to trace all the copyright holders but if any have been inadvertently overlooked the publishers will be pleased to make the necessary arrangements at the first opportunity.

1. Introduction

1.1 INTRODUCTION

The nature of universities in Europe has changed dramatically since the mid-1990s. A number of events have precipitated this change. First, following the drop of federal funding for research at universities in the US, the public research funding of research at universities in Europe has also decreased (Etzkowitz, 1983). Second, a public debate has emerged about the role which universities have to play in society. Third, many countries in Europe have adopted a Bayh–Dole type of Act on university patenting activity. These environmental changes are believed to increase the pressure and incentives to commercialize university research (Bank of England, 1996; Confederation of British Industry, 1997; Siegel, et al., 2003). Traditional emphasis has been upon the licensing of innovations (for example, Thursby and Thursby, 2002) but greater attention is now being addressed internationally to the creation of new ventures that involve the spinning-off of technology and knowledge generated by universities (Table 1.1).

According to the Association of University Technology Managers (AUTM), US universities spun out 4543 start-ups between 1980 and 2003 (AUTM, 2005). In the 1980s, US universities created fewer than 100 start-ups per year. In 2004 they created 462 start-ups, taking equity in 240 of them. For many analysts, this growth is explained by the passage of the Bayh–Dole Patent and Trademark Amendments Act of 1980 which permitted performers of federally funded research to file for patents on the results of this research and to grant licences for these patents, including exclusive licences, to firms. Although there is some debate about the direct effects of the Act (Mowery, 2001), patent activity in academia has seen exceptional growth, for example from 1584 patent applications in 1991 to 10 517 in 2004. During the same period, university revenue from patents licences jumped from $200 million to $1.3 billion (AUTM, 2004). This Act made it easier for universities to license and commercialize inventions, facilitating the creation of spin-off firms interested in licensing and developing these inventions (Mowery et al., 2004). More generally, the Bayh–Dole Act legitimated the involvement of universities in technology commercialization and spin-off activities at US universities.

Table 1.1   University spin-offs internationally (selected countries)

Country	Period	Number of spin-offs
US	1980–2003	4543*
Canada	1962–2003	1100
France	1984–2005	1230
Netherlands	1980–1990s	300
Australia	1984–1999	97
UK	1981–2003	1650+
Belgium	1980–2005	320
Sweden	Up to 1990s	3000–5000++
Germany	1997–1999	470–4000 p.a.**++
	2001	900–8000

Notes:
   *   Includes 462 for 2004 relating to US and Canada.
   +   Different number of respondents in different years.
  ** Estimates vary depending on definition and methodology.
 ++ For Sweden and Germany estimates difficult due to IP ownership residing with the
academic rather than the university.

Source: Authors' review.

Within Europe, there is some debate about whether too many (Lambert, 2003) or too few (Williams, 2005) spin-offs from universities are being created. As in the US (O'Shea et al., 2005), university spin-off activity in Europe is highly skewed. UK evidence (Wright et al., 2003) shows, for example, that 57 per cent of 124 responding universities did not create any spin-offs in 2002 and only nine universities created five or more. Similarly, a pan-European survey covering 172 universities in 17 countries found that 103 provided spin-off services. Only half of the universities providing spin-off services created one or more spin-offs in 2004 (Proton, 2005).

In principle, university spin-offs benefit society and universities in a variety of ways, including their effects on local economic development, their ability to produce income for universities, their tendency to commercialize technology that otherwise would be undeveloped, and their usefulness in helping universities with their core missions of research and teaching (Shane, 2004). There is clear evidence that some university spin-offs are highly successful. For example, in the US, 18 per cent of all spin-offs from the Massachusetts Institute of Technology (MIT) in the period 1980–86 went public (Shane and Stuart, 2002) and in the UK there were 20 public listings of spin-offs in the period 2003–04 (UNICO, 2005). In Belgium, the InterUniversity Institute for MicroElectronics has realized a multiple of 36 on a trade sale of a ten-year old spin-off sold for 50 million euros, while the first spin-off from the University of Gent was sold in 1994 for slightly over 2 billion euros after an initial investment of 75 million euros over a ten-year period. Yet, many spin-offs are not successful and they do not generate substantial wealth even though they appear to have high survival rates (Nerkar and Shane, 2003). While it is relatively straightforward to create a legal entity, the act of creating a company does not necessarily mean that it will subsequently create capital gains or income. There is, therefore, a major need to understand the spin-off creation process and, in particular, how wealth can be generated in the traditionally noncommercial environment of universities.

The focus of research and policy attention has predominately been on a small number of successful US institutions such as MIT and Stanford (Colyvas et al., 2002; Shane and Stuart, 2002). These cases are atypical even in the US because of the resources they can command and because they are located in regions that are effectively quasi-incubators. Although cases such as Cambridge, Leuven, Heidelberg and Chalmers may be considered successful high-tech centres by European standards, the geographical context of MIT and Stanford is not replicated in any part of Europe. Rather, many universities and public research organizations (PROs) in Europe have traditionally operated in an environment where high-tech entrepreneurship is relatively new or undeveloped. The spin-off process in such contexts is likely to be very different from that in more developed high-tech entrepreneurial environments such as Boston or Silicon Valley (Roberts, 1991; Roberts and Malone, 1996; Saxenian, 1994a, 1994b) where the capability to select the best projects and allocate resources to them already exists. Here the spin-off process can follow a 'business pull' strategy that is not dependent on the activities of the PRO, but benefits from high levels of innovation within the surrounding region. In contrast, in environments with less demand for innovation, characterized by a weak entrepreneurial community and few other key resources, PROs may need to play a more proactive incubation role. This strategy is best described as 'technology push', where the PRO exercises selection and provides venture creation and development support throughout the stages in the spin-off process.

The purpose of this book is to examine the spin-off venture creation process in a European context. We encompass a range of institutional environments both in terms of different countries and in respect of different regions and universities within individual countries. Our analysis adopts a multi-level approach. We focus on evidence from spin-offs in Belgium, France, Germany, Sweden and the UK. These countries provide a range of institutional environments within the European context in which there is variation in the general institutional context (La Porta et al., 1998; Reynolds et al., 2003), the ownership of intellectual property (IP) in universities and the processes and policies relating to the stimulation and funding of spin-offs.

The structure of this chapter is as follows. First, we outline the definition of spin-offs used in this book. Second, we review key indicators of institutional differences between the US and European countries. As the institutional context may impact the nature of commercialization activities and processes, we are particularly interested in how the elements of countries' national innovation systems, research activity and funding, structure and management of public sector research, entrepreneurial and business environments, and availability of private equity capital may differ.

1.2 DEFINITION OF UNIVERSITY SPIN-OFFS

Our study includes a wide range of companies that originate from universities. We define university spin-offs as new ventures that are dependent upon licensing or assignment of an institution's IP for initiation. This definition is consistent with that used by the AUTM in the US. In some cases, where permitted, a university may own equity in the spin-off in exchange for patent rights it has assigned or in lieu of licence for fees. This is a narrow definition of a spin-off, but also the one which is most often used in empirical studies, although not every researcher clearly specifies that his/her study exclusively looks at these spin-offs. The reason for this is that in general these spin-offs are the easiest to keep track of for the Technology Transfer Office (TTO) since they are by definition based upon university IP.

However, if we only focus on spin-offs using the first part of the definition, we would miss a substantial part of the reality. At some universities in some institutional contexts, IP is not necessarily owned by the university. Moreover, many companies are created that *do not* build upon formal, codified knowledge embodied in patents. Therefore, we also include start-ups by faculty based in universities which do not involve formal assignment of the institution's IP but which may draw on the individual's own IP or knowledge. It is hard to assess how many of these academic start-ups exist in comparison to the number of spin-offs. The relative proportion of both categories will depend upon the research composition at the university, the institutional context, the university policy with regards to IP rights and, finally, the entrepreneurial activity of the academics themselves. Some evidence from our Belgian sample suggests that in that specific context about half of the companies created by university faculty are spin-offs; the other half are academic start-ups.

However, we exclude companies that may be established by graduates after they have left the university and companies established by outsiders that may draw on IP created by universities. The former are only loosely connected to the university and are very difficult to identify in empirical studies. Most universities do not have an idea about the companies that were created by graduates from their undergraduate or master programmes. Even if they do, it is usually not clear whether the start-up can be linked to specific knowledge created and transferred in the university setting or whether it is based on knowledge which the graduate cumulated outside the university. Although we do not include them in this book, their number should not be underestimated. Some empirical evidence collected by the University of Twente suggests that companies created by graduates might outnumber the spin-offs by 20 per cent.

1.3 INSTITUTIONAL DIFFERENCES

Institutional differences between the US and European countries may have a general contextual bearing on the extent and nature of university spin-off activity in Europe. In this section, we examine different indicators of these contextual differences. First, we explain how the European Innovation Paradox forms the basis of the recent changes in Europe's innovation policy. Second, we discuss the intensity of research and development (R&D) in each of the countries in the study and pay particular attention to the so-called 3 per cent norm in terms of gross expenditure on research and development as a percentage of gross domestic product (GDP). Third, we analyse how the university system differs in each of the countries included in the book with a particular focus on differences between Europe and the US. Fourth, we discuss briefly the legal-institutional framework within which professors operate. This framework, which encompasses the regulation of IP and the public status of professors, differentiates Europe from the US. Fifth, we outline differences in entrepreneurial and the national business environment, which are relevant to explain the academic spin-off activity. Finally, we discuss differences in the availability of equity capital.

The European Innovation Paradox

In Europe, a discussion about spin-offs cannot take place without having a look at the innovation system in which these spin-offs are created. This innovation system comprises all the actors that play a role in the development and commercialization of knowledge. The innovation system in Europe started to change after the European Commission introduced its famous concept of a 'European Innovation Paradox' (Caracostas and Muldur, 1998). In their seminal work, Caracostas and Muldur have shown that the productivity rate of academics in terms of scientific papers is higher than that of their US colleagues, when we take language-related issues into account. However, in terms of patents per capita, all European countries lag significantly behind the US. The European Union plays a leading role in top-level scientific output, but lags behind in the ability to transform this strength into wealth-generating innovations. In other words, Europe performs well in science but badly in innovation. This idea of a *technology gap* with the US is however not new in Europe. In France, it appeared for the first time in 1964 in a publication of the *Direction Générale à la Recherche Scientifique et Technique*. It shows how Europe perceives the US innovation system.

The US innovation system is expected to have a strong ability to convert its scientific research into technologies and practical applications through the creation of high-tech start-ups. The strengths of the US innovation system have been identified as: a favourable IP system, universities as a source of a large number of spin-off firms, strong links between university and industry, strong relationships between large companies and new firms, the availability of venture capital and of business angels, and last but not least, public policies to support these new spin-offs through the Small Business Administration (SBA) and the Small Business and Innovation Research (SBIR) programme. Seen through a European lens, the US has created world leaders such as Intel (created in 1968), Microsoft (1975), Cisco (1984) and Dell (1984) who appear among the 25 larger American companies, whereas SAP (created in 1987) is the only 'young' firm to appear among the top 25 European companies. If one looks at the companies created after 1980 among the 1000 larger companies in the world, 64 are American and only nine are European (Worms, 2005). Since 1980, American small and medium-sized enterprises (SMEs) generated seven times more new world-leading companies than the SMEs from the whole of the European Union (CEC, 2004).

In Europe, the national systems of innovation seem traditionally to have been much more unfriendly to new firms. The weaknesses of these systems are explained largely in terms of institutional, organizational and cultural factors. Intellectual property regulation is still quite weak and the single European Patent is blocked by ethnic minorities in the European Union. This results in high translation costs and expensive court trials. Most universities are publicly owned and thus embedded in the bureaucratic nature of any national administration. They have to overcome a number of legal barriers in order to be even allowed to spin-off companies. Collaboration between small and large firms is hindered by the absence of technology agglomerations such as Silicon Valley and Route 128 (Saxenian, 1994a, 1994b). The financial markets experienced a strong growth in the mid-1990s with different alternative markets such as the European

Association of Securities Dealers Automatic Quotation System (EASDAQ), the Alternative Investment Market (AIM), Neuer Market, le Nouveau Marché being launched in different countries, but each of these markets – except maybe AIM – suffered from illiquidity of the small cap stocks that were quoted on these markets, and the secondary markets in Germany and France as well as the Brussels-based EASDAQ simply collapsed after the dotcom bubble. On top of this, some of Europe's flagships in the new economy, such as BAAN Company and Lernout & Hauspie, both successfully quoted on the New York Stock Exchange (NYSE) at a certain point in their lifetime, experienced fraud and eventually went bankrupt in very spectacular ways, receiving lots of adverse media attention in most of Europe.

However, European policy-makers are increasingly aware that economic growth depends strongly on the development of technology transfer from public research to industry, especially through the creation of new knowledge-based firms. As a result, policy-makers clearly have perceived a need to develop new policy instruments and change the legal and institutional environment of the mid-1990s to develop a system of innovation in which new technology-based firms (NTBFs) and particularly spin-offs or start-ups from public research play a crucial role in new technologies. Because these changes are so numerous, we devote a chapter to them. Chapter 2 describes the development of policy priorities and instruments in this area in European countries.

Research Input and Output and the 3 Per Cent Norm

Within the context of the European Innovation Paradox, the European policy-makers have agreed that not only the system of innovation should be transformed, but also that the intensity of innovation efforts should be increased in each of the member states. Since a simple metric to quantify the innovation intensity in a country does not exist, the general idea was to turn back to a widespread and very objective measure: gross domestic expenditure on R&D (GERD). Through consensus building, the key goal in Europe for European Union (EU) member countries is to achieve a target ratio of GERD to GDP of 3 per cent by 2010. There are large structural differences, both between European economies and the US and within European countries in terms of the extent of R&D funding in relation to national income, who funds the expenditure and who performs the research.

Comparing GERD to GDP, there is a substantial gap between the US and the EU: 2.66 per cent for the former and only 1.86 per cent for the latter (Table 1.2, column 3). As the ratio was relatively stable between 1999 to 2002 (respectively 21 per cent and 20 per cent), this gap seems likely to persist, with Europe still having much to do to catch up with the US.

Table 1.2   R&D expenditure

	Gross domestic expenditure on R&D Volume (billion $) (2002)	Gross domestic expenditure on R&D Evolution % 1997/2002	Gross domestic expenditure on R&D as % of GDP (2002)	% of GERD carried out by the public sector	% of GERD carried out by the private sector
Belgium	6.4	+ 33	2.24	26.7	73.3
France	37.9	+ 17	2.26	36.7	63.3
Germany	54.2	+ 19	2.53	30.8	69.2
Sweden	10.2	+ 36	4.27	22.4	77.6
UK	31.1	+ 19	1.87	33.0	67.0
EU	202.0	+ 21	1.86	36.2	63.8
US	277.0	+ 20	2.66	28.0	72.0

Source: Data OECD, Eurostat, OST estimations and computation (OST, 2006).

In 2002, EU member states spent $202 billion on R&D. Nearly two-thirds was spent by three countries: Germany ($54.2 million), France ($37.9 million) and the UK ($31.1 million). In absolute amounts, Sweden ($10.2 millions) and Belgium ($6.4 millions) are some distance behind (Table 1.2, column 1). But, when research spending is expressed in terms of each country's GDP, Sweden, with 4.27 per cent of its GDP devoted to R&D, becomes the leading European country. When ranked by this indicator, the gap between Germany, France and Belgium is notable (2.53 per cent compared to 2.26 per cent and 2.24 per cent, respectively). But the depth of activity in these three countries is markedly greater than that of the UK (1.87 per cent).

In 2002, nearly two-thirds of European R&D effort was carried out by the private sector (63.8 per cent) and one-third (36.2 per cent) by the public sector (Table 1.2, columns 4 and 5). Looking at how the national R&D effort of the five countries studied in this book is distributed between the private sector and the public sector notable differences appear. In Sweden and Belgium, R&D is chiefly carried out by the private sector (77.6 per cent and 73.3 per cent, respectively). In Germany and the UK, the role of the private sector is a little less strong (69.2 per cent and 67 per cent, respectively). France is the country where the private sector activity (63.3 per cent) is the closest to the EU average.

There are about 5.3 million full-time-equivalent researchers in the world: 1.26 million of them work in the US and 1.13 million in the EU. When this number of scientists is expressed as a ratio of the labour force, a major difference emerges, with the density of researchers in the US (8.62 researchers per thousand workers) being considerably ahead of that in the EU (5.39) (Table 1.3, column 1).

The distribution of researchers between the private (laboratories of private firms and enterprises) and public sectors (laboratories funded by the state, universities and other institutions of higher education, and not-for-profit organizations) varies greatly from country to country.

In the US, less than a fifth of researchers work in the public sector (17.7 per cent), while in Europe this figure is around a half (50.6 per cent) (Table 1.3, column 2). Among the five European Union member states studied in this volume, a disparity exists but is less important ranging from France, where 48.9 per cent of researchers work in the public sector, to the UK and Sweden, where 39.8 per cent and 39.4 per cent of researchers, respectively, are in the public sector.

Scientific publications are one of the main products of research activity. By using the information contained in bibliographic databases that record all articles published in a selected set of scientific journals, it is possible to count articles by country (as well as by the discipline, region or institution). In 2003, nearly 35 per cent of world publications were produced by the EU and 27.5 per cent by the US (Table 1.3, column 3). The EU's scientific output is concentrated in a small number of member states: Germany, France and the UK account for over half of EU scientific production. The UK is the EU member country with the largest publication share at 6.9 per cent of the world total, followed closely by Germany with 6.7 per cent. The share accounted for by France is noticeably smaller at 4.8 per cent but this figure is some way ahead of Sweden and Belgium (1.4 per cent and 0.9 per cent, respectively).

Last but not least, even though they have their limits, patent data are the best available basis for indicators of the technological activity of a country or set of countries. Two very different patent systems coexist: the European system and the American system. In the European patent system, patent requests are published after 18 months. Under the American system, only successful applications are published, after a variable waiting period. In the European patent system, EU members states' patent share dominates, unsurprisingly, accounting for 40.2 per cent of all applications (Table 1.3, column 4). The US accounts for less than one-third of the patents in this system (31.7 per cent). Germany leads all European member states with a world share of 16.7 per cent, compared with 5.6 per cent for France, 5 per cent for the UK, 2 per cent for Sweden and 1 per cent for Belgium. In the US Patent and Trademark Office, the US accounts for 47.9 per cent of filings, and Europe for only 17.6 per cent (Table 1.3, column 5). Here also,

Table 1.3 Science and technology indicators

	Number of researchers Ratio per thousand labour force (2002) [1]	Public % of total full-time equivalent researchers (2002) [2]	World share (%) of scientific publications 2003 [3]	World share (%) of European patent applications (2003) [4]	World share (%) of US patents (2003) [5]	Scientific density per labour force (2003) [6]	Technological density per labour force (2003) [7]
Belgium	7.39	44.9	0.9	1.0	0.5	131	117
Germany	6.71	41.5	6.7	16.7	7.4	102	222
France	6.90	48.9	4.8	5.6	2.6	109	110
Sweden	10.27	39.4	1.4	2.0	1.1	192	230
UK	5.80	39.8	6.9	5.0	2.5	141	87
EU	5.39	50.6	34.8	40.2	17.6	100	100
US	8.62	17.7	27.5	31.7	47.9	n.a.	n.a.

Notes:

[1] Data OECD, Eurostat, Ricyt and other sources, OST estimations and computation.
[2] Data OECD, Eurostat, Ricyt and other sources, OST estimations and computation.
[3] Data ISI-Thomson Scientific, OST computing; world publication share is determined using fractional count based on the bibliometric version of the Web of Science.
[4] Data INPI and EPO, OST computing.
[5] Data USPTO, OST and CHI-Research computing.
[6] Data ISI-Thomson Scientific, OST computing; relative scientific density is calculated as the ratio of the quantity of a nation's publications to the size of its labour force, normalized to 100 for the European Union.
[7] Data INPI, EPO and Eurostat, OST computing; technological density is calculated as the ratio of the quantity of a nation's patents to the size of its labour force, normalized to 100 for the European Union.

Source: OST (2006).

Germany largely dominates its EU partners, with a world share of 7.4 per cent, nearly three times that of France and the UK. Sweden and Belgium account for 1.1 per cent and 0.5 per cent, respectively.

Morgan et al. (2001) find in the US that the patent success rate for academic researchers was lower than for those from industry but that a significant fraction of patent activity in universities results in commercialized outputs. Comparative estimates of the number of patents issued by academic establishments suggest that the UK performs less well than the US when gross patenting numbers are deflated for differences in the size of the countries (Wright et al., 2003). For example, while in 2002 the US universities generated 31.4 patents per $100 billion GDP, the comparative figure in the UK was 23.0 patents per $100 billion GDP.

The ranking of the countries looks quite different when one looks at their world shares of scientific production and at their world share of patents. For example, the UK led the other countries in scientific production, with a world share of 6.9 per cent ahead of Germany (6.7 per cent) and France (4.8 per cent). However, its ranking looks quite different when world shares of patent applications are considered, with Germany dominating and the UK in third place. This demonstrates that there is no automatic relationship between scientific output and technological capacity of the countries.

The above data have shown that the five countries differ widely by size and R&D potential. Using indicators of scientific and technological density is a way of countering the effect of country size. The scientific density (Table 1.3, column 6), which relates the number of scientific publications to the size of the labour force, is higher for Sweden (192), the UK (141) and Belgium (131) than for France (109) and Germany (102). The Sweden performance is remarkable: its density is nearly double the European average (100).

When technological density – that is, the number of European patent applications by a nation compared to its labour force – is calculated for the five countries (Table 1.3, column 7), once again Sweden (230) is at the top, followed by Germany (222). France, Belgium and particularly the UK trail at some distance.

In conclusion, the figures show that most European countries perform very well in terms of publication and patent output. So, the innovation paradox in these measures seems to disappear. However, this has not yet translated into growth-orientated spin-offs. It remains questionable whether the actions taken will accomplish the 3 per cent target or result in the desired objective increasing spin-offs. A lot of effort seems to be put in to subsidizing research which is mainly performed by the industry sector. However, innovation efforts in terms of commercialization tend to be overlooked, although some countries like Belgium consider public venture capital as part of the R&D budget. Belgium has set up a public pre-seed capital fund with an almost 7 million euros budget to invest in spin-offs and other technology-based start-ups. This amount of money is considered to be R&D budget. The structure of the R&D sector will also determine the extent to which spin-offs can be realized. In the next paragraph we discuss these structural differences.

Structure of the Public Research Sector

The structure of the public research sector varies considerably between the US and Europe and within Europe. The US is differentiated from Europe by the higher percentage of private universities, among which commercialization activity may be quite significant (Owen-Smith and Powell, 2001).

In Germany, the public research sector consists of two main types of PROs: universities and research institutes. Of the 350 universities, 271 are state owned with many private universities not having research bases. Within the state sector, the technical universities have historically had close connections to industry, notably engineering. The 63 general universities comprise all higher education institutions without a clear engineering background that offer a broad variety of disciplines. The 144 universities of applied sciences (in German, *Fachhochschulen*) have a strong orientation towards practical needs with a disciplinary focus of engineering, computer sciences and business administration. A further 128 universities specialize in specific disciplines such as the arts, medicine, education sciences, business administration, public administration, sports or theology. Outside the university sector are several hundred individual public research institutes (PRIs) the vast majority of which belong to one of four large trade organizations. First, the Hermann von Helmholtz Gemeinschaft Deutscher Forschungszentren (HGF) comprises 15 large research centres mainly engaged in natural science and engineering, including nuclear research and space research. Second, the Max Planck Gesellschaft zur Förderung der Wissenschaft (MPG) runs 77 Max Planck Institutes (MPIs, including two institutes outside Germany). Third, the Fraunhofer Gesellschaft zur Förderung der angewandten Forschung (FhG) consists of 58 research institutes mainly engaged in applied research in engineering, a few of which carry out military-related R&D. Fourth, the Wissenschaftsgemeinschaft Gottfried Wilhelm Leibniz (WGL) unites 80 research institutes that cover a range of disciplines and types of research, including some institutes with service function (such as museums and scientific libraries). These institutes receive a greater proportion of their funding from government than the universities. In addition to direct state funding, a major funding body is the German Research Foundation (DFG) financed jointly by the Federal and the local state (*Länder*) governments and providing grants for scientific research based on a peer review system (both for small projects and long-term research networks and centres of excellence). Funding by companies is almost entirely project based, either in the course of contract research or collaborative projects. Funding for scientific research is provided by company foundations such as Volkswagen-Stiftung, Fritz-Thyssen-Stiftung, Bosch-Stiftung, Bertelsmann-Stiftung and hundreds of other private foundations. Until the 1990s, public funding severely restricted investment by universities into spin-offs. Latterly, the environment has changed as more universities are becoming subject to global budgeting, enabling university managers to decide where to allocate the institutional funding received from the state government.

In Sweden, only 11 out of 39 higher education establishments have a university status. Two are broadly diversified in the field of science, the remainder being more or less specialized. Three are private: Chalmers University of Technology, Stockholm School of Economics and Jönköping University. Ten out of the 39 dominate the R&D carried out. The 30 public research institutes and industrial R&D institutes cover diverse fields of science. Two-thirds of the institutes' finances come from individual companies. The state, through such bodies as NUTEK[1] and VINNOVA,[2] provides an important one-third of the finances.

The public research sector in the UK consists of 167 organizations that have university status (there are three additional private universities), though not all are engaged in research. There are also 85 government laboratories/public research institutes. Financing for university research is provided by seven discipline-based autonomous state-funded research councils[3] which are part of the Office for Science and Technology (OST) and the Higher Education Funding Councils (HEFCs), which finance the main operating costs of universities. The allocation of HEFCE money is influenced by the (approximately) five-yearly Research Assessment Exercise (RAE) under which a range of discipline-based panels of peers rates the research of each university department. Falling Higher Education Funding Council for England (HEFCE) funding for research universities has contributed to increased fund-raising from the commercial sector. In addition, major foundations like the Wellcome Trust and other charities finance research, in particular in the medical field.

At the extremes, the management of universities may be centralized or decentralized. In the decentralized model, universities retain a high degree of autonomy and effectively compete against one another (Goldfarb and Henrekson, 2003). It has been argued that as a result of the highly decentralized system in the US, where there are proportionately more private universities than in European countries, universities have been more able to become responsive to the economic needs of society (Argyes and Liebeskind, 1998). In the centralized model, the state plays an important, and highly visible, role in managing the overwhelmingly public university sector, such as in mainland European countries. Under this system academics have traditionally been civil servants with high degrees of pay uniformity. The UK is probably best described as a hybrid model, a mixture of both the decentralized and centralized systems. In particular, competition has been encouraged within the state sector for research funding through the RAE and the Research Councils. Although the academic labour market has become relatively flexible, rigid pay scales are still imposed at all levels below full professor.

In France, the public research sector consists of three main types of PROs: 90 universities, 25 public research organizations and around 180 grandes écoles (public engineering or agronomic schools and management schools). The main public research organization is the CNRS (Centre national de la recherche scientifique – the National Centre for Scientific Research), a multidisciplinary institution with a mission to undertake fundamental research. The other main important PROs are the CEA (Commissariat à l'énergie atomique – research on nuclear energy), INRA (Institut national de la recherche agronomique – agricultural research), INSERM (Institut national de la santé et de la recherche – Health and medical research) and INRIA (Institut national de la recherche en informatique et automatique – research on computer science and artificial intelligence). All these public research organizations have autonomy in decision-making and research strategy. In contrast, the universities lack autonomy both in recruiting (which depends upon a national competition) or managing their personnel or in implementing a strategy. The universities, the CNRS and the grandes écoles represent academic research activity, while the other PROs represent what is referred to as 'la recherche finalisée' (OST, 2004).

Recent years have seen the disappearance of dualism, the separation between the CNRS and the universities, and the existence of the grandes écoles without research activities, which had been a particular feature of the Colbertist model in France (Mustar and Larédo, 2002). The CNRS could now be considered, following the example of the Anglo-Saxon research councils or the National Science Foundation (NSF), as a research support agency or, more specifically, an agency concerned with structures, which makes its contributions in the form of human potential and large technical rather than financial resources. For example, CNRS staff and university staff collaborate closely, since 90 per cent of CNRS personnel are employed in laboratories located in the universities. Traditionally, the universities have weaker links with industry. Most of the best PhD graduates traditionally obtain positions in the public sector. The grandes écoles have strong links with industry and most of their graduates obtain high-level positions in industry. Currently, across all disciplines, one in every five PhD theses in France is produced in the research centres of these schools, although they only contain barely 6 per cent of all teacher-researchers.

These changes have occurred in the wider context of governments increasingly disengaging from large military and civil programmes, and looking towards the support of SMEs and high-tech firms, using public sector research as a major vehicle. In 2005, two new agencies were created. The first is the Agence de l'Innovation Industrielle (AII), which will finance the new Programme Mobilisateurs pour l'Innovation Industrielle. The first six large research programmes involving 600 million euros of funding, 236 million euros of which are to be provided by AII, were launched in April 2006. These programmes focus on the Internet (Quaero), biotech (BioHub), telecommunications (TVMSL), the built environment (Homes), transport (NeoVal) and the green car. The second agency is the Agence Nationale de la Recherche (ANR), whose objective is to increase the number of research projects across the scientific community, which will be financed after peer evaluation of competitive bids. The main idea behind the creation of this agency is that project-based research funding is wide-spread in many foreign countries and constitutes a factor of dynamism to explore the borders of science. The ANR is effectively envisaged as a French NSF, with a budget for 2006 of 800 million euros for research projects of a duration of four years maximum.

In Belgium, there are 17 universities and 59 polytechnic schools active in the field of research and education. These universities have increasingly suffered from budgetary cuts. The result of this unfavourable policy is that research has increasingly become financed by external sources, which in turn leads to difficulties in attracting permanent staff. However, in the mean-time the number of students is increasing annually. For example, the two largest Dutch-speaking universities Katholieke Universiteit Leuven (KUL) and Universiteit Gent (UG) saw their number of students increase from, respectively, 23 659 and 19 920 in the academic year 1997–98 to 28 058 (+18 per cent) and 22 052 (+11 per cent), in the academic year 2000–2001. Conversely, the personnel at the KUL decreased over the same period from 5720 to 5038 (−12 per cent) while it increased only slightly at Ghent University from 3562 to 3772 (+6 per cent).

The legal framework for industry science relations is particularly complicated since the country is divided into three 'regions' (Brussels, Flanders and Wallonia), that are delegated to organize industry matters such as R&D subsidies (including joint R&D–university projects) or issues concerning intellectual property. In a kind of matrix structure, the country is divided into two 'communities': the Flemish and the French (Walloon) community. Each of these regions and/or communities has its own policy and regulations. In this book, we will examine the situation in Flanders.

In addition to the universities and polytechnics, there are four important independent Flemish research institutes: the Flanders Interuniversity Institute for Biotechnology (VIB), the Interuniversity Institute for Microelectronics (IMEC), the Flemish Institute for Technology Research (VITO) and IBBT. The VIB specializes in biotechnology research, the IMEC specializes in microelectronics, and the VITO conducts orientated contract research and develops innovative products and processes in the fields of energy, environment and materials. The IBBT is the recently created Institute in Broad Band Technology. The importance of these institutes for spin-offs is great since they cumulate research efforts across universities. In other words, the Flemish government has chosen to build a critical mass across universities in particular technological domains. The IMEC, for instance, unites research groups from four different universities and also has its own campus. In total it employs over 1000 researchers. The VIB and the recently created IBBT follow a model of virtual cooperation. This means that the research groups stay within the different universities but a holding structure coordinates their efforts.

In conclusion, we can state that the university system in Europe is mainly dominated by the government, both in terms of management and research funding. This will have severe consequences for the way in which the universities are managed and, relatedly, on their degrees of freedom in terms of recruitment, promotion, commercialization efforts, and so on. In addition, in some countries such as France, Germany and Belgium, public research has been concentrated in government-based research laboratories, which cannot be neglected in a study on spin-offs. These research laboratories are created by government to concentrate the research efforts and build up a critical mass. Often, they compete with the universities in terms of research funding and employees or, as in Belgium, they simply draw resources from the different universities.

One of the most important environmental changes in Europe which is supposed to have had an impact on the way in which spin-offs are conceived is change in legislation relating to IP rights. This is the topic of the next section.

Management of IP

The ownership of IP has important implications in terms of the creation of incentives for academics, and other related parties, to commercialize technology. Where property rights are weak and knowledge is tacit, the transfer of technology can be highly problematic due to the problems of hold up. As licensing may be problematical in such circumstances, it may be preferable to create a spin-off company and incentivize the academic through the provision of an equity stake (Shane, 2001).

The Bayh–Dole Act (BDA) in the US played an important role in the development of policy relating to IP. Proponents of the BDA argue that by granting universities control over their own IP they effectively gave incentives to universities to invest in their own technology. Mowery et al. (2001) argue that the rise of the biotechnology industry, the legal change that made it possible to patent 'engineered molecules' and the general policy for the strengthening of property rights for IP in the US, have also been important influences on the commercialization of technology developed in universities.

Belgium adopted a Bayh–Dole-type of Act in the second half of the1990s, while France has had this type of regulation for a long time. Although the UK has no formal Bayh–Dole-type Act, in public research organizations the IP strictly belongs to the university who will commonly grant the academic inventor a right to a proportion of the income stream from it. As a result there is no formal requirement to disclose inventions. In contrast, in both Sweden and Germany the academic has traditionally been the sole owner of the IP. This position changed in Germany in 2003 and a system more similar to that of the US has been introduced. In Sweden, however, this position prevails and is thought to be a major impediment in technology transfer occurring from Swedish universities, as the universities have nothing to gain from commercializing IP if all the gains accrue to the individual scientist. Although the position has not yet changed in Sweden, it is subject to considerable debate. The relatively recent changes in Germany and Sweden also imply that the universities did not keep track of the spin-off activity.

Next to the regulation of IP, an important determinant of the success of spin-off companies concerns the involvement of the academic scientist in the company (Jensen and Thursby, 2001). This creates interesting issues relating to the structure of academic careers and the extent to which universities can/will be willing to be flexible in terms of the career progressions of academic entrepreneurs. Academic entrepreneurs, who are expected to spend time commercializing their IP, will not be able to dedicate the same amount of time to the traditional areas of teaching, research and administration. There is a need to ensure that the right financial incentives for the academic are present on the upside and a need to accommodate the problems associated with the potential downside for the entrepreneur's academic career (Goldfarb and Henrekson, 2003).

The US and the UK both have much more fluid labour markets than the top-down countries. In the US, where salary levels are much more market driven, there is a greater dispersion of academic salaries compared with other countries. In Sweden, Belgium, Germany and France rigid pay scales have meant that it has often been in the interest of universities to discourage interaction between academics and industry.

Although academic labour markets are much more flexible in the US and the UK than many other countries, technology transfer may still create its own tensions for university management. A particular concern is the extent to which involvement with commercial projects such as spin-off companies is valued in terms of the promotion system. In the US and the UK, the focus of academic tenure and promotion decisions has historically been on the basis of publication (and citation) records and research funding. Similarly, the academic labour market is more fluid in terms of mobility, with academic faculty competing for posts on an individual basis.

In Germany, France and Belgium staff at state-owned universities are either civil servants (that is, with a permanent contract, including all professors) or administrative employees of the state government. In Germany, professors are recruited based upon a central quota system. For instance, the whole of Germany employs 46 marketing professors. One can only become a marketing professor after one of these 46 leaves the cohort and a position becomes available. Hence, there is extreme competition among young graduates to become a professor. Once one reaches the level of a professor, one has research funds and young researchers at one's disposition and a central institute such as Steinbeisch regulates all kinds of consulting activities that might render an extra income to the professor. In contrast, young researchers have non-permanent contracts (typically running for five or six years) and are urged to quit the universities after finishing their PhD or their Habilitation (post-doctoral degree). It is not surprising that in this context it is extremely difficult to create spin-offs.

In both France and Germany, there is a central recruitment system organized by government. Only the candidates who pass the 'concours' can be employed in a French university.

In Belgium, recruitment is decentralized to the individual universities as well as the promotion decisions. However, salaries are fixed by government. Professors are evaluated based upon their scientific output, their teaching qualities and, finally, their involvement with society.

Again, the spin-off activity discussed in the remaining chapters of this book has to be seen in the context of these different legal and institutional environments.

Entrepreneurial Activity

Renault (2006) showed in a study of 98 professors in 12 universities in the US that the entrepreneurial attitude of the academics had most explanatory power in predicting their commercialization activities, including their involvement in licensing out technology, spinning off companies and being involved in contract research. The general entrepreneurial attitude of people is an indicator which is known to vary between countries within Europe and between Europe and the US in particular. Without going into the details on what drives entrepreneurial activity, we describe in this paragraph how entrepreneurial activity differs, using data drawn from the Global Enterprise Monitor (GEM). This monitor collects data on the total entrepreneurial activity (TEA) in a country. This is an index that measures the degree to which adults are involved in nascent or new firms with growth ambitions. It indicates that entrepreneurial activity is considerably greater in the US than in Europe, especially in relation to continental European countries (Table 1.4, Panel A). There are several reasons, given in the General Entrepreneurship Monitor, about why entrepreneurial activity is so low in many European countries. A rigid social security system and inflexibility on the job market are two main reasons, the relevance of this for academics having already been discussed above.

In addition to these constraints, the administrative difficulty in actually setting up a business is also considered to be an indicator of entrepreneurial activity. The US is ranked the world's third easiest economy in which to start a business. The UK economy is ranked ninth, whereas the German economy is only ranked at forty-seventh. Other secondary indicators have to do with the easiness of running a business in each of these countries. Differences between countries with respect to enforcing contracts may be particularly important in the case of high-tech companies which are based on legally protectable IP. The US is the highest ranked of the countries we have highlighted, ranked tenth in the world. The lowest ranked country we focus on is the UK, which is ranked thirtieth. The US and UK have far more flexible labour market laws compared to Germany and France. There are also big differences in terms of businesses' ability to raise credit (Table 1.4, Panel B). In particular, the UK and German economy rank highly with first and fifth place respectively, while the French economy lags considerably.

We can conclude with the observation that creating spin-offs or academic start-ups in Europe will be a much more laborious process than in the US, and may not render the same kind of social esteem as in the US. In continental Europe, the number of people simply starting up a business is much lower than in the US or the UK. So, it seems less generally accepted to get involved in this kind of activity. Academics who still want to start up a company not only face resistance within the university system but also have to convince their friends and family about such a career move. As the idea develops, in countries such as France, Germany and Belgium they will also encounter a rather complex process administratively. So, they will need an

Table 1.4 Entrepreneurial indicators

Panel A	US	UK	Sweden	Germany	France	Belgium
	No. adults per 10 000 in nascent/new firm expecting ≥19 jobs in 5 yrs	No. adults per 10 000 in nascent/new firm expecting ≥19 jobs in 5 yrs	No. adults per 10 000 in nascent/new firm expecting ≥19 jobs in 5 yrs	No. adults per 10 000 in nascent/new firm expecting ≥19 jobs in 5 yrs	No. adults per 10 000 in nascent/new firm expecting ≥19 jobs in 5 yrs	No. adults per 10 000 in nascent/new firm expecting ≥19 jobs in 5 yrs
Total entrepreneurial activity with growth ambitions 2005	141.36	70.60	49.30	46.11	37.71	16.32

Panel B	Doing Business world rank	Doing Business world rank	Doing Business world rank	Doing Business world rank	Doing Business world rank	Doing Business world rank
Doing business (overall)	3	9	14	19	44	18
Starting a business	3	9	20	47	13	34
Dealing with licences	17	29	13	20	23	31
Hiring and firing	6	15	86	131	142	43
Getting credit	15	1	30	5	115	45

Protecting investors	7	9	95	57	56	13
Enforcing contracts	10	30	14	25	13	17
Closing a business	17	10	18	30	32	9

Notes: The ease of doing business index ranks economies from 1 to 155. The index is calculated as the ranking on the simple average of country percentile rankings on each of the ten topics covered in Doing Business in 2006. The ranking on each topic is the simple average of the percentile rankings on its component indicators.

Source: Entrepreneurship indicator: GEM (2005). The World Bank – Doing Business: Benchmarking Business Regulations,' http://www.doingbusiness.org.

accountant and other advisers to help them in this start-up process, which creates both a psychological and a financial barrier to starting up a venture. The financial part is exactly the topic of the next paragraph.

Availability of Finance

Wright et al. (2006b) have shown that a lack of venture capital is often seen as a major barrier to start-up activity by technology transfer office (TTO) managers. This kind of equity finance is used to finance concept-testing activities and to value the IP at start up. In addition to the rational explanation of a need for equity finance, starting up a company with a substantial amount of capital might also be seen as a more solid basis for a career than bearing all the entrepreneurial risk as an academic.

Again, marked differences are evident between the US and Europe in the availability of personal capital to start businesses. The personal capital of young entrepreneurs is generally higher in the US, with funding from 'family, friends and fools' (3F) being more in evidence than in Europe. High-tech entrepreneurs in the US stress the importance of networking as a source of finance prior to seeking venture capital finance (Roberts, 1991). In the US education system, there also appear to be greater opportunities to encounter individuals from a variety of backgrounds. In particular, scientists and people with a financial or Master of Business Administration (MBA) background may get to know each other more easily, forming a basis for a willingness to invest in high-tech ventures.

In addition to personal funds and so-called 3F money, the US model of technical entrepreneurship is linked to the availability of venture capital to select and to finance the best projects (DiGregorio and Shane, 2003; von Burg and Kenney, 2000). A major premise for the introduction of policies to stimulate the development of venture capital in European countries was that the gap in high-tech entrepreneurship between European countries and the US was a financial one (Edwards, 1999; European Commission, 2000a). These developments have had mixed success.

In the UK, whose financial system most closely resembles that of the US, a venture capital sector developed ahead of those elsewhere in Europe. Although there were long established venture capitalists (VCs) such as 3i, the VC sector began to develop in earnest at the end of the 1970s following the Wilson Committee inquiry into the role of financial institutions (Wilson, 1979; Wright and Robbie, 1999). However, the greater emphasis of the UK venture capital market has been on later-stage and management buy-out investments. Evidence from the early 1990s suggested that new high-tech firms had to meet more rigorous selection criteria than equivalent non-technology projects (Murray and Lott, 1995). While there had been some improvement by the late 1990s, the problem still persisted (Lockett et al., 2002a).

In Germany, the public authorities attempted to foster a venture capital market from the 1970s by mobilizing banks' investment. However, the first German venture capital fund created in 1975, the Deutsche Wagnisfinanzierungsgesellschaft (WFG) never succeeded in inducing larger market development (Becker and Hellmann, 2003). Creating a venture capital market in a bank-based financial system proved particularly difficult and slow (Black and Gilson, 1998; Wright et al., 2005).

A number of venture capital initiatives were introduced in France from the early 1970s, such as the creation of Sociétés financières d'innovation (innovation finance companies) to facilitate the industrial application in France of technological research and the promotion and exploitation of inventions, the establishment of the Société Française de Garantie des Financements des PME (SOFARIS) as a fund to guarantee the risks relating to their equity investment in innovative SMEs, and measures to enable the creation of Sociétés de Capital Risque (venture capital companies) with attractive tax benefits for shareholders. Following only modest development of the venture capital industry up to the mid-1990s, it came to be recognized that there was a need to create a new and specific stock market for high-growth firms that would contribute to the development of venture capital by improving the liquidity of the shareholders in innovative growth companies. In 1996, le Nouveau Marché was created. A year before, the AIM had been created in London with the same objective, some months after the EASDAQ was created in Brussels. At this time a consortium was created with the French Nouveau Marché, the EASDAQ and the German Neuer Markt and the Belgian New Market (the latter two both created in 1997). In Sweden, two new markets established for small technology companies the Stockholm Bourse Information (SBI) and the Innovationsmarknaden (IM) were merged in 1998 (OECD, 2003), These markets enabled innovative firms to raise capital to accelerate their growth, and venture capitalists to make their equity capital in these firms more accessible. However, the success of these markets has been mixed with, for example, the Neuer Markt closing in the aftermath of the bursting of the dotcom bubble.

Focusing on the provision of venture capital for new and early stage ventures, it is not surprising that the US has the highest formal venture capital to GDP ratio (Table 1.5). Reflecting their emphasis on later-stage and buy-out investments, although the UK and France are the most developed private equity and venture capital markets in Europe, they have considerably lower levels of early stage VC investment per percentage of GDP. Sweden's early stage formal venture capital markets figure relatively highly, while those in Germany and Belgium are very low. However, a remarkable

Table 1.5   Formal and informal venture capital 2003

	Informal investment per GDP %	Formal VC per GDP %	VC and informal investment per GDP %
France	0.62	0.082	0.71
UK	0.66	0.089	0.75
Belgium	0.86	0.039	0.90
Sweden	0.80	0.118	0.92
US	0.96	0.164	1.12
Germany	1.09	0.028	1.12

Source: GEM (2004).

difference is that the informal venture capital industry appears highly developed in Germany in relation to GDP. In contrast, both France and the UK have the lowest involvement from informal VC investment per percentage of GDP capita, with 0.62 and 0.66 respectively.

1.4   THE ISSUES AND STRUCTURE OF THE BOOK

Our examination of the issues involved in developing spin-offs is based on several levels of analysis – the policy context, the types of spin-off firms, the incubation processes involved in developing spin-offs at the university and public research organization level, the processes involved at the spin-off firm level, the role of individual entrepreneurs and entrepreneurial teams, and the role of financiers.

In Chapter 2, more specific policies relating to the promotion of innovation and the development of spin-offs in universities and public research organizations are examined.

Understanding of the nature of spin-offs is important in designing approaches to address the challenges in their creation and development. The heterogeneity of spin-offs is analysed in Chapter 3. The chapter maps the literature on spin-offs through the development of a matrix aimed at identifying general dimensions of the typologies of research-based spin-offs. Three broad conceptual perspectives are identified which relate to differences in the resource endowments, institutional links, and business models of spin-offs. A distinction is made between the process of spin-off creation and the process of spin-off development.

In addition to heterogeneity in the nature of spin-offs, there may also be variety in the incubation processes adopted in order to develop these ventures. Chapter 4 presents a systematic analysis of the different approaches.

The chapter uses evidence from 50 universities and public research organizations across Europe to identify five incubator models. Three of these, identified as Low Selective, Supportive and Incubator models, involve approaches where the organization has the resources and activities to meet their objectives but with distinctly different types of spin-offs and levels of involvement. The other two models, labelled as Resource Deficient and Competence Deficient, are unable to meet their objectives because of shortcomings in their resources and activities, respectively.

Chapter 5 examines the phases that spin-offs go through in their development, and analyses the key challenges these ventures face. The analysis indicates that spin-offs pass through a number of different distinct phases of activity in their development and that, between the different phases, ventures face critical junctures that need to be addressed before they can progress to the next phase. Each phase can be characterized as an iterative process of development. The phases are identified as the research phase, the opportunity framing phase, the pre-organization phase, the reorientation phase and the sustainability phase. The critical junctures that are encountered in moving between each of these phases are identified as the opportunity recognition juncture, the entrepreneurial commitment juncture, the credibility juncture and the sustainability juncture.

Chapter 6 examines the key issues in identifying individual entrepreneurs and entrepreneurial teams who can create and develop the spin-off. More specifically, we focus on how teams are created in the pre-start-up phase. The role of the TTO officer, who is often some sort of privileged witness, is highlighted. Further, we discuss the team composition in spin-offs and link it to the possibility of being successful in terms of growth in revenues and employees. Teams that are artificially composed at the moment a business opportunity is spotted by the TTO seem to be very fragile. They are able to attract venture capital at start-up because the team fits the criteria used by the VC, but this early growth is seldom sustainable. This is in contrast to companies that are created by teams who have both shared social or working experience and a heterogeneity in terms of skills and/or backgrounds. Finally, solo entrepreneurs or teams that have no heterogeneous composition seem to be the least successful in terms of growth.

Accessing finance to establish and grow the spin-off poses major challenges. Chapter 7 examines issues relating to accessing finance for spin-offs. We triangulate evidence from spin-off companies, university TTOs and venture capital firms in the UK and continental Europe to identify the problems in accessing this form of finance. We compare perceptions of high-tech venture capital firms that invest in spin-offs with those that do not, and also consider VCs' views on spin-offs versus other high-tech firms. We identify a mismatch between the demand and supply side of the market.

In line with the pecking-order theory, venture capitalists prefer to invest after the seed stage. However, in contrast to the pecking-order theory, TTOs see venture capital as more important than internal funds early on.

Finally, Chapter 8 presents some conclusions and policy implications

1.5   DATA AND METHODOLOGY

The analysis in this book is based on a multi-level programme of studies of spin-offs carried out across Europe. The programme covers issues relating to universities, technology transfer offices, spin-off firms, academic entrepreneurs, financiers and government policy. As a result, the programme involved a set of interrelated studies using different research approaches. The research posed major challenges in data collection in terms of identifying appropriate universities, firms and individuals as well as persuading appropriate respondents to take part in the study.

In order to identify trends and developments in the policy context, we used archival data from a number of sources. To review the heterogeneity of spin-offs we conducted a detailed review of the relevant literature.

Data relating to the activities of technology transfer offices were identified using both quantitative and qualitative means. In March 2002, a survey of university technology transfer activities comprising quantitative and qualitative questionnaires was sent to the top universities in the UK as ranked by research income, accounting for 99.8 per cent of this revenue. As the survey was conducted with the support of the two associations of technology transfer officers in the UK, the Universities' Companies Association (UNICO) and the Association of Universities Research and Industrial Liaison officers (AURIL), we were able to identify the most suitable respondent through their membership. We conducted an initial telephone exercise to identify the most suitable person to complete the questionnaire. This person was typically the head of the TTO or their designate. We received information from 98 of these universities. We returned to these institutions in the spring of 2003, and obtained full data on the level of their spin-off activity in financial year 2002 from 124 universities. Tests showed that the respondents were representative of the population of universities that are active in commercialization of university research.

This quantitative survey of TTOs was followed in 2003 and 2004 by a series of detailed interviews with a selection of TTOs in order to enable insights to be gained regarding the processes used to get projects investor ready. We approached TTOs in institutions within the context of maintaining coverage that reflected a range of age, experience, geographical spread and size. The universities in our sample are drawn from a wide range of geographic regions across Europe. The universities also display a substantial age range. The sample includes both some of the longest-established universities as well as more recent technologically focused universities.

To examine the different incubation processes in universities and public research institutes we adopted a two-stage process. First, We identified 13 regions at the EU NUTS2 level, that is, the regional classification system adopted by Eurostat, which according to the *European Report on Science and Technology Indicators* (1994, p. 152; 1997) contained 80 per cent of all research laboratories and enterprises of the EU at that time:[4] Île de France and Centre-Est (Rhône-Alpes) in France, Vlaams Gewest and Région Wallonne in Belgium, Eastern (East Anglia) and East Midlands in the UK, Oost-Nederland and Zuid-Nederland in the Netherlands, Bayern, Baden-Württemberg and Hessen in Germany, Northern Italy (Nord Ovest, Lombardia, Nord Est and Centro) in Italy, and Southern and Eastern Ireland (see Table 1.6).

For each region, a university researcher based in the region was asked to identify, for their region, technology transfer units according to the following criteria: (1) they needed to be founded before 1997, (2) they needed to

Table 1.6   Research institutions and regional economic data

Name of Scientific Regions of Excellence in Europe	GERD as a percentage of GDP, 1998	Number of patents applications per capita, 2000	Number of high-tech patents applications per capita, 2000
Vlaams Gewest	1.9	159.6	26.8
Région Wallonne	1.9	134.9	12.6
Baden-Württemberg	3.8	527.4	57.5
Bayern	2.7	480.6	124.0
Hessen	2.2	350.4	31.5
Île-de-France	3.4	296.3	68.1
Centre-Est (Rhône-Alpes)	2.3 (2.3)	197.2 (221.3)	32.7 (39.5)
Northern Italy (Nord Ovest, Lombardia, Nord Est, Centro)	1.4	104.6	8.0
Oost-Nederland	2.0	136.3	17.2
Zuid-Nederland	2.3	521.7	192.9
East Midlands	1.8	114.3	15.5
Eastern (East Anglia)	3.6	238.8 (309.9)	77.1 (120.2)
Southern and Eastern Ireland	1.4	103.6	28.8

have a documented record of spin-offs and (3) the local researchers had to consider them as examples of processes of spin-off activity that were successfully achieving their objectives. Seven cases matched the criteria: Scientific Generics and TTP in the UK, Leuven R&D and IMEC in Belgium, BioM in Germany, University of Twente in the Netherlands and Crealys in France.

Data on each case was collected through personal interviews with several persons in the institutes and secondary data sources such as annual reports, websites and descriptions of the institutes in the local press. Using a structured questionnaire, we assessed to what extent and how each spin-off service was organized or was engaged in the particular activity. We also analysed the resources developed to organize these activities on the bases identified by Brush et al. (2001): human, social, financial, physical, technological and organizational. We examined to what extent the resources that were present were crucial to organize the activities described above.

To validate the models developed in stage 1, we selected a range of different cases from the regions identified in stage 1. First, we identified a sample frame of universities and research organizations in these regions. Second, the universities and research institutes (RIs) were screened for the existence of a spin-off service. Third, a preliminary analysis of the effectiveness of the initiatives set up by the spin-off service took place. Based on this analysis, the most active spin-off services in each region were selected. This analysis produced a sample of 43 RIs. The selected cases were actively pursuing a spin-off strategy, but did not necessarily meet the three different criteria used as selection conditions in stage 1. Data were collected on each RI as for stage 1.

To examine *university spin-off* (USO) development, qualitative data were collected using in-depth face-to-face and telephone interviews with representatives from 12 USOs in the UK, as well as each of their financial investors and seven associated universities over the period July 2001 to July 2002. These universities were selected on the basis that they are among the top ten research elite universities in the UK and that they are actively pursuing a programme of university technology transfer. Each university was at a different point in transforming its policies, routines and incentive mechanisms towards commercialization through USOs. We selected a range of different ventures in terms of their technology and stage of development. Interviews were carried out with the head of the TTO – or equivalent – business development managers (BDMs) and the members of a spin-off company who had taken the venture through the process, including both the academic entrepreneur and the 'surrogate' entrepreneur where applicable. We also gained access to the seed-stage investors in each of the USOs. In addition, we interviewed the head of each department from which the

USO originated. The interviews lasted from one to two hours and were openly recorded and transcribed afterwards.

For the analysis of the *spin-off team* processes, a detailed field study was carried out of ten academic spin-offs located in Flanders, Belgium. These spin-offs were stratified in particular stages of their development. A longitudinal process approach was adopted (Burgelman, 1983). Cases were selected on the basis of at least two spin-offs being present in each of four stages: research commercialization and opportunity screening, organization-in-gestation, proof of viability and the maturity phase. The projects in the first two stages were selected based on contacts with TTOs, which helped us to obtain some understanding of which seemed to be potential spin-off opportunities. Teams that had got in touch with the TTO in order to protect their IP and that had recently filed or obtained a patent were selected. At the time of the study, the teams at the first stage were considering the options they had to commercialize their IP, of which a spin-off was only one possibility. The teams in the second phase had identified a market opportunity and had decided to create a spin-off. The companies in the last two stages were selected from a list of spin-offs in Flanders, with founders/chief executive officers (CEOs) being contacted to identify their stage of development. Those in the third stage had founded a legal entity and had brought together the necessary resources to develop it. Ventures showing persistence were identified as cases in the fourth, maturity phase. Data relating to teams were collected using a number of methods. First, for projects still located at the university, the head of the research team was contacted to provide data on the research and the team involved. For each selected formally incorporated venture, either the founder or the CEO was asked about the start-up history of the firm and particularly how the team evolved over time. During these interviews, we also asked for the exit/entry dates of individuals involved. For both the head of the research team and the founders/CEOs, the questionnaire was handed to the head of the research team and appointments made to collect the questionnaire. Second, for those teams still in the project stage, all members of the research team were asked to fill out the questionnaire. Each member of the management team of the formally incorporated ventures was asked to fill out the questionnaire. This questionnaire consisted of a part asking for background information on education and experience, and a part aimed at identifying the personal orientation required to realize venture success based on Van Muijen et al. (1999). Third, we collected background information on all individuals entering and exiting the team to allow us to evaluate the experiential diversity of the team at different stages during the spin-off process. The number of persons filling out the questionnaires ranged from two to eight per firm, depending on the phase in which the project/venture was positioned. In all cases, all the members of the entrepreneurial team were involved in the study. Persuading team members to complete the questionnaire posed major challenges for the researchers.

To examine issues relating to the perspective of *financiers*, a questionnaire was sent in November 2003 to the 56 venture capital funds in the UK that identified themselves as being active investors in technology-based small firms according to the British Venture Capital Association (BVCA) definition of technology (BVCA, 2004). We aimed to examine the attitudes and perceptions of venture capital investors and to analyse the factors affecting the supply of finance from venture capital funds for spin-offs. The questionnaire sought both quantitative and qualitative information as well as presenting the opportunity for respondents to offer 'write-in' comments. We received 27 fully completed questionnaires plus nine nil responses/partially completed returns; that is, 50 per cent of the active VCs in the high-tech market. This response rate is in line with other surveys of VCs in the UK and very encouraging for a mail survey. To supplement the UK data, we conducted face-to-face interviews with 65 VC firms located in six European countries which mentioned in their local venture capital association directories that they invested in high-tech start-ups. To maximize the intra-sample variety of these VC firms, the sample frame of VC firms was divided into four groups: funds with more than 50 per cent public capital, captives which belong 100 per cent to a financial institute, multinational VC firms and local VC firms. In each category a random selection of four firms was made. From the 96 identified VC firms, 65 (60 per cent) agreed to participate in the study.

NOTES

1. NUTEK, the Swedish Business Development Agency, is a national agency under the charge of the Ministry of Industry, Employment and Communication that handles issues concerning industrial policies.
2. VINNOVA, the Swedish Agency for Innovation Systems, integrates research and development in technology, transport and working life. VINNOVA's mission is to promote sustainable growth by financing R&D and developing effective innovation systems.
3. Medical Research Council (MRC), Biotechnology and Biological Sciences Research Council (BBSRC), Natural Environment Research Council (NERC), Engineering and Physical Sciences Research Council (EPSRC), Particle Physics and Astronomy Research Council (PPARC), Economic and Social Research Council (ESRC), Council for the Central Laboratory of the Research Councils (CLRC) and the Arts and Humanities Research Board (AHRB).
4. EU refers only to the 12 original EU member states. The Northern European countries – Sweden, Finland and Denmark – joined the EU much later and were not included in the *European Report* due to lack of regional R&D statistics compiled by Eurostat.

2.   Public policies to foster academic spin-offs

2.1   INTRODUCTION

For the past 15 years or so, academic research spin-offs have received increasing attention by government authorities in the leading scientifically developed countries. The capacity of prestigious US universities to generate new companies from Genentech to Google has highlighted the strategic role of public-sector research, not only in the generation of new knowledge and technology but also in the creation and development of high-growth technological firms. Spin-offs from universities and public-sector research institutes have become a key issue in government research and innovation policy in many countries. Although the creation of academic spin offs is nothing new, what is original is the extent of the phenomenon and the fact that public policies have being introduced to encourage the commercial exploitation of public-sector research results through new businesses.

The genesis of this public policy, which is directly orientated towards the stimulation of spin-offs, can be found in the broader technology policy actions that were developed in the early 1980s in most European countries, following the single European Treaty at the EU level. This treaty launched the first framework programme through which the public finance of R&D was organized (European Report on Science and Technology Indicators, 1994). The general idea was that European companies should catch up in terms of R&D with their US equivalents. It was stipulated that especially the so-called new or emerging technologies needed some public support, so action programmes in biotechnology and information and communication technologies were set up.

The emergence of the US biotech industry in the early 1980s and the success of technology clusters such as Silicon Valley and Route 128 often seemed to be a source of inspiration (Saxenian, 1994) for these initiatives. A flourishing venture capital industry in the US is referred to as an important engine for the success of these industries and regions. Hence, in addition to technology subsidies, several national countries have tried to emulate the venture capital success story of the US. Since the first wave of venture capitalists faced difficulties in the early 1990s to exit their portfolio companies, several European countries facilitated the creation of new stock markets for high-tech firms on the model of the National Association of Securities Dealers Automated Quotations (NASDAQ). The EASDAQ in Brussels, the AIM in the UK, le Nouveau Marché in France and the Neuer Markt in Germany were some examples of these markets. This resulted in the mid-1990s in the extremely successful, visible and profitable initial public offerings (IPOs) of some high-tech firms created in the mid and late 1980s. Among the most notable were Lernout & Hauspie in Belgium and Ilog in France. These successful and visible IPOs received a lot of media attention and alerted universities that the technology developed inside their research laboratories might be much more valuable than they had initially thought.

In order to structure the development of technology and accelerate the start-up of IP based spin-offs, universities started to lobby for the introduction of Bayh–Dole-type of acts in the different countries. Along the same lines, they asked for financial support to professionalize the technology transfer services and, subsequently, to financially support the creation of the spin-offs themselves. This policy in the mid-1990s led to an immediate boost of spin-offs. The spin-offs that were created were based on projects that were already inside the university. However, after the sudden boost, few projects were able to make it into a venture despite the abundant amount of public pre-seed finance. Policy-makers and university administrators have therefore become convinced that there was not only a need for financial support programmes, but that researchers also lacked the knowledge to prepare a business plan and to start a company. Since the end of the 1990s, governments have introduced a large range of programmes to help researchers starting up spin-offs.

This chapter examines the specific national policies related to the creation and the development of spin-offs in universities and public research organizations (USOs) in selected European countries. Its focus is mainly the national-level policy because the national governments have played a crucial role in the design of these policies, although we do not ignore the fact that the regions have often played an important role in their implementation.

Section 2.2 presents an overview of the measures taken to promote spin-offs in five countries. In section 2.3 we present two extreme cases with very different research systems, UK and France. Finally, section 2.4 critiques the idea of a convergence of policies towards spin-offs in Europe and discusses the limits of public intervention in this field.

2.2 POLICIES TO SUPPORT THE CREATION OF USOS IN EUROPE

Since the early 1990s, different forms of support for technology-based spin-offs have been set up by most of the scientifically developed European countries (Table 2.1). The creation and development of many of these start-ups are linked to universities and public research organizations, and they demand a wide range of support measures, including incubators, seed money, competitions for funds and other aid, and authorization for civil servants to participate in the creation of a company without losing their status.

In Table 2.1, we give an overview of the most important actions that have been undertaken by the different countries included in the study. A first focus of interest among most countries has been on the regulation of IP. Germany and Belgium have recently changed the law, granting the IP rights on technology developed within the university (and financed by public sources) to the institute instead of to the individual researcher. In Sweden, this debate is in progress, while in the UK the universities themselves have, in most cases, developed an internal regulation which grants them the IP rights. There seems to be a general consensus that this IP legislation is necessary to accelerate the professionalization of TTO offices.

In addition to changes in IP legislation, most countries in Europe have taken a vast number of initiatives to bridge the so-called 'knowledge' and 'finance' gaps (see Table 2.1. for a selected overview). In the UK (challenge funds), Sweden (innovation bridge) and Belgium (Vlaams Innovatiefonds – VINNOF), public funds were set up that specifically invest in spin-offs and high-tech start-ups in general. In France, Germany and Sweden, national incubator programmes were launched to provide active coaching to various spin-offs in each of these countries. The Swedish national incubator programme has as an objective to coordinate the different incubation initiatives taken by the various universities and to professionalize these initiatives. It is illustrative of the strong belief that European governments have in the need for coaching, counselling and advice for spin-offs.

The TTOs are always expected to play a major role in this process. Accordingly, in the different European countries a number of initiatives have been taken to professionalize the staff and the modus operandi of these TTOs. In Belgium and the UK, various financing schemes have been developed to financially support the TTOs and train their managers (see Table 2.1). Also the National Incubation Programme in Sweden has, among others, a mission to accomplish this.

Table 2.1   National policies in Europe (selected countries)

Milestone	Germany	Belgium	UK	France	Sweden
I. Country-specific version Bayh–Dole (BDA) type of Act	2002 Employer Invention Law: invention belongs to the employer not to the professor	1999	No formal BDA. In the case of UK public research organizations the IP is owned by the institution and the royalties associated with the IP are distributed between the relevant parties. The distribution of royalties is organized on an institutional basis	Not relevant since all IP belongs to universities/public research institutes following the 'code de la propriete intellectuelle'	No formal BDA. Discussion going on about whether this Act is desirable
II. Public forms of public support to spin-offs	2000 EXIST: public programme that assists spin-offs through preseed capital and management support 2002 EEF-Fund: researchers can receive a scholarship to start a spin-off	1997 First Public–Private University Capital Fund 2002 Spin-off Post-Docorates: special type of post-docorate which can be used to start a spin-off 2005 Innovation Fund: public fund which supports academic	1998 University Challenge Funds: universities were granted a challenge fund to support spin-off and limited incubation support 2005 De Medici Scheme	1999–2000 11 (pre-) seed capital funds were created to invest in innovative start-ups and take equity 1999 First national competition for the creation of technologically innovative start-ups (30 million euros per year)	2003 Launch of National Public Incubator Programme, sponsoring the coordination between different public incubators 2005 Launch of the Innovation Bridge (a spin-off from VINNOVA)

III. Financial support to TTOs	2002 22 TTOs (*patentverwertungs-agenturen*) were established which take care of IP management	spin-offs in collaboration with the university preseed funds	2002 Each TTO in a Flemish (Belgian) university receives a public financial support to professionalize its activities	2001 HEIF (Higher Education Innovation Fund) provides a permanent flow of financial support. Initiatives include UCF (University Challenge Funds total £60m) and SEC (science enterprise challenge, total £28.9 m), with goal to establish a network of centres in UK universities to teach entrepreneurship and science commercialization to scientists and engineers at all stages of their careers	1999–2000 31 incubators were supported to offer support in training, consultancy and finance In 2004, six Houses of Entrepreneurship were created on university campuses to raise student awareness	Since 1994 seven broker institutions called Technology Bridging Foundations (*Teknikbrostiftelser*) have been established in major university regions. Their role seems to be to perform the functions undertaken by university TTOs in other countries. In addition, four foundations, such as the Foundation for Knowledge and Competence Development, have been established which, among other things, are intended to provide a bridge between the

Table 2.1 (continued)

Milestone	Germany	Belgium	UK	France	Sweden
IV. Invention disclosures	1999 Researchers are obliged to disclose inventions to universities		In principle, researchers obliged to disclose inventions to universities	2000 Each professor is obliged to disclose inventions to the TTO	university and industry. No obligation for disclosure as academic owns the IP

In conclusion, most government initiatives aimed at the promotion of spin-offs share the idea that economic growth depends heavily on the development of technology transfer between public research and industry, especially through the creation of new technology-based firms. These policies are often part of a broader range of measures aimed at bridging the gap between academia and industry. As illustrated by the selected examples in Table 2.1, most of the policy focus lies in the pre-commercial or pre-founding phase of spin-off creation. Some examples are: project identification in laboratories, business training for researchers; advice and counselling; business plan competitions; incubator support; seed money and financing for high-tech start-ups.

The following section describes the general framework within which these government initiatives are taken.

2.2.1 Creation of a Framework

The measures taken in recent years were intended to create a framework to promote an 'entrepreneurial culture' and 'a better exploitation of basic science and technology' in (universities, research institutions, engineering schools, and so on. There are many examples of how different countries took actions to create these framework conditions (Callan, 2001; Clarysse et al., 2000). In the UK, for example, the government published a white paper at the end of 1998 on competitiveness (*Our Competitive Future: Building the Knowledge Economy*) and one in 2000 on research and technology transfer (*Science and Innovation: Excellence and Opportunity*) (DTI, 1998; 2000). These two reports define 'a new approach to industrial policy based on knowledge, competencies and creativity' and propose measures that primarily concern 'technology transfer and the creation of high-tech firms'.

In France, the Innovation Act of 12 July 1999 aims primarily at 'promoting the creation of technologically innovative firms'. In Italy, the 27 July 1999 decree enables university researchers and academic staff to be seconded to start-ups, and the industry ministry's November 2000 white paper defines the mobilization of financial resources for technology spin-offs from research. In Germany, the EXIST programme ('creators of firms from higher-education institutions') was set up 'to create a favourable climate for university research spin-off and to increase the number of start-ups from academic institutions' (Bmb+f, 2000) (see Box 2.1).

Also in Sweden, the public authorities have done a lot to change attitudes and provide a framework for universities to commercialize new technology.

BOX 2.1   A FRAMEWORK TO FACILITATE
SPIN-OFFS AND START-UPS FROM
UNIVERSITIES AND PUBLIC RESEARCH
ORGANIZATIONS: THE GERMAN EXIST
PROGRAMME

In 1998, the Federal Ministry of Education and Research launched the 'EXIST – University-based start-ups' programme. The aim is to increase the number of innovative start-ups and to establish a culture of entrepreneurship in higher education institutes. The 'EXIST – University-based start-ups' programme has four main objectives:

● to create a 'culture of entrepreneurship' in teaching, research and administration at higher education institutions
● to increase knowledge spillover into economic value added – in line with the responsibility of higher education institutions for technology transfer, newly formulated in the Federal Higher Education Framework Law (1998), which introduced technology transfer as a third mission to the two traditional missions of teaching and research
● the goal-directed promotion of the large potential for business ideas and entrepreneurs at higher education institutions and research establishments
● to increase significatively the number of innovative start-ups and to create new jobs accordingly.

Source: various official documents and BMFT website: http://www.bmbf.de/en.

In the second half of the 1990s, changes in legislation have emphasized the cooperation with the surrounding community. Important resources were allocated to two governmental agencies: Teknikbro stiftelserna (Foundation for technology transfer) and VINNOVA (the Swedish agency for innovation systems). Their purpose is to help universities to transfer technology and new knowledge in various ways to the community with an emphasis on the creation of academic spin-offs (Delmar et Sölvell, 2004). In Belgium, the situation is more complex since the country consists of three regions each of which have their own government responsible for most of the matters related to innovation and technology policy. In

Flanders, the largest autonomous region in Belgium, an Innovation Decree was passed in 1999 which specifically approved and encouraged the public support of innovation instead of technology development activities. In this Decree, there was a section on public support of innovative start-ups. In addition, separate funding to professionalize the TTO services at the universities in the region was approved.

In line with the legal framework that was created, administrators in the various countries have developed a range of programmes to nurture start-ups. These programmes can be grouped into five different categories: first, a number of programmes deal with the status of the researchers; second, specific attention is devoted to business training for academics; third, various governments have stimulated regional initiatives through public financing of bottom up project; fourth, a range of programmes specifically focus on incubation activities and, finally, some programmes are related to the (pre-)seed financing of spin-offs. We describe each of these in the following paragraphs.

Researchers' status

In several countries, the civil servant status of an academic prevents him from participating in the creation of a private enterprise in order to transfer their research results. In France this status has been amended, so that state employees can now create a firm and leave their laboratory without losing their status (with the possibility of returning to the institution in case of failure), or participate in the creation of a firm without leaving their laboratory. In Italy a recent Decree allows academics–researchers to be seconded to industry, primarily to SMIs (small and medium-sized industries) and start-ups, for a period of four years, renewable once. A similar programme has existed since 2002 in Flanders and since 1999 in Wallonia. In these autonomous regions in Belgium, the post-doctoral researchers can make use of a scholarship to get involved in the start-up process of a spin-off company. In Germany, France and Flanders a return to the parent institution in case of failure of the start-up is provided for. For example, this is the case with the Max-Planck Institutes in Germany (Ambassade de France en République Fédérale d'Allemagne, 2000).

Business training for academics

Although researcher status is without doubt a condition sine qua non to create spin-off activity, it is not sufficient in itself. Therefore, a number of countries have developed specific programmes that train and coach researchers to become an entrepreneur (especially young PhDs). Several classes on entrepreneurship open to researchers, have been set up in universities, primarily in Northern European countries. The entrepreneurship programmes of the universities of Linköping and Chalmers in Sweden and the KUL in Belgium, are entrepreneurial training schemes orientated towards the training and coaching of entrepreneurs to write a business plan and set up a business. Usually, they are financed by regional or national government funds. Examples include universities in the UK which, since 1998, have been receiving funds from the Science Enterprise Challenge. This programme assists the creation of entrepreneurship centres in universities for training scientists in the commercialization of research results (see below).

The organization of entrepreneurial training courses for researchers might contribute to the awareness of the latter about entrepreneurship and entrepreneurial programmes. However, it remains a rather passive form of giving incentives. Therefore, countries decided to create pull factors to encourage researchers into entrepreneurial activities and to financially support business plan competitions that could pull researches into entrepreneurial activities.

Public support of incubation and spin-off support activities
Competitions to stimulate the creation of innovative firms are proliferating and, at regional and national levels, constitute an important tool of policies to financially support those projects judged as the most promising. In Germany, innovation and technology transfer, especially through start-ups, are a government priority. Many competitions are held to finance German universities and their regional partners that create a network of support for high-tech start-ups, primarily in biotechnology or to select and to finance new academic start-ups (see Box 2.2).

In France, the 'National competition for the creation of technologically innovative firms', launched by the research ministry in 1999, has drawn over 9500 candidates. Close to 1400 have been rewarded in the 'emergent' and 'creation-development' categories. In addition to this financial aid, the award winners are put into contact with various partners. Some of the winning projects are then hosted in a government incubator.

The European Commission the Gate2Growth Programme launched through which incubators, technology transfer offices, pre-seed capital funds and alike were financed to exchange their experiences and analyse best practices.

Incubators and support structures for projects
Following the creation of science parks in the 1980s (the majority of which have maintained few ties with universities, even if they are geographically close), business incubators have been the main tool used in the 1990s by universities and research institutions to promote the creation of new enterprises. These incubators (which offer premises and advice to new

---

BOX 2.2   EXAMPLES OF COMPETITION : THE NATIONAL COMPETITIONS OF THE GERMAN BMFT IN THE FIELD OF BIOTECHNOLOGIES

The Federal Ministry of Education and Research has launched different national competitions in the field of biotechnologies: some to stimulate fundamental research, some to facilitate the technology transfer and innovation, but the majority are orientated towards the creation of start-ups (BioRegio, BioChance, BioChancePlus, ExistGO-Bio, BioFuture).

BioRegio: to mobilize the regions to foster the creation of start-ups and technology transfer in the field of biotechnology. The 29 bioregions coordinate financial sources and R&D potential at the regional level. They create the necessary structures of interface for the transfer of technologies. 90 million euros have been invested by the BMBF between 1997 and 2005.

BioChance: to give support to young enterprises for industrial R&D in biotechnology (50 million euros invested by the BMFT and 150 million euros from private parties between 2004 and 2006).

BioChancePlus: for the consolidation and growth of young enterprises through industrial R&D in modern biotechnologies. 100 million euros invested by the BMBF between 2004 and 2006.

BioFuture: competition in fundamental research to encourage the work of young researchers and to give them the opportunity to create a company. Fifty-one projects have been helped with 75 million euros between 1998 and 2005.

ExistGO-Bio: support for the creation of new companies in the field of biotechnology and the commercialization of new processes in biosciences. 150 million euros will be invested by the BMBF between 2005 and 2010.

Source: www.bmft.de; www.bioregio.com; Ambassade de France à Berlin (2006).

---

firms) are generally financed by regional or national governments. New incubators are usually attached to research laboratories. They provide start-ups with access to a range of services, from premises and equipment to financing, consultancy, training, contacts with varied partners (Phan et al., 2005).

In France, Belgium, the UK, Germany and Sweden, the majority of these incubators were created in the early 2000s. For example in Sweden, legislative changes and the availability of resources led to the establishment of an important number of incubators at the end of the 1990s and the beginning of the 2000s. These incubators typically use a four step programme: (1) screening of rough idea, (2) turning the idea to a commercial offer and training the entrepreneurs, (3) establishment of a new venture,

---

BOX 2.3   INCUBATION MANAGEMENT IN SWEDEN

For a long time, incubators were run more on the basis of enthusiasm than professionalism. Many times, the incubators were managed by former students that had an interest in entrepreneurship and who wanted to get some practical experience before seeking a job in the commercial sector. However, with the changes in legislation and the availability of resources the profiles of the employees have shifted. During the 2000–2002 period managers of incubators were recruited from academic administration, banking and the consultancy sector. Most of the managers do not have a substantial business or entrepreneurial background. However, this is not necessarily a problem as most of the tasks are related directly to consulting or supporting specific ventures. Work rather focuses on the daily management of the incubator, interacting with university administration, ensuring financing, contacting teachers and relevant ad hoc personnel for the training programs, and promoting the incubator within the university and outside the university. Hence, the role of incubator manager is that of manager and network broker. He or she has to develop the network of stakeholders around the incubator, such as entrepreneurs with a background in the specific university, legal aid, and business developers, and investors. Much of the practical work of due diligence of projects, courses and support in specific areas are provided by others than the incubator managers. Recently, there has been a trend for incubator managers to become more professional and directed towards the work of the incubator. The reason is that incubators have become players that are taken for granted by all stakeholders after three to four years of operations.

Source: Delmar and Sölvell (2005).

and (4) the growth and expansion of this venture (Delmar and Sölvell, 2004). They have a small number of employees and are mainly financed by public money. Across Europe, these incubators have strong links with the regional or local authorities. Several studies have shown that one of the difficulties of the European incubators is the personal background of the people in charge of their management (for example, Siegel et al., 2003b).

The value added of the various incubation initiatives remains questionable however. In a study of three of the five countries covered by the book (Germany, Belgium and Sweden), we identified a 'prominent' incubator which was selected by the local government sponsors of incubation programmes as a 'best practice'. We analysed the value added of these incubators both from the incubator tenant point of view and from the company point of view. It was clear that the only value added of the incubator was related to facility management. None of the so-called important coaching activities such as business plan guidance, business coaching, and so on were found by the entrepreneurs to be important. A summary of this evaluation is discussed at the end of this chapter.

In addition to the more traditional incubators that offer basic facility management services, some research incubators have been created which specifically focus on spin-offs as tenant companies. Examples are the IMEC in Belgium, Chalmers Innovation in Sweden and INRIA in France. They have set up specific structures to nurture the process of business creation and to accumulate the capital necessary for investments (a detailed example of Chalmers is presented in Box 2.4). These incubation activities are much more closely linked to the research base on which the start-ups are created. As such, in depth knowledge of the technology is provided. Incubation usually implies the development of a good IP Regime to optimize the chances of a trade sale, the establishment of contacts with the downstream industry and pre-seed financing of preliminary business plans (Moray and Clarysse, 2005).

Pre-seed capital funds and stimulation of funding for USOs
Since most venture capital firms are not prepared to finance the early phases of university spin-offs, government authorities in many countries have set up (pre)-seed capital funds within public-sector research institutions. Since the 1990s, various government initiatives have been implemented in several European countries to stimulate funding for new high-tech firms. These funds are supposed to enable universities to commercially exploit their own research results. In most European countries, the financial opportunities for pre-seed capital funds are multiple.

In general, the different initiatives can be divided into six types of measures: (1) publicly owned (100 per cent) funds focused in pre-seed and

BOX 2.4   CHALMERS INCUBATOR IN SWEDEN

Chalmers Innovation was founded based upon a donation of 5 million euros by the Sten A Olsson Foundation for Research and Culture in 1997. The donation enabled the development of a new centre for 'innovation related activities' near the Chalmers University of Technology – a business incubator – in 1999. Chalmers Innovation's mission is threefold. First, the incubator offers a modern workplace where people, ideas and companies are encouraged to grow and to develop. The office facilities are flexible and can be arranged in such a way they meet every company's needs. Secondly, Chalmers Innovation offers a wide variety of competences to the start-up companies. More specifically, a team of three senior and three junior business developers/coaches focuses on fast-growing technology-based start-up companies. The last part of Chalmers' mission, providing access to external financing, is probably the most important issue for young companies. The success of most technology-based start-ups depends on external financing at some point in time.

Chalmers Innovation started with a capital of 5 million euros. Seventy per cent of the total amount was used to build the business incubation centre. This left only 1.5 million euros available to cover working expenses, such as maintenance of the facilities and the staff's salary costs. Therefore, the incubator needed some additional sources of income in order to be sustainable. It has three sources of revenue. As for most incubators, a first important source of income is the rent for office space. However, spin-offs in the pre-incubation phase (12 in 2003) do not pay any rent! The second source of income is the support Chalmers Innovation receives from government agencies. For example, the centre received 400 000 euros from VINNOVA and the Technology Bridge Funds and 20 000 euros from Nutek in 2003. The last income flow is much more uncertain, namely the return on equity held by Chalmers Innovation in the companies. Chalmers Innovation holds between 5 and 20 per cent equity in the companies housed at the incubator. After some time, the incubator hopes to make a couple of profitable exits which will generate new revenue. Up till now, Chalmers has not received any significant revenues through exits.

The incubation of the companies at Chalmers Innovation consists of two phases. The first phase is the pre-incubation phase.

This six-month period is used to develop a solid business plan, attract people with business experience and start looking for external investors (especially Chalmers Invest). Once the company is founded, a three-year incubation period at Chalmers Innovation begins.

Chalmers incubation offers several services to its tenant spin-offs. During pre-incubation, the incubator staff looks for a suitable entrepreneur to complete the (often) inexperienced teams. They typically look for a person who started a company, was quite successful and wants a new challenge. In most cases, this person will not invest in the company. Chalmers Innovation has 300 000 euros (soft money) available to support teams during the pre-incubation period. The money is provided by Chalmers Invest and the Technology Bridge Foundations, and the government provides 50 per cent. There are no conditions attached to this sum; it is similar to a grant. With this 'public relations' fund, Chalmers Innovation can support ten teams (30 000 euros per team). The teams use the funds for market research, IP feasibility studies and so on. Besides the rent-free incubator's facilities, the teams are coached by Chalmers Innovation staff. A business coach is responsible for two teams at the same time. Their task is to guide the team through the business plan development process, for which no fee is charged. Instead, Chalmers Innovation gets 5 per cent of the equity in the newly established company. The focus during the incubation phase is to provide capital to the newly founded, high-tech companies. The start capital of the companies is provided by several parties (seed funds and business angels). The most important capital provider at start-up is Chalmers Invest. This closely related venture capitalist invests typically 200 000 euros in a company. The incubation centre sometimes invests between 10 000 and 50 000 euros per company (typically 30 000 euros) to persuade other investors to invest in the company.

From the moment growth takes off, a lot of companies need additional money. To make this accessible for the companies, Chalmers Innovation works together with InnovationsKapital. However, not all companies have the same growth path nor want to take venture capitalists on board at an early stage. Those companies would face a financing gap if it was not for cooperation with the Connect business angels network.

Source: Clarysse and Bruneel (forthcoming).

seed stages, (2) public–private partnerships with the same focus as the previous, (3) small business investment companies (SBIC)-type of refinance schemes, (4) guarantee schemes (risk sharing), (5) fiscal incentives in the form of tax reduction on value added or income tax deduction and (6) incubation schemes (see Table 2.2). Some of these schemes are common across Europe while others relate to particular countries.

Some governments have created public funds with the specific aim of financing (high-tech) spin-offs at a very early stage. These funds only have public parties as institutional investors and are therefore publicly owned, such as the Flemish (Belgian) VINNOF. This fund has a budget of 100 million euros and is involved in *pre-seed, seed* and *early stage venture capital.* In the pre-seed and seed stage, additional coaching is given to improve business plans and finance market research activities. France is another country in our study, which has created a 100 per cent public fund (one-third Caisse des Dépôts et Consignations [CDC],[1] one-third French State and one-third European Investment Fund) to finance the pre-seed and seed stage (Fonds de co-investissement pour les jeunes entreprises [FCJE]. The objective of this fund of co-investment for young companies, managed by CDC-Entreprises, is to take minority stakes in French technological companies that are less than seven years old, alongside VC funds established in European countries. The FCJE intervenes in the sectors where private financings are most difficult to mobilize, in particular in the biotechnology sector.

A second category of policy initiatives involves the establishment of public–private partnerships set up to finance (high-tech) start-ups. Public investment in these funds varies from 10 per cent to over 90 per cent. Almost every European country has its own public–private partnership fund. A specific category of such partnerships are the university funds. Pressure from government on universities to commercialize IP (HM Treasury and DTI, 1998) has been accompanied by the establishment of various programmes to facilitate the process. Usually, the establishment of seed and pre-seed funds associated with the university are part of this process. University funds almost always invest exclusively in start-ups that are based on technology developed at the parent institution with which they are associated. The degree of public involvement varies from country to country. Programmes such as University Challenge Fund (UCF) in the UK comprise up to 77 per cent public capital, while the University Seed Funds in Belgium (Flanders) only have 20 per cent public capital, on average.

A third, much less popular, set of initiatives is inspired by the US Small Business Investment Companies (SBIC) scheme. In these schemes, the VC fund that invests in a (high-tech) spin-off can co-finance its investment by a

Table 2.2   Types of public finance support programmes

Type of programme	Description	Example
Public fund	100% publicly owned funds focused on pre-seed and/or seed stages	Twinning Growth Fund and Biopartner (Netherlands)
Public/private equity fund	Fund in which government and private sector co-invest with same focus as previous	University Challenge Funds (UK) Technologiebeteilung-gesellschaft (Germany) Fonds d'amorçage (France)
SBIC-type of refinance schemes	Schemes which leverage the deals made by adding public money to the private investment	Arkimedes (Belgium) SBIC (USA) Kreditanstalt für Wiederaufbau (Germany)
Guarantee schemes	Insurance schemes which guarantee (part) of the VC money in case of bankruptcy	Various, in each country
Fiscal incentives	Tax reduction scheme on value added or income tax deduction	Aunt Agaath Scheme (Nl) 'Jeune Entreprise Innovante' status (France) Trust Capital Funds (UK)
Incubation scheme	Scheme which pays the salaries of coaches, which offers facilities and/or which offers network opportunities	National Incubator Programme (Sweden) DIILI Programme (Finland) Innovationsmiljoer (Denmark) Exist (Germany) Incubateurs Publics (France)

loan which is granted by the government. As the loan is to be reimbursed at a fixed, usually below market rate, the scheme increases the potential profit that can be made on such an investment. It does not, however, decrease the risk for the venture capital fund. In Europe, only Germany (Kreditanstalt für Wiederaufbau) and Belgium (Archimedes) have such programmes in place.

The fourth category of policy measures aims to reduce the risk to the venture capital firms through guarantee schemes. If a start-up fails, the government can reimburse the venture capital firm which qualifies for the scheme for (part of) its lost investment. There is no consensus about the effectiveness of these schemes since some tend to argue that they give an incentive to VC funds to let their portfolio companies go bankrupt in order to recover at least part of their money invested instead of trying to save these companies. Despite this lack of consensus, such a guarantee scheme exists in almost every European country.

A fifth form of policy measure comprises the 'fiscal incentives'. These provide tax reductions on capital gains created by investments or they allow investors in venture capital funds that qualify for the scheme to offset (parts of) their investment against taxes. In the UK, VC Trusts and the Enterprise Investment Scheme provide private investors with tax relief on income and capital with venture capital firms involved in managing the trusts. In the Netherlands, private investors who invest in small businesses created by relatives receive a significant deduction in income taxes through the Tante Agaath Scheme. In France, the status 'Jeune Entreprise Innovante' (JE – Young Innovative Enterprise) provides a tax advantage consisting of a total exemption of profits for three years, followed by a partial exemption of 50 per cent for a further two years. Companies qualifying for the JEI are exonerated from payment of the employers' share of social security payments for researchers, technicians, managers of R&D projects and the lawyers in charge of industrial protection. In Belgium (Privak system), the surplus value on shares invested in venture capital companies that qualify under specific criteria is subject to a much lower tax scheme.

Finally, a sixth form of support refers to business incubation schemes. In the late 1990s, the governments in France and Sweden launched their National Incubation Programmes (Jacob et al., 2003). Also the German EXIST programme and the Danish Innovationsmiljoer are incubation-like initiatives. In these initiatives, governments usually do not provide direct pre-seed or seed capital, but provide infrastructure and management support for high-tech start-ups. Often, the incubator is linked to a university or public research institute.

To sum up, this section suggests an apparent convergence between the different types of action implemented by national and regional governments and public-sector research institutions, in countries as different as the UK, Germany, Scandinavian countries, France, Belgium, and so on. Distinct differences exist between these countries, but they seem secondary compared to the goal and range of interventions presented above. The great difference between the liberal model and the centralized model with extensive government intervention seems to be neutralized by an imitation effect. The terms and types of government intervention relating to spin-off of public-sector research are often the same in very different national configurations.

The following sections describe the UK and the French case, respectively, in detail.

2.3 POLICIES TO FOSTER THE CREATION OF ACADEMIC SPIN-OFFS IN THE UK AND FRANCE

2.3.1 The UK

Since the end of the 1990s, the UK government has launched different funding schemes to support universities in developing the commercialization of their research. The main emphasis has been upon the establishment of an entrepreneurial culture in which scientific capabilities are exploited through start-up and spin-off companies (Georghiou, 2001). Four main initiatives have been taken to foster the creation of start-ups based on public-sector research: the University Challenge Fund, the Science Enterprise Challenge, the Public Sector Research Exploitation Fund and the Higher Education Innovation Fund. The impact of these initiatives has been evaluated by the Department of Trade and Industry (SQW, 2005).

Researchers' status
Unlike the French, UK academics are not civil servants but are directly employed by the universities to which they are attached. Academics in the UK can create companies and hold equity stakes in those companies. These companies may or may not be related to the formal IP generated as part of the academic's employment. Traditionally, the approach to enforcing ownership of IP was fairly loose, but more recently universities have asserted their ownership rights. This is in line with the provision of the UK Patent Act 1997 which states that inventions of employees who may reasonably be expected to make inventions are clearly owned by their employer, as long as this is stated in an employment contract. The approach to spin-off creation is decentralized, which enables universities to adopt different approaches to negotiate the relative equity stakes division between the university itself and the researcher or academic.

Business training for academics
To decrease the knowledge gap, specific efforts were undertaken to provide entrepreneurial training to academics. The Science Enterprise Challenge scheme in the UK addresses the need for training.

The Science Enterprise Challenge (SEC) was launched in 1999. It is a part of the government's strategy to introduce a 'third mission' for higher education, alongside teaching and research, to encourage the transfer of science and technology innovation to the business sector. Its goal was to establish a network of centres in UK universities to teach entrepreneurship and science commercialization to scientists and engineers at all stages of their careers. The SEC resulted in the creation of 13 science enterprise centres involving over 60 UK universities and higher education institutes, which provide educational, training and financial services to would-be academic and graduate student entrepreneurs. A total of 43.35 million euros has been allocated so far by means of a challenge competition. As for the UCFs, the majority of the centres are collaborative (three exceptions are Cambridge University, Imperial College and Oxford University). The centres focus on two main areas of activity: teaching of enterprise and entrepreneurship to science and technology students; encouraging the growth of new businesses by supporting start-ups, including spin-off companies based on innovative ideas developed by students, and faculty within the universities.

These centres are essentially engaged in promoting the exploitation of IP, by licensing or spin-off formation and by introducing entrepreneurship into the curriculum, at both undergraduate and postgraduate levels. On the issue of IP exploitation, three approaches have been adopted: no support provided (where the university has an established IP support office), delivery by staff located in the centre, and subcontracting to existing support services. The innovative aspects of the science enterprise centres relate more closely to a wide diversity of curriculum development. This diversity includes student modules at different levels, workshops about technology commercialization at the postgraduate level, business plan competitions, summer schools, business-related project work and postgraduate degrees with an enterprise focus. The majority of these modules are on a voluntary basis and have been incorporated into existing modules. With the centres, entreprises modules are embedded in the curriculum of a substantial number of science and engineering students. The centres have established an infrastructure for enterprise education, the know-how to design and deliver programmes and enterprise education for substantial numbers of students. However, it is too early for this to be reflected in economic impacts (SQW, 2005).

Incubators and support structures for projects
Both universities and public research institutes are encouraged in the UK to set up various sorts of incubation and support schemes. Both the Public Sector Research Exploitation Fund (PSRE) and the Higher Education Innovation Fund (HEIF) have been launched to financially support this kind of activity.

Higher Education Innovation Fund   The HEIF builds on and follows the third stream of funding initiated by the Higher Education Reach-out to Business and the Community Fund (HEROBC). Alongside their traditional roles of teaching and research, the public authorities asked to higher education institutions and public-sector research establishments to adopt a further role as stimulators and facilitators of knowledge transfer to business and society. Funds are awarded to support universities and colleges in this third stream engagement, increasing their capability to respond to the needs of business, public services and the wider community, and to transfer knowledge.

A total of 136 bids were submitted in July 2001 for funding up to August 2004, 89 awards were confirmed under the HEIF ranging from 300 000 to 7.5 million euros, paid over three years, including 16 collaborative projects. The HEIF provided around 120 million euros to English higher education institutions over the period 2001–04.

Unlike the two previous initiatives, the HEIF – which is only available to English institutions – will not focus on start-ups but is encouraging proposals across the full range of academic activities: the establishment and strengthening of industrial liaison offices, internal promotion of commercialization, IP expertise, incubation support, dialogue with businesses, business advice and mentoring. The HEIF provides direct financing support for a project that strengthens connections between universities and firms. In this sense, the HEIF provides a framework and facilitates the creation of university spin-offs and start-ups.

A second round of HEIF (HEIF 2) has been allocated for the period 2004–06. This round took into account one of the conclusions of the *Lambert Review* (Lambert, 2003) in relation to technology transfer offices. The *Lambert Review* noted that a 'barrier to commercialising university IP lies in the variable quality of technology transfer offices. Most universities run their own technology transfer operations, but only a few have a strong enough research base to be able to build high-quality offices on their own' (p. 5). The review recommended the development of shared services in technology transfer on a regional basis and to improve the recruitment and training of technology transfer staff. The HEIF2 continues and develops the work of the first round of the HEIF, supporting interactions between higher education institutions (HEIs) and business, and between HEIs and the wider community. The HEIF 2 also incorporates activities based on current Science Enterprise Challenge and University Challenge initiatives in England. The HEIF 2 therefore represents a consolidated third stream of funding, complementing core funding to institutions for research, and for learning and teaching. After extensive discussions with academic, business and other stakeholders, the goverment has confirmed the scale of funding for

HEIF 3 – up to 349 million euros to HEIs in England, to be allocated over the period August 2006 to July 2008. This is to be allocated substantially on the basis of a formula in order to make the HEIF funding more stable and predictable, and hence more embedded in HEIs' strategic planning.

The major impacts of the HEIF have been on knowledge transfer strategy and organization, the generation of a more positive attitude among scientific staff towards working with businesses, and the improvement and simplification of access by business to resources in higher education (SQW, 2005).

Public Sector Research Exploitation Fund   Public-sector research establishments that are not universities receive similar government funding through the PSRE. This fund was a response to the Baker Report (Baker, 1999) on realizing the economic potential of public-sector research establishments. The PSRE initiative was set up to help public-sector organizations other than universities make the most of their research. It is open to all public-sector organizations that carry out research, including Research Council Institutes, NHS Trusts, research institutions owned by government departments, and major museums. A total of 37.5 million euros was provided in first (October 2001) and second rounds to enable public-sector research establishments to develop their capacity to exploit their science and technology potential and to provide seed funding to support the very early stages of business formation from ideas emerging out of research in the public sector science base. Third-round awards worth 37.5 million euros were announced in January 2006.

The PSRE projects are focused on knowledge transfer though licensing and spin-offs. Many PSREs were previously involved in knowledge transfer activities but the timescales and uncertainties attached to intellectual property commercialization, together with limited core funding in some cases, meant that IP exploitation expertise was limited, and in some institutions non-existent prior to PSRE (SQW, 2005). Although funded institutions have established an infrastructure for IP exploitation appropriate to their needs, the revenues generated are still at a low level and activities are unlikely to be sustained without further funding rounds (SQW, 2005).

Ultimately, UK policy is characterized by a large number of initiatives to develop this third stream engagement of HEIs, increasing their capability to respond to the needs of business, public services and the wider community, and to transfer knowledge. The HEIF, the UCF and the SEC form part of a systematic process to create this third stream of funding for universities, in addition to revenue derived from teaching and research.

The HEIF and the PSRE provide direct financing support for the establishment and strengthening of industrial liaison offices, internal promotion of commercialization, IP expertise, and projects that strengthen connections between universities and firms. They provide a framework that is complemented by different schemes that have been designed to develop entrepreneurship and business skills and to take ideas from the laboratory to the market. These initiatives try, first, to fill the *knowledge gap*, as with the Science Enterprise Challenge's aim to develop the teaching of entrepreneurship in the sciences and engineering curricula, and provides the opportunity for university researchers and people with business experience to work together. Secondly, these initiatives aim to address the *financial gap*, as with the University Challenge Funds' attempts to provide funding for the first stage of research commercialization, such as for scoping research, market studies, prototypes development and setting up spin-off firms.

In the UK, academic spin-off firm support forms part of a larger policy that tries to develop knowledge transfer between the universities and business and society. However, there is a general consensus emerging in the UK that although spin-offs are an important means for the commercialization and exploitation of new knowledge and the transfer of technology, they are not the only way. This point was emphasized with the publication in December 2003 of the *Lambert Review of Business–University Collaboration*. This report suggested that there has been too much emphasis on developing university spin-offs, a good number of which may not prove to be sustainable, and not enough on licensing technology to industry. The recommendation was that the balance needed to be redressed towards licensing as this is less resource-intensive and has a higher probability of getting technology to market. The *Lambert Review* also recommended increasing the availability of proof of concept funding to establish whether a new technology is commercially viable or not.

Pre-seed capital funds and stimulation of funding for USOs
Finally, we discuss a very specific scheme which has been developed in the UK to financially support spin-offs in the pre-seed and seed phase.

University Challenge Fund the UCF provides VC funding for university-based spin-offs. Its purpose is to increase the availability of early stage funds for universities to overcome the perceived finance gap. The aim is for universities to establish their own seed funds with the help of the University Challenge money and for the seed funds to enable academics to scope out the commercial potential or research outcomes and take the first steps towards commercializing the research, thus addressing the seedcorn-funding gap (Georghiou, 2001). The UCF was launched in March 1998 as a 67.5 million euros seed capital fund to encourage the exploitation of scientific discoveries in universities. The government contributed 37.5 million euros to the

UCF while additional funding was provided by the Wellcome Trust (27 million euros) and the Gatsby Charitable Foundation (3 million euros). In October 2001, the second round, a further 27.5 million euros was awarded.[2]

This total funding of 90 million euros was apportioned to 15 successful bids in the first round, and a further five in the second (one fund got first and second round money). Nineteen different UCFs are in operation across the UK. These funds are associated with different universities (involving between two and six universities or research institutions), except Imperial College and Oxford University. Universities were required to contribute a minimum of 25 per cent of total fund value. The maximum total investment in any one project was restricted to 375000 euros.

2.3.2   France

Policy-makers in France have tried to replicate the US model of technology transfer. During the first half of the 1990s, the government improved the environment for technology start-ups. Various tools were modified to support research and innovation in SMEs, such as intellectual property law, turnover tax, and legislation on venture capital. A new Research and Innovation Act to promote the creation of technological firms from the public research sector was adopted in 1999. This law introduced a new legal framework for the creation of companies by academics. This new researchers' status was accompanied by three main incentives for the creation of companies by the Ministry for Research: competitions, incubators and seed capital funds.

Researchers' status
In France, the civil servant status of academics traditionally prevented them from participating in the creation of a private enterprise to transfer their research results. In 1999, this status was amended, so that state employees or civil servants[3] can now create a firm and leave their laboratory without losing their status (with the possibility of returning to the institution in case of failure), or can participate in the creation of a firm without leaving their laboratory. The Research and Innovation Act 1999 is dedicated to facilitate the involvement of researchers in the creation or development of innovative companies or to provide scientific assistance and even participate on the board. With this Act, researchers, teacher-researchers, engineers, young PhD students, technical and administrative staff can be involved in the creation of a company to exploit their research work. They are authorized to participate as a partner or manager of the new company, for a period of time (a maximum of six years) at the end of which they can choose between returning to the public sector or staying in the company. The law,

therefore, allows the public sector (university or research laboratory) to pay the salary of the creator of the company during the start-up phase. The law also prevents those who are involved in starting up companies from being penalized in terms of their research careers. A contract defines the links between the company and the research establishment whose work is being exploited. Research staff can provide their scientific support for a company that develops their research work, while they remain in the public sector. The law also allows a research employee to contribute to the capital of a company that commercializes his/her research work. His share could initially be up to 15 per cent of the capital of the company, although in March 2006 this percentage was raised to 49 per cent. The employee agrees, in return, not to take part in any negotiations between the university or research laboratory and the spin-off company. Researchers and teacher-researchers can be members of the management of a company but they cannot be the chief executive officer or the chief operating officer of the firm nor be a member of the board. The request must be submitted to the authority (organization, university, and so on) responsible for the research staff. The authority must then notify, for approval, the National Public Sector Ethics Committee (Commission Nationale de Déontologie). This committee can (or not) enable the academics to take part in a new firm project according to the three cases below. The goal of this committee is to avoid conflicts of interest, which can easily occur in the commercial exploitation of public research results or in the spinning off of activities from public research results, and to guarantee the interest of the public side in these commercialization activities of public research results.

Business training for academics
In recent years, the French Ministry for Research has supported actions aimed at raising awareness and providing entrepreneurship training for young people. In 2001, an Observatory of Teaching Practices in Entrepreneurship (OPPE) was created by the Ministry for Research, the Ministry of Industry, the Agence Pour la Création d'Entreprises (APCE) and the Académie de l'Entrepreneuriat (an association of academics working in the field of entrepreneurship). This Observatory has three main objectives: to carry out an inventory of actions relating to the teaching of entrepreneurship in various establishments, to diffuse this knowledge, methods and practices, and to evaluate the effects of the training programmes in the field of entrepreneurship and to carry out specific studies on related topics. In 2004, Maisons de l'Entrepreneuriat were created in six universities and higher teaching institutions. These establishments are encouraged to enforce the links with companies, to lay down specific policies to develop entrepreneurship, and to establish publicity campaigns

about entrepreneurship for students, researchers and academics. The Maisons provide courses, entrepreneurship clubs for students, a resource centre, business plan competitions, entrepreneurial forums and guides for the student entrepreneur, and develop partnerships with local economic actors and involve the latter in the projects. They have integrated different national or international networks on the topic of entrepreneurship.

Incubators and support structures for projects
The first 'National competition for the creation of technologically innovative firms', was launched in 1999. The competition is open to people residing in France or in a member state of the European Community, as well as to French people residing abroad whose project fits the requirements. In 2005, the seventh of these competitions will have a total budget of 30 million euros provided by the ministry in charge of Research (18 million euros) with the support of the European Social Fund (7 million euros) and of ANVAR (the French Agency of Innovation) (5 million euros). The categories of the competition make it possible for people either to validate a project at the idea stage or to make the idea more concrete by creating a company.

The French Innovation Act allowed higher educational and research establishments to set up incubators for the purpose of providing premises, equipment and material for those hoping to create companies or for young companies. This measure encourages in particular, the creation of high-technology companies by research staff and students. The Research Ministry, with the support of the European Social Fund, subsidizes these incubators for a three-year period and covers 50 per cent of their expenditure. The remaining 50 per cent is financed by local and regional authorities.

A call for tender, initiated in 1999 and renewed in 2000, aimed to encourage the implementation of new structures for incubation, coming in particular, but not only, from higher education establishments or research. The scheme's main preference was to provide support for new projects set up in partnership. A company incubator is defined as a place hosting and assisting holders of innovative firm start-up projects. It offers them support in training, consultancy and financing, and accommodation until they join a technology park, and can support the cost of industrial premises.

Pre-seed capital funds and stimulation of funding for USOs
In France, one of the characteristics of seed capital funds is to combine public and private funding. Five national funds, dedicated to biotechnology and information and communication technologies, and six regional funds were created in 1999. The seed capital funds provide finance at the first stage of funding. Higher education and research institutions participate in most of these funds, along with investors from the public

sector (primarily CDC Enterprises) and from the private sector (mainly investment capital firms).[4] These new structures bring together the local actors of the technology transfer offices, research centres and universities to facilitate close links between the investors and their laboratories. As investors, the managers of these funds form a close relationship with the company's founders.

A chain of measures from idea to market   The government support measures described above are based on the objective of creating an integrated process of developing spin-offs that will both increase the number of spin-offs created from the public research sector and enable them to generate sustainable growth. This results in the following process: public researchers who want to transfer their research results by creating a company ask for an authorization from the public ethics committee; they then present a file to the national competition where the best projects are identified and grants awarded; these best projects are then hosted in public incubators; once they have developed they are financed by seed money funds; and finally, the best projects are selected for venture capital investments.

2.4   EVALUATION OF SPIN-OFF SUPPORT POLICY SCHEMES

Performing a specific evaluation of the spin-off support schemes is difficult since most programmes, especially in France and Belgium, are not specifically orientated towards spin-offs only, but most innovative start-ups can benefit from them. Moreover, many of these public policy initiatives are too young to be evaluated. In the following paragraphs, we provide some evaluation data that was available in each of the countries covered in our study.

Researchers' Status

First, in France the Observatoire des Sciences et des Techniques (Office for Science and Technology – OST, 2003) has undertaken an official review of the impact of the Innovation and Research Act which allows researchers to transfer their research results by creating a start-up. The review found that between 1999 and 2004 450 people received authorization. A quarter of them function in a new venture as a partner or take an executive function as a CEO. The others provide consultancy services. Allowing for the fact that several people often participate in the same project, close to 250 firms were involved (Direction de la technologie, 2005).

Business Training for Academics

Analysis of the impact of the 12 Science Enterprise Challenge funds located in universities across the UK, shows that with respect to both post-graduate and undergraduate training, most exceeded their targets and have been able to initiate a major positive change compared to before the pro-gramme (SQW, 2005). Nine SECs recorded creation of spin-offs, five SECs applied for patents and only three granted licences. Segal, Quince and Wicksteed Limited (2005) note that only four SECs reported new business links, but in all but one case this equalled or exceeded targets.

In France in 2005, the Direction de la Technologie of the French Ministry of Research has produced a first account of the actions of the six Maisons de l'entrepreneuriat plus those of the Maison de l'entrepreneuriat at Grenoble which was created in 2002 (Direction de la technologie, 2006). The report found that 2696 students had followed an entrepreneurial train-ing module during their university courses. A total of 1977 students had participated to an awareness workshop or a business creation game. There were 37 university diplomas in entrepreneurship. The number of students who had taken part in conferences relating to entrepreneurship was 4552. A total of 214 students had been involved with the Maisons de l'entrepre-neuriat regarding an idea or a plan to create a company.

Incubators and Support Structures for Projects

In France, about 31 incubators were created between 1999 and 2002. Each incubator had an agreement with the Ministry of Research which fixes some obligations in return for a public grant. The Ministry of Research has reaffirmed its commitment by allocating 25 million euros with the assis-tance of the FSE (European Social Funds) over the period 2004 to 2006.

By December 2004 the 28 active incubators had hosted 1139 projects, resulting in 612 start-ups employing more than 2000 people. Just under 40 per cent of these firms were created by the winners of the national entrepreneurship competition, which shows significant complementarity between these two programmes. The available data show that 50 per cent of the projects in these incubators result from public research and 50 per cent are not based on public research but have a link with a public laboratory (Direction de la technologie, 2005).

Since the start of Chalmers Innovation in 1999 in Sweden, the number of companies grew from 13 to 49 new, technology-based companies at the end of 2003, most of which are spin-offs. The number of people employed in the companies has risen from a little more than 100 to 220 people in 2003. In total, the companies have attracted 63 million euros in external financing from private venture capitalists, and 6 million euros in public seed financing.

As mentioned previously, we performed a detailed evaluation of three selected incubators related to universities and research institutes in Belgium, Germany and the UK. Erasmus European Business and Innovation Center (EEBIC) is a research incubator located in Brussels, Belgium. It recruits companies from the universities in Brussels. Jülich TZ is located in the science park in the research park of Jülich, located between two main cities in the north-west of Germany (Aachen and Cologne). Chalmers was described above in Box 2.4. The following services were mentioned by the managers of the incubators as being offered to spin-offs: (a) pre-incubation support such as business plan coaching and assistance in searching pre-seed capital; (b) entrepreneurship training and business courses; (c) assistance in accounting and legal matters; (d) assistance in market research and sales support: (e) support in internationalization; (f) support in new product and/or service development and, finally, (g) support in recruiting new personnel. The results are interesting (Table 2.3). It is astonishing how poorly each of the incubators scores in terms of offered services (average values of 4.5 on a score of 7). Although these services are considered by the companies as very important incubation activities, only Chalmers Innovation scores highly among the tenant companies in terms of satistfactory service support. The other two incubators usually claim that they support the companies but in the end do not provide this support in a satisfactory way. This raises the question of whether incubators are an effective policy tool to provide spin-off support.

Pre-seed Capital Funds and Stimulation of Funding for USOs
An initial evaluation of the impact of the UCF initiative in the UK shows that up to July 2003, 413 projects benefited from a UCF investment and almost half the projects (48 per cent) were in the biomedical area (SQW, 2005). Almost 40 per cent of the commitments to projects were for 15000 euros, reflecting the widespread use of pathfinder projects for activities such as market assessments and securing the IP position. Fifty-five projects received the maximum (total) commitment of 375000 euros, which involved cases which had gone through the initial stages of development and for which the fund considered there was real commercial potential.

These investments in 413 projects have translated into 59 spin-off companies and four licences. SQW (2005) note that these figures relate to a fairly early stage in the pipeline and that it will take some time for current projects to mature to the commercialization stage. For the SQW report, one measure of success of the funds is the extent to which projects were able to attract additional external funding. At July 2003, 103 projects had secured

Table 2.3   *Different incubation models: a comparison of perceived importance and perceived effectiveness of services offered (by the tenant companies)*

	EEBIC N = 9		Chalmers Innovation N = 8		Jülich TZ N = 10	
	Imp	Effec	Imp	Effec	Imp	Effec
Pre-incubation services	3.43	2.57	5.00	4.62	4.60	4.40
(business plan development)	(2.70)	(2.15)	(2.33)	(1.69)	(2.61)	(1.95)
Business training and coaching	2.42	1.25	3.65	4.00	3.40	(NA)
	(2.15)	(0.50)	(2.26)	(0.99)	(2.19)	
Legal and accounting assistance	4.00	3.67	3.63	3.33	2.80	(NA)
	(2.71)	(3.10)	(1.92)	(0.82)	(1.79)	
Market research, marketing,	3.00	3.00	4.63	3.00	3.60	(NA)
sales support	(1.83)	(0.00)	(1.92)	(1.41)	(3.13)	
Export assistance	2.67	1.67	3.50	(NA)	3.50	(NA)
	(1.86)	(1.15)	(1.69)		(2.51)	
Support to develop new	4.50	4.50	4.75	4.17	2.80	(NA)
products	(1.87)	(2.65)	(1.83)	(1.94)	(2.49)	
Recruitment advice	4.29	(NA)*	4.74	4.00	3.20	(NA)
	(2.14)		(2.13)	(2.31)	(2.49)	

Notes:
Scale = 1–7 semantic differential scale.
* This form of support is not offered as a service.

co-funding, but two projects accounted for almost a quarter of this and the top ten for 60 per cent. The two major sources in terms both of the number of projects and the average size of investments were venture capital and industrial funding. As the SQW report notes, flexibility over size of investment is important. The funds have the ability to make small investments in order to test the commercial potential of an investment in which the private sector is uninterested. Further, UCFs have reduced the pressure on universities to establish companies at a very early stage, even earlier than would be optimal, with the hope that these companies that are established after a period of development of the idea will be of higher quality.

Last but not least, the management of the funds is dicussed. The UCFs have established advisory boards (comprising university staff and members with business and venture capital experience). The board specifies the overall framework for investment criteria, monitors investments and decides on investments (sometimes it is undertaken by a subcommittee). A fund manager makes proposals to the board or committee but often has discretion to approve small investments. Those universities which were active previously in promoting and funding spin-offs and licensing have tended to recruit an in-house manager for their funds. The others, which were less involved in these activities, have recruited an external specialist.

Segal, Quince and Wicksteed Limited (2005) conclude that there is little doubt that the UCFs met a gap in the UK for early stage funding of technology-based ideas. Several UCFs still have significant funds uncommitted but the number of research ideas that have been taken closer to commercialization has increased significantly

In France, the national competition for the creation of technologically innovative start-ups, received applications from 9500 candidates between 1999 and 2004. A total of 1377 candidates received a grant and contributed to the creation of almost 700 new companies, which themselves generated more than 3000 highly qualified employment. Candidates could enter the competition under either an 'emergent' or 'creation-development' category. The former receive around 45 000 euros for technical, legal or financial research to consolidate their business plan. The latter receive a grant of up to 450 000 euros to finance a part (around 50 per cent) of their innovation project. In addition to this financial aid, the award winners are put in contact with various partners. Some of the winning projects are then hosted in a government incubator. It is important to note that more than 90 per cent of the companies created with this support still exist, a survival ratio higher than usual for the creation of companies. This competition seems to contribute largely to the economic transfer of public research, since a third of the prize winners have projects resulting or linked to public research results (Direction de la technologie, 2005).

In conclusion, in France the most general analysis has been of the different policy support initiatives. Since 1999, the four measures presented above have resulted in the creation or support of 1236 firms. However, a large proportion of these firms were not research spin-offs. Surveys of incubators show that 55 per cent of the firms created from the hosted projects were founded by staff from public-sector research institutions. Another survey, this time on winners of the national competitions for the creation of innovative firms, shows that only slightly more than one-third of these are spin-offs involving public-sector research. Surveys and estimations have also been done for the Ethics Committee and the seed money funds. The Direction de la technologie (2005) estimates that half of the firms that benefited from these measures are public-sector research spin-offs. In six years, close to 620 start-ups were spin-offs of public-sector research, an average of over 100 per year.

Compared to the situation before, the changes to the legislation were introduced, these developments appear to represent a marked increase in activity. Mustar (1988) studied 145 companies created by academics in 1988. To examine the changes in these spin-offs and to identify subsequent new technological companies created by researchers in France, a second enquiry was carried in 1994. These two enquiries estimated that over the six-year period at least 40 firms were created in France each year by researchers (Mustar, 1994). Is the law on innovation a success? At least 40 spin-offs were created each year prior to the introduction of the law and 100 afterwards. The Innovation Law and the related support measures described below have increased the trend that was starting to emerge in the 1980s and 1990s, but only to a limited extent.

However, closer examination of these data suggests a strong decrease in the number of USOs created each year from 1999 to 2004. In 2004, only eight requests for authorization made to the Ethics Commission involved researchers at a public research institution or professors at a university deciding to leave their laboratory to participate in a new venture as partner or director. Indeed, this is the continuation of a downward trend observed over the preceding four years (37 in 2000; 30 in 2001; 26 in 2002; 23 in 2003 and 8 in 2004). In the light of the findings of Mustar (1988; 1994), this rate of applications indicates that the creation of new ventures is not more numerous before the law of 1999.

Rather, the great majority of the demand of authorizations concerns researchers or professors who bring their scientific advice to a company created from their research results. The Civil Service Ethics Committee received 91 demands in 2002, but 76 in 2003 and 46 in 2004. Hence, the number of scientists who engage in the creation of a company is more limited than hoped for by the political decision-makers and has been decreasing since 2000.

With respect to the 2005 national competition for the creation of techno-logical innovative firms, only 4.6 per cent (51) of the 1120 proposals involved academics or researchers (civil servant or not). The same phenomenon can be observed with the public incubators. In 2001, public projects represented 75 per cent of the total of projects hosted in the incubators. In 2002, the cor-responding figure was 60 per cent, in 2003, 50 per cent and even lower in 2004. Finally, only around 7–8 per cent of the firms hosted in incubators have received investment from the seed capital funds.

In summary, these trends indicate that the National Innovation Law has simply provided a legal environment for a phenomenon and behaviour that have already existed for at least 20 years in the French research system. The reason for these disappointing effects may partly lie with a policy con-structed on an anticipated linear trajectory from the creation of a firm by a scientist on the basis of a licence or patent from a public sector institution to a venture-backed firm that will be able to float on a stock market, and the lack of autonomy of the actors to adapt to the specific context of individual spin-offs, many of which are likely to remain small.

2.5 CONCLUSIONS

In this chapter, we have reviewed the attempts by European governments to fill the gap between the US and Europe with respect to the creation of academic start-ups. Analysis of the contrasting cases of the UK and France, shows that there is no convergence of national policies to foster the creation of firms by academics. Rather, the two countries demonstrate different rationales and approaches to policy in this area. In the UK, the rationale for spin-off policy is mainly to develop a third stream of financing. Spin-offs are a part of a policy to commercialize technology and knowledge created by universities. Universities in the UK have to find a balance between licensing and spin-off creation, and the universities can take equity in these new firms. In the UK, policy is at the university level, leading to the creation of diverse structures, as we show in more detail in Chapter 4. Moreover, the public schemes that have been introduced bring public money directly to the universities.

In France, the framework is totally different. The rationale for policy towards the creation of new ventures by academics is economic growth, the development of a high-technology sector and job creation. The notion of a third stream of financing is an argument that is never advanced. Typically, French universities do not take shares in the spin-offs that emerge from the research they generate, with some exceptions for some public research institutions. Again in contrast to the UK, universities do not have discretion to act independently and centralization is high. The evaluation of applications for authorization, of competitions and of the incubators is at national level, with a strong homogeneity effect. Public funds for the incubators or for the seed capital funds are not for the universities but for these new structures. This results in a paradox or a syllogism: the attempt to create entrepreneurial universities in a system without autonomy. This is a system far removed from the US context it purportedly seeks to emulate.

But behind these differences some common features can be stressed. In each country it was necessary to develop framework conditions in order to facilitate the process of start-up creation in general. These countries' experience has shown that neither this framework, nor money alone (VC funds) were enough to create a dynamic spin-off sector. It was necessary to invent diverse micro (or meso) schemes or instruments. These measures concern the ownership of IP, the creation of the possibility and the capabilities for academic to create a company, support for a project or firm, and the development of TTOs, incubators and seed capital funds in or around universities and public research institutions.

Although there is debate about the end of national-level initiatives and the growth of regional and European initiatives, in the two cases decribed here, the national level was the engine of policy to encourage spin-offs. In these two countries, the ministry or the department in charge of research launched the programmes: the OST in the UK, and the Ministry of Research in France. This is also the case in Germany, that is, a country where the *Länder* play an important political role (Audretsch and Beckman, 2005).

One important policy concerns the complementary between the diverse initiatives taken to promote spin-offs. The SQW (2005) evaluation report shows that in July 2003, less than 50 per cent of the funded HEIs in the UK received funding from more than one programme. On the other hand, 51 HEIs received only HEIF funding, seven only SEC funding and three only UCF funding. However, SQW (2005) note that the additional activity of all programmes is high in terms of the recruitment of extra staff, which the institutions would not have funded on a similar scale from their own budgets, and the generation of additional commercialization of research ideas and company formation. In the French case, there appears to be a degree of complementary, with 32 per cent of the creators being involved in more than one of the four incentives measures. The most important overlap is observed between the competition and the incubators. Of all the companies resulting from the competition and the incubators, 23 per cent of companies are common to both measures; the 315 companies concerned accounting respectively for 47 per cent of the companies created from the incubators and for 45 per cent of the companies resulting from the competition.

However, our analysis of the available data and our discussion with the people in charge of the incubators and the public seed capital funds show that there is a large gap between these two instruments. The government intervention model in its present form functions only partially. The linear model adopted by the government is limited, as only a very small percentage of the start-ups financed by seed capital funds are from public-sector incubators. Although the French government perceived there to be complementarity in its measures concerning incubators and start-up funds, this complementarity did not materialize since only eight of the 344 firms created from incubators by the end of 2001 had benefited from seed capital funds. Indeed, 77 per cent of the firms supported by the seed capital funds (that is, 27 out of 35) were not created from incubators. Conversely, only 2 per cent of the firms created in incubators (8 out of 344) benefited from seed capital. At the end of 2005, the 11 public seed money funds resulting from the call for projects in 1999 (five national funds and six regional funds) had invested in 106 companies. Among these 45 companies, 43 per cent came from the incubators. There is thus a complementarity between the funds and the incubators. However, these companies accounted for only 6 per cent of the total of 844 companies generated by the incubators at the end of 2005 (Ministère délégué à la recherche, 2006). As far too few projects are financed by seed capital, this cuts across the main premise of French policy towards spin-offs.

While UK initiatives are characterized by the fact that they bring money to the higher education institutions, French initiatives do not. The UK has placed the universities at the heart of policies aimed at the creation of spin-offs; this may be less the case in France.

NOTES

1. Via specialized funds CDC Entreprises invests directly in new ventures, whatever their branch of industry or their stage of development. CDC Entreprises intervenes also indirectly in the financing of the capital companies while subscribing to investment funds or by taking participations in VC companies. The total amount of funds managed within CDC Entreprises is 4.2 billion euros. One of its missions is the promotion of the VC funds for technological companies.
2. The following information is from Segal, Quince and Wicksteed (SQW) Limited's (February 2005) interim evaluation of knowledge transfer programmes funded by the office of science and technology through the science budget (http://www.ost.gov.uk/enterprise/knowledge/unichal.htm).
3. In France, academics in universities are civil servants and researchers in public research institutions are generally civil servants or have a similar status.
4. In national seed money funds, three types of subscriber can be distinguished: private subscribers (30–50 per cent of the funds), CDC-Enterprises (20–30 per cent), and public research organizations (15–30 per cent). The Regional Councils and universities are also subscribers to regional funds.

3. Types of spin-offs

3.1 INTRODUCTION

The key to designing approaches to address the challenges in creating and developing spin-offs is understanding their nature. Spin-offs have been studied from different conceptual perspectives. Some authors have taken the link with the parent institute as a point of departure and studied the institutional environment in which spin-offs emerge and they study differences in the link between the spin-off and the parent-research organization. For example, in Chapter 4, we describe different incubation models and the way in which they can impact the starting configuration of a spin-off. A second stream of researchers have used a resource-based lens to study spin-offs. They make distinctions between those spin-offs which have looked after external equity versus those that have not. Others have categorized spin-offs based upon their technological resources and identify technology platform spin-offs versus product or service spin-offs. Still others in this literature stream make a distinction between those spin-offs that are able to attract management experience in a founding team and those that are founded by individual researchers. A third stream of literature has distinguished between different types of spin-offs based upon their business and revenue model. These researchers have made a key distinction between those spin-offs that are exit orientated and envisage a trade sale, and those that are revenue orientated and require time to break even.

Based upon the insights generated by the different conceptual perspectives, we develop a taxonomy of different types of spin-offs. We distinguish between venture capital-backed spin-offs, prospectors and lifestyle spin-offs. Each of these spin-offs is quite different at start-up in terms of institutional link, resource base and business model. We extract 12 different criteria from the literature, which can be used to categorize the spin-offs. Venture capital-backed spin-offs are exit orientated, often have a formal link with the parent institute and this is reflected in a resources base which provides a sufficient amount of external financing, a balanced team and a disruptive technology (see section 3.3.3) basis. In contrast, prospectors often are early in the product development cycle but do not have a disruptive technology to start from. Their link with the parent institute is formal, though less closely involved than that of a VC-backed spin-off. They often need external capital to define the business model that suits their needs. Finally, lifestyle companies most often are the result of a single initiative of the researcher-professor-entrepreneur who wants to commercialize a close-to-market product or his or her own knowledge. The starting resources imply little external capital and do not embody a disruptive technology. The business model is clearly revenue driven and the link with the parent institute is informal at most.

The chapter is structured as follows. Section 3.2 outlines conceptual perspectives that inform differences among spin-offs. Section 3.3 describes the taxonomy. The concluding section considers implications for practitioners, policy-makers and researchers.

3.2 CONCEPTUAL PERSPECTIVES

Our review of papers that either focused on research-based spin-offs (RBSOs) as a subpopulation of new technology-based firms (NTBFs) or tried to explain the diversity among the NTBF population identified three main theoretical research traditions. A first category of papers mainly focuses on the resources of the firm as a differentiator and a predictor of competitive advantage (Barney et al., 2001; Brush et al., 2001). We label this group the resource-based perspective. A second category of papers describes the activities that are developed by NTBFs, the sectors in which they are located and other key indicators that make these companies different from other start-ups. We label this the 'business model perspective'. A third group of papers focuses on the link with the parent institution. We label this group the 'institutional perspective'. The following sub-sections review each of these themes.

3.2.1 The Resource-Based Perspective

In recent years, the resource-based theory, which attributes superior performance to organizational resources and capabilities has emerged as one of the most influential frameworks in strategic management research (Barney et al., 2001). Resource-based scholars define resources rather broadly as all tangible and intangible assets semi-permanently tied to the firm. As a result, a variety of alternative resource classifications exist. Most of these resource typologies are developed in the specific context of large, established firms.

Barney (1991) classifies resources as physical capital, human capital and organizational capital resources. According to his classification, physical capital resources include the physical technology used in the firm, a firm's plant and equipment, its geography and its access to raw materials. Human capital resources, on the other hand, include the training, experience, judgement, intelligence, relationships, and insights of individual managers and workers in the firm. Finally, organizational capital resources include a firm's formal reporting structure, its formal and informal planning, controlling and coordinating systems, as well as informal relationships among groups within a firm and between a firm and those in its environment. Lichtenstein and Brush (2001) developed the resource-based perspective in the context of new ventures. They found that capital, organizational systems, management know-how, employees, owner's expertise and reputation, technology, physical resources, leadership, organizational structure and culture or informal systems are the most relevant for new ventures. Further, Brush et al. (1997; 2001) categorized the resources of early stage ventures into six types: technological, human, social, financial, physical and organizational resources. Other researchers, who explore resource-based theory in new and/or small firms, adopt the same typology (for example, Borch et al., 1999). We build on previous work of Barney (1991) and Brush et al. (2001) and adopt four resource categories in the remainder of the chapter: technological, social, human and financial resources. Each of these resource categories is described below.

The category 'technological resources' refers to the firm-specific products and technology (Borch et al., 1999). Spin-offs might vary in degree of innovativeness, scope of their technology, (perceived) quality or legitimacy of the firms' research and development (R&D) and position of the firm in the product-development cycle. The category 'human resources' refers to attributes of the founding team, the management team and the personnel of the company. Human resources usually are measured as: size of the founding team, background of the founders, professional management experience, and organizational size. Brush et al. (2001) define 'social resources' of a company as its industry and financial contacts. Others refer to these social resources as the network or the social capital of the company (for example, Elfring and Hulsink, 2003; Lee et al., 2001). Lee et al. (2001) make a distinction between 'partnership-based linkages' and 'sponsorship-based linkages'. The 'financial resources' usually refer to the amount and type of financing of the firm. A distinction is made between capital, loans, subsidies and reserved profits. Further, having personal funds, which can be invested in the very early start-up phase, can be an advantage for spin-offs. Therefore, it makes sense to split the variable 'capital' by two indices, namely, the amount of external capital invested in the firm and the amount of personal funds (money invested by the entrepreneurs or their personal friends and family).

According to studies in this literature that have focused on human resources, the initial competencies of new ventures basically coincide with the competencies of the founders (see Cooper and Bruno, 1977). Therefore, they mainly link the diversity of spin-offs with the characteristics of their founders. Other studies have focused on financial and technical resources. An interesting aspect of the analysis of these taxonomies inspired by the resource-based view is the evolution in the investigation of financial aspects. For a long time, classifications of RBSOs based on this dimension have distinguished firms only according to the presence of venture or industrial capital (Heirman and Clarysse, 2004; Mustar, 1997; Shane and Stuart, 2002).

As will be seen in Chapter 5, creating a spin-off company as a joint venture with an industrial partner, may be a means of overcoming some of the potential problems associated with managing resource weaknesses and inadequate capabilities that may be difficult to achieve as a free-standing spin-off company, with or without venture capital backing.

Technical resources have not been well explored. Hindle and Yencken (2004), studying the conditions of knowledge transfer between the public research organization (PRO) and the spin-off, considered different types of technology, that is, patented technology versus technical knowledge, without formal protection. Heirman and Clarysse (2004) examined the technical resources of RBSOs focusing on the stage of the technology development cycle and the scope and innovativeness of the firm's technology.

Whereas resources are assets, either owned or controlled by a firm, capabilities refer to the ability to exploit and combine resources through organizational routines in order to accomplish its targets (Amit and Schoemaker, 1993). In Chapter 5 we show that RBSOs go through a number of distinct phases in the development of resources and dynamic capabilities. An RBSO has to overcome critical junctures at the intersection of each consecutive phase, which can be labelled as research, opportunity framing, preorganization and reorientation phase. It is only when they can overcome certain resource hurdles, that RBSOs are able to go from one phase to the other.

3.2.2 Business Model Perspective

Although consultants often refer to the 'business model' adopted by a start-up, the academic literature largely ignores it (Chesbrough and Rosenbloom, 2002; Zott and Amit, 2005). Chesbrough and Rosenbloom (2002) defines the business model as the articulation of the value proposition, the identification of the market segment, the position which is taken in the value chain and the estimated cost structure and profit margin. Bower (2003) was probably the first to explicitly refer to the business model of RBSOs as a subject of study. Druilhe and Garsney (2004) more systematically analysed the different business models at start-up in a sample of RBSOs from the University of Cambridge. In the same vein, Heirman and Clarysse (2004) linked business model to growth in a sample of Belgian NTBFs. Studies within this perspective can be divided into three groups.

The first group focuses on what activities are undertaken. Stankiewicz's (1994) pioneering study made a distinction between RBSOs that are mainly *consultants*, those that are *product orientated* and, finally, those that have a *technology asset orientated mode*, which means that they basically develop technologies which are sold through licences and partnerships. The latter group does not engage in market-orientated activities. The conceptual distinction between service and product orientated RBSOs has been confirmed in various empirical studies. Chiesa and Piccaluga (2000) find, in a sample of Italian RBSOs, that about half the RBSOs are service orientated and about half are product orientated. Mustar (2002) derives a typology that comprises five spin-off categories and is focused on the nature of the firms' output, that is, whether it is for final customers or not and whether it is service, production or research orientated. Pirnay et al. (2003) report similar prevalence rates of product-orientated and service-orientated RBSOs in a sample of Belgian spin-offs. Bower (2003) highlights the technology asset orientated mode as a dominant mode in the emerging phase of a new technology such as biotechnology in the late 1980s or plant biotechnology in the early 1990s. The aforementioned studies are typically atheoretical in nature and explorative in approach.

The second group of studies distinguishes NTBFs (and RBSOs as a subsample) based upon the *growth orientation* which these companies establish. In contrast with the US success stories as described in Saxenian (1994a), Autio and Lumme (1998) conclude that most high-tech start-ups in Finland do not grow at all. They argue that their results might have more external validity for the rest of Europe than the US studies. Also Wtterwulghe (1998) describes how Belgian and French NTBFs tend to be mostly one-man small and medium-sized enterprises (SMEs) with a limited ambition to grow and without a clear commercial strategy. In an exploratory article, Tiler et al. (1993) reported that NTBFs start up in three different growth modes. The fast and slow growers as described above and, finally, the transitional growers. They might start up as consulting companies, R&D boutiques or niche players and eventually turn into high-growth companies. The difference with the low growers is that the latter already have the *ambition to grow* at start-up, but for a variety of reasons they postpone exponential growth plans for a few years. Degroof (2002) builds on this analysis to explore the growth ambitions of 42 Belgian spin-offs at start-up. He also found these three different types.

The reason possibly lies in the limited theoretical guidance which can be found in the third group of studies that examine how technologies or knowledge can be transformed in commercial value.

One approach to transformation can be distinguished as 'infrastructure companies' (Branscomb and Auerswald, 2001; Druilhe and Garsney, 2004; Heirman and Clarysse, 2004). These companies have an exit-driven strategy, which is focused on seeking investor acceptance during most of their early growth path. Heirman and Clarysse (2004) show that most of these high-growth RBSOs have increasingly negative cash flows and spend the largest chunk of their capital on technology development and platform building and not on business development, marketing or sales. Agarwal and Bayus (2002) argue that the commercialization of technology platforms takes, on average, over 14 years, which is much longer than the time horizon of most venture capital firms. This immediately shows the vulnerability of the platform model.

A second transformation approach concerns ventures that offer goods and services that customers quickly choose to buy and are thus able to grow their revenues at a faster rate in the early years (Chesbrough, 2003). These ventures are more likely to turn profitable sooner, consume less cash and rapidly achieve a profitable liquidity event for their investors (Bhide, 1992). The long lead times to market, as described by Agarwal and Bayus (2002), might also be a major reason why some RBSOs start up as consulting companies in software or contract research start-ups in biotechnology (Bower, 2003). Usually, these quick revenues are needed to become more attractive as a company. In general, concrete business plans for smaller but focused markets/applications are found to be more successful than 'large-scale/ broad' product introductions (Golder and Tellis, 1996; Moore, 1991).

A third transformation model focuses on product oriented spin-offs (Chiesa and Piccaluga, 2000; Degroof, 2002; Mustar, 2002). Heirman and Clarysse (2004) consider new technology based firms that start as a one-product company and only later develop a customer-driven technology base. Usually the founders of these companies have business experience and became interested in a close-to-market product, which the parent company does not support. The reasons for this might be various. Either the product does not fit into the mainstream strategy, the market size does not meet the minimum requirements for the parent company or the top management cannot be convinced. The founders leave the company with a marketable product and spend the first years after company start-up commercializing the product. After a few years, they are quite familiar with their customers' needs and develop new products for their established customer base. By doing so, they change their strategy from a one-product company towards a multi-product company with several products that suit their customer base.

A fourth transformation model is inspired by the work of Druihle and Garnsey (2004) who base their typology on the interplay between the entrepreneur's prior knowledge and experience and the intensity of resource requirements, and is in line with Heirman and Clarysse (2004) and Degroof (2002). Interestingly, in contrast to the other studies, Druihle and Garnsey (2004) adopt a dynamic perspective on how these interrelationships yield a business model and suggest that business models are altered as entrepreneurs improve their knowledge of resources and opportunities. This means that many RBSOs start up without a clear idea of how they will create value in the beginning, especially if these entrepreneurs are researchers or professors and are unfamiliar with the transformation approaches that are used in the industry. They spend considerable time searching for the right approach to value creation during the first years after start-up and can be considered 'prospectors'. Usually they continue to develop the technology in the meanwhile and test various assumptions in the marketplace. Often pre-seed capital and incubation funds linked to universities provide a first investment in these companies to finance their search for viable mechanisms to create value.

3.2.3   The Institutional Perspective

The institutional perspective is based on the recognition that RBSOs are founded to exploit intellectual property emerging from science and are typically embedded in a parent organization, although the nature of the embeddedness may vary. This parent organization has its own culture, incentive systems, rules and procedures (Moray and Clarysse, 2005). Scholars, who study RBSOs from this perspective, are particularly interested in how the institutional context shapes the starting configuration and later development of the RBSO (Dacin, 1997). Studies may combine insights from institutional and neo-institutional theory (for example, Boeker, 1989) with reference to organizational theory (Debackere, 2000), resource dependency theory (Meyer, 2003) and even strategic management (Moray and Clarysse, 2005) to explain their findings.

Roberts (1991: 103–7) noted the variety of linkages between science-based entrepreneurial firms and the Massachusetts Institute of Technology (MIT). He questioned entrepreneurs about the link between the firm and the research organization and, more specifically, about the importance of technology transferred to the new firm. The author asked respondents to rate the degree of dependence on source technologies: direct, partial and vague. Where technology is transferred directly, the company would not have been started without the formal transfer of intellectual property rights (by means of a licence agreement or transfer of a patent). 'Partial' means that the company was founded based on the formal transfer of intellectual property (IP) rights; however, this know-how needed to be expanded with some other source of know-how (that is, IP coming from another institute than the parent institute). The category 'vague' represents those companies that are categorized as research-based start-ups (RBSUs) by the parent institute for other reasons than formally transferred technology. Building on this pioneering work, the Association of University Technology Managers (AUTM)[1] adopted a more pragmatic approach labelling those companies which have received a formal transfer of technology 'spin-offs', while the others are start-ups. Formal means that there is some kind of licence relation, be it equity based or not, with the parent organization. Informal means that the relation is not institutionalized. Moray and Clarysse (2005) have found that the degree to which the technology is 'formally' transferred from the parent organization to the RBSO has both a direct impact on the starting resources of the RBSO and on the later growth path of the RBSO.

A number of scholars in this institutional tradition do not limit their analysis to the *institutional link*, but analyse how the *strategic choices* made by the parent institute might have a lasting effect on the RBSOs that are created (Boeker, 1989). In a pioneering study, Radosevich (1995) focuses on the inadequate incentive systems at universities to induce inventors to become involved in the commercialization of their inventions. Instead of having a lasting effect, universities and public research institutes are still considered a barrier. Steffensen et al. (2000) were probably the first to make a clear distinction between those RBSOs that result from an organized effort by the parent organization and those that occurred spontaneously, sometimes even despite the university. In this study, they describe the efforts of research centres to provide facilities to new firms. Along the same lines, Franklin et al. (2001) examine universities' attitudes to using surrogate entrepreneurs in the development of spin-offs in order to compensate for the lack of entrepreneurial culture. Debackere (2000) indicated that universities can also have a positive and stimulating impact on the creation and growth of RBSOs. In an in-depth case study, he clearly describes how the University of Leuven created a separate organization to foster RBSOs and support them in their early growth path. Lundqvist and Hellsmark (2003) performed a similar study, describing the entrepreneurial university support system of Chalmers University in Sweden.

Building on the insights of previous studies, Mustar (2002), Meyer (2003) and Clarysse et al. (2005a) suggested that the policy choices made by the parent institute might not only affect the number of spin-offs but also the 'type' of spin-off. The previous chapter has elaborated the distinction between three kinds of organization models at the level of the parent organization: the Low Selective model, which is orientated towards maximizing the number of entrepreneurial ventures regardless of the start-up size and configuration; the Supportive model which is orientated towards generating spin-offs as an alternative to licensing and tries to set up RBSOs with an average resource intensity; and the Incubator model focused on RBSOs which are viewed as tradable assets.

3.3 INTRODUCING A SPIN-OFF TAXONOMY

In the previous section, we have described the different theoretical perspectives that have been used to analyse spin-offs. In this section, we derive a spin-off taxonomy from these different perspectives. The taxonomy is built upon the different perspectives and distinguishes three main types of spin-offs based on a list of 12 indicators derived from the literature, which fit into the three theoretical perspectives: (a) the institutional point of view; (b) the business model perspective and (c) the resource-based point of view. Drawing on the insights derived from these theoretical streams, we have defined three types of spin-offs: (a) the venture capital backed spin-off; (b) the prospector spin-off and (c) the lifestyle spin-off. Each of these spin-offs differs significantly for the variables that belong to the different domains as identified above (Table 3.1). In the next paragraphs, we describe the types of spin-offs and the underlying variables that distinguish them.

3.3.1 The Institutional Link

Formal involvement
The first category of variables belongs to the institutional perspective. A distinguishing item in this category is whether the spin-off has a 'formal' link with the university after start-up. The AUTM explicitly makes the distinction between those spin-offs that have a contractual agreement with the parent institute based upon the formal transfer of technology embodied in a patent and those that do not have such an agreement. Lifestyle companies, which are mostly consulting companies in an academic context, seldom involve the formal transfer of technology and hence do not belong to the spin-off category strictly speaking as defined by the AUTM. Moray and Clarysse (2005) further distinguish between spin-offs that are based upon one patent and those that are the result of a careful trade-off between licensing out part of a technology and spinning it off in an independent legal entity. In the latter case, not one patent but a family of patents,

Table 3.1 Taxonomy of spin-offs

	VC-backed	Prospector	Lifestyle
I. Institutional link			
1. Formal involvement	Equity relation based upon complex IP system	Equity relation based upon one patent or none	Licence contract informal relation
2. Prestige of research group	Worldwide recognition in broad domain	Worldwide recognition in focused subdomain or local recognition	Various
II. Business model			
3. Investor vs market acceptance	Investor acceptance	Both	Market acceptance
4. Mode of value-capturing	Clear IP maximizing strategy or value chain acquisition strategy to prepare trade sale/IPO	Optimize time to break even and future trade sale value, no clear exit yet	Optimize profit
III. Resources			
IIIa. Technology resources			
5. Degree of innovativeness	Disruptive technology or market	New product based upon non-disruptive technology	New product/service addresses clear unmet market need
6. Stage of product/service development	Early, sometimes not even defined	Early, alfa prototype	Almost market ready product/service
7. Broadness of the technology/concept	Can be broad	Narrow	Not relevant

Table 3.1 (continued)

	VC-backed	Prospector	Lifestyle
IIIb. Financial resources			
8. VC involvement	Able to attract 1–5 million euros in the first 18 months after founding	Lower amounts of business angel, baby VC or public fund type of investment	Usually no external equity, some business angel involvement possible
9. Financing mix	High amount of external equity, some debt financing, intensive use of subsidies	Mix of external capital, soft loans and subsidies	Internal funding, debt and some soft loans
IIIc. Human resources			
10. Balanced team	Surrogate entrepreneurs or hired guns	technical scientists act as entrepreneurs	Technical scientists
11. Sectoral experience	Management experience, research excellence	Little experience	Quite a lot of sector experience
IIId. Social Resources			
12. Partnerships at start-up	Formal partnerships with stakeholders such as VCs and technology providors	None	Formal availability of lead user

contractual arrangements and other IP rights are usually the technological assets to start from.

Prestige of research group
Apart from the mode of technology, spin-offs are different depending on the scientific quality and prestige of the parent institute. Moray and Clarysse (2005) show that institutes or departments which have a large critical mass of researchers in a specific technological domain can more easily attract the attention of venture capitalists (VCs) to invest in the start-up and more easily find lead users because multinational companies often have invested embedded laboratories on the campuses of these universities and research institutes. As such, we assume that VC-backed companies will more easily emerge from departments within universities that have enough critical mass and scientific excellence to be spotted on the radar of world-wide financial and corporate investors. Alternatively, prospector companies make less progress in these environments since they do not pass the highly selective nature of deals to be supported by the parent research institute (Clarysse et al., 2005b). In contrast, these companies seem to emerge from mid-range universities that clearly opt for a spin-off policy in favour of licensing out patents to large companies. Finally, lifestyle companies are founded at the initiative of individual entrepreneurs based upon their personal knowledge or based upon a specific product they have developed internally which is market worthy. Hence, the prestige of the parent seems not to be so relevant here.

3.3.2 The Business Model

As aforementioned, the business model is probably one of the most difficult to assess. Heirman and Clarysse (2004) refer to the growth model of a company as a basis to describe its business model. They distinguish between those companies that mainly look for investor acceptance in their first years after start-up and those that are pursuing market acceptance.

Investor vs market acceptance
Figure 3.1 shows the three types of companies and their relevant growth path according to their business model. The VC-backed companies look for investor acceptance and therefore optimize the value created by the company and the tradability of its assets. Selling products or services to customers and end consumers is not always a top priority. An example of such a company is a plant biotechnology company which develops an applied gene technology platform to be able to improve genetically the crop yield of corn, rice, wheat or other. The goal in the first years of this

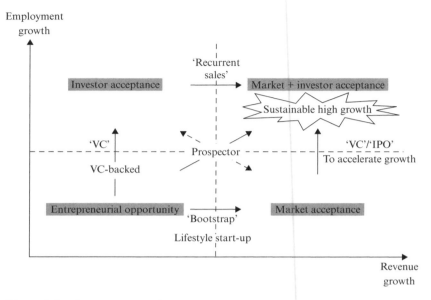

Figure 3.1   Investor vs market acceptance

company is not to generate revenues but to prove that the technology works. Eventually most of these companies will be subject to a trade sale. In the case of the plant biotechnology company, this trade sale might be to a large seed company. In a few cases, the start-up looking for investor acceptance will make a move itself and become a revenue-generating company. However, this is not an easy process. Tellis et al. (2003) show that only 6 per cent of the pioneers are able to become market leaders afterwards. Lifestyle companies are making a horizontal move in Figure 3.1, looking for market acceptance. They typically 'bootstrap' (develop through their own initiative and effort) and look for minimal costs and a fast time to break even. A typical example of such a company is a professor who has developed a biological test to analyse the quality of water. He starts a company and becomes successful in a niche market, which in this case might be geographically limited. Others start a company in consulting and are internationally active in a very specific niche which is determined by the borders of their in-depth knowledge. A few of these companies move, after some years, from a start-up looking for market acceptance towards one looking for investor acceptance. There may be several reasons for this shift: beneficial stock markets, customer pulls or other reasons can change the window of opportunity. Finally, we identify the category of prospectors. These companies still have to refine their business model. An exit through trade sale belongs to the opportunities. However, it is not the only possible company outcome. Revenues also are generated and the start-up might well turn out to be a profitable niche company. The most important is that neither of these two avenues is excluded.

Mode of value-capturing

The mode of value-capturing is quite different between VC-backed spin-offs and others. A useful way of thinking about value-capturing is the framework developed by David Teece (1987). According to Teece, the degree to which an innovator or innovative start-up can capture value is a function of its appropriability regime and its ease of acquiring complementary assets to bring its idea to the market. The appropriability regime includes the degree to which the start-up can protect its idea. Venture capital-backed companies are mostly positioned at places where the appropriability regime is more tight than average and the complementary assets are important and difficult to acquire (see quadrant III in Figure 3.2). In those industries where the appropriability regime is very strong, such as biotechnology, the focus of VC-backed companies is to develop a patent portfolio. Because the complementary assets are important to reach the end consumer and because they are tightly held by a limited number of seed companies, chances to succeed as a company and capture most part of the value chain are limited. The future of most plant biotechnology start-ups is a trade sale to a large seed company. In industries where the appropriability regime is weaker, such as information

Complementary assets

APPROP-RIABILITY		Free available or unimportant	Tightly held and important
	L o w	Difficult to make money	Holder of complementary assets
	H i g h	Inventor	Inventor or party with bargaining power

Source: Teece (1987).

Figure 3.2   The Teece framework

technology (IT), we often observe that acquisitions are made downstream in the value chain to increase the organization's bargaining power *vis-à-vis* the companies that hold the marketing or distribution power (for example, OEMs – original equipment manufacturers). Branding and name recognition based upon technological excellence are used. In both cases, value is created through building up a portfolio of 'intangible' assets in order to sell the company to potential buyers downstream in the value chain.

In contrast, lifestyle companies clearly belong to quadrant I in Figure 3.2. This quadrant is characterized by a weak appropriability and a relatively easy way to access customers. The result is that no superabundance of financial gains can be made. The typical consultant company reflects this very well. The income of the company is sufficient to earn a good living (for example, lifestyle) but repetitive sales are difficult. Finally, prospectors are situated at start-up in quadrant IV in Figure 3.2. The idea is not easy to protect and it seems difficult to build up a position in the value chain. Therefore, time and money is needed to find out how to position the company in the value chain and capture (part of) the profits.

3.3.3   The Resources

Technology resources: degree of innovativeness
The degree of innovativeness reflects whether or not the technology on which the spin-offs is based is disruptive (Christensen, 1997). A disruptive technology means that a new technological S-curve is started which has the potential to completely outperform the old technology. For instance, in the period 2000–2003 it was feared that the WIFI technology would completely surpass the UMTS technology in which a lot of telecommunications companies had invested. WIFI technology based start-ups were sold in that period at a very high price premium to telecom incumbents. Each time a new technology emerges, incumbents are nervous and interested to buy, eventually, the pioneering companies. Not surprisingly, VC-backed spin-offs usually have a rather innovative technology at start-up. This disruptive technology justifies venture capital investments that might lead to a visible trade sale.

Technology resources: stage of new product/service development (NPD/NSD)
By definition VC-backed spin-offs that are based upon a disruptive technology are extremely early in the new product or new service development process. Often, these companies still have to identify applications for the new technology, so the product/service development has not started yet. Also prospectors tend to start early in the NPD/NSD process. They have developed an alpha-prototype which needs considerable customer testing

or similar. As such, this means that further investments are needed in product development and engineering which force the start-up to look for extra capital in the form of soft loans, R&D subsidies or business angel money. Finally, lifestyle companies start very late in the NPD/NSD process. In the case of consulting companies, they often already have a first customer to start with. In the case of product start-ups, the professor has developed some form of product for a customer base, which he knows through contract research, and starts with a beta version rather than an alpha prototype.

Technology resources: broadness of the technology/concept
A final distinguishing factor is the broadness of the technology. The technology of a typical VC-backed spin-off can be quite broad. The broader the technology, the more risk can be diversified over different application domains and the more potential buyers can be found for an exit. However, broad technologies – usually known as platform technologies – also have a drawback: a large amount of capital is needed to develop them. Prospectors usually are looking for product excellence rather than technological excellence. Hence the technology is at start-up already embodied in a product idea. The same holds for the lifestyle companies. Sometimes, technology is not even relevant for these. Knowledge rather than technology is the core for the company.

Financial resources: VC involvement
There is a large difference between those spin-off proposals that are able to attract professional venture capital within the first 18 months after legal incorporation and those that do not. Venture capitalists always have a significant impact on the business and growth model, and select only those proposals of which they expect a favourable exit. Heirman and Clarysse (2006) have shown that successful high-tech start-ups usually attract 1 million to 5 million euros of VC money within 18 months of incorporation. Because of the size of the capital required, not only public VCs participate in the capital but also larger VC companies become interested. Often the VC consortium that commits itself to provide the first round of financing contains at least one VC that specializes in the technological domain of the start-up. The specialization also implies that the consortium might involve VCs from outside the country and certainly from outside the region.

In contrast to VC-backed spin-offs, prospectors do not collect the same amount of start capital and can thus focus themselves upon a much broader range of 'local' VCs, such as public funds, university funds, business angel funds or individual business angels. These investors might have different expectations, in terms of exit and multiples to be realized upon exit, from those of the professional VCs. Public funds and university pre-seed funds often take higher risks and are not concerned only about financial returns. Business angels also have non-financial motives to participate. Still, the prospector obtains external equity and has to conform its organizational structure to that form of investments. This means a board of directors will be formed and the pressure to grow or pursue an exit-orientated strategy might still be substantial, even if the market seems quite narrow and the potential buyers are not clearly identified.

Finally, lifestyle companies very seldom start with external investors. Only in those cases where a business angel wants to play an active role or has a large value added, is some external capital used.

Financial resources: financing mix

The financing mix is broader than the use of venture capital as a financing mechanism strictly speaking. It includes the use of soft loans, subsidies, various forms of debt financing, and so on. Venture capital-backed spin-offs usually optimize the financing mix in a way very similar to large companies. Because of the relatively high amount of external venture capital, these companies receive substantial credibility among the banks, which are important for various sorts of loans and also among R&D-granting institutes, including the European Commission. Clarysse (2004) showed in a study of Belgian spin-offs that VC-backed companies often received more than half their total capital as R&D subsidies. These subsidies could be as high as 40 million euros over a ten-year period. Prospectors often have much less credibility. Although they might have some form of external capital, it is generally not sufficient to convince banks to allow debt financing of working capital. As a result, the financing mix of these companies is rather limited. Even suppliers will be very careful to guarantee payment periods or to provide leasing contracts. The spin-offs are usually considered not to be sustainable during the first one or two years after start-up. We also observe that it is more difficult for these companies to access R&D grants, especially at the European level. The lifestyle companies have totally different needs. They usually need cash to finance the working capital of the company but this can be done through debt financing. Since they do not really develop new products anymore, financing is much more short-term orientated. We also observe that personal and family capital is used to a larger extent here.

Human resources: balanced team

Founding teams of VC-backed companies tend to be balanced in terms of functional background and experience. Venture capitalists do not want to invest in spin-offs where the founding team consists only of researchers without business experience. So, universities try to attract surrogate entre-preneurs to partner-up with the founders and present the proposal to a VC. If no surrogate entrepreneur is available, VCs might suggest looking for a manager and recruiting the manager as the condition of investing. This means that the deal only goes ahead if a manager can be recruited to com-plement the founding team. Depending on the quality and experience of the VC, the quality and experience of the founding team will be different. Prospectors also sometimes start up with surrogate entrepreneurs, but much less with managers since there is no money to pay them. Also, surro-gate entrepreneurs are not always paid in these prospector companies. They sometimes come on the payroll of the university or incubator and get support from there. In the VC-backed spin-off the surrogate entrepreneur also receives a decent management fee according to the industry standards. In the prospector company, a trade-off will be made in that the surrogate entrepreneur will be replaced by coaching the researchers if the available surrogate entrepreneurs turn out to be too expensive. The founding team of life-cycle companies is more limited and can be one or two researchers and/or professors. Team balance is less of an issue unless a product is marketed. In that case, a technical and commercial researcher tend to partner-up.

Human resources: sectoral experience
In both the VC-backed and the prospector type of company the sectoral experience of the founding team is quite limited. Even if a manager is hired or a surrogate entrepreneur enters the team it is very seldom that these people really have the sectoral experience and network to guarantee a fast launch of the company. Paradoxically, lifestyle companies usually are founded by researchers/professors who have considerable consulting experience with the incumbent companies they offer services to. Even in the case of a product start-up, it seems that they are very familiar with the market segment they want to target.

Social resources: partnerships and lead users
Networks and partnerships are often referred to as important accelerators of growth for innovative start-ups. However, we observe that prospectors often completely lack these networks. Prospectors look for opportunities to sell their product downstream in the value chain. This is exactly the area that they are unfamiliar with. The small-scale VCs that invest in these companies very rarely can offer contacts to the founders, nor do the surrogate entre-preneurs have a relevant network. Venture capitalist-backed start-ups, on the other hand, make use of the partnerships which their VC and often their research department can offer. Since these companies do not immediately

target market acceptance, the VC network is of much relevance to obtain investor acceptance and successfully enter subsequent rounds of capital increase. Also, the prestige of the research department they spin off from is very important to attract capital and increase the credibility of the company. Lifestyle companies that sell services usually have one or more formal contracts with customers to start from. Lifestyle companies that sell products usually have a beta version of a product that is co-developed at the site of a lead user. This lead user might be a company with which they had contacts before they started the new business. The idea is that the lead user helps them to customize the product for the market segment they want to target, and even finances this customization exercise.

3.4 CONCLUSIONS

In this chapter, we have discussed the literature on spin-offs and distinguished between three conceptual streams which have approached the spin-off phenomenon: the institutional, the business model and the resource-based perspective.

The institutional perspective studies how parent organizations facilitate spin-off creation and development. Researchers in this stream focus their attention on direct support mechanisms, ignoring indirect ones. Yet, public research institutions can support their spin-offs indirectly through staging and contractual arrangements aimed at sharing the cost of qualified personnel between the RBSO and the parent organization, or through the signalling effect of the reputation of the research organization to investors, potential partners and potential high-quality personnel. The parent institution can also be a source of network links that are key in reducing the costs of the search for partners, thus favouring establishment of alliances (Nicolaou and Birley, 2003a; Scholten et al., 2001).

Typologies of RBSOs based on the business model have tended to neglect aspects relating to the influence of the degree of vertical integration and outsourcing decisions on the structure of the value chain; and the influence of cost leadership and international expansion strategies on the spin-off organization.

Resource endowment perspectives have emphasized the importance of the human capital characteristics of founders on the diversity of spin-offs. There has been growing emphasis on the importance of different financial resources. Spin-offs can be distinguished in terms of the relations between the resource configuration of a spin-off and the resource base of their venture capitalist or industrial finance partner (see Wright et al., 2004b). There has been some examination of the technical resources of RBSOs, focusing on the stage of the technology development cycle and the scope and innovativeness of the firm's technology.

In the literature, there remains limited incorporation into typologies of the different resource requirements, business models and institutional linkages required as RBSOs evolve through their different phases of development, so we addressed this gap by developing a taxonomy derived from the different insights generated in the various conceptual streams. In these conceptual perspectives, we identified a set of 12 variables on which spin-offs tend to differ significantly: institutional link, prestige of the parent institute, growth model, appropriability regime and complementary assets, innovativeness of the technology, broadness of the technology, stage in the NPD/NSD cycle, VC involvement, financing mix, degree of founding team balance and experience. Based upon these different variables, we generated a taxonomy of three different spin-off types: the VC-backed type, the prospector type and the lifestyle spin-off.

NOTE

1. For a description see www.autm.org.

4. Processes at the institutional level: incubation models[1]

4.1 INTRODUCTION

In this chapter we explore the processes for the incubation of spin-offs at different European universities and public research organizations. Many public research organizations, especially in Europe, operate in environments where high-tech entrepreneurship is relatively new. The spin-off process is likely to pose different challenges in these contexts compared with more developed high-tech entrepreneurial environments such as Boston or Silicon Valley (Roberts, 1991; Roberts and Malone, 1996). In contrast to a developed environment with a strong entrepreneurial community, in less developed environments there may be an important need for a proactive incubation role by public research organizations. A university or public research organization (PRO) engaging in spinning-off companies can adopt a range of support activities to provide the venture with the resources and capabilities it needs to develop through its different phases (see Chapter 5). The ability to provide necessary support activities and resources may vary between public research organizations and may be associated with different types of spin-offs. The number of spin-offs created with external equity investment appear to be significantly associated with expenditure on intellectual property protection and the business development capabilities of technology transfer offices, rather than the number of technology transfer staff, the age of the technology transfer office or the available technology (Di Gregorio and Shane, 2003; Lockett and Wright, 2005; Siegel et al., 2003a). However, the differing nature of incubation strategies is not well understood.

In this chapter we examine the different incubation strategies employed by public research organizations to achieve their goals regarding the spin-off process in terms of the resources utilized and activities undertaken. Different public research organizations may differ in their goals and objectives for creating new spin-off ventures. Our analysis is based on detailed examination of the spin-off process at seven initial cases and 43 randomly selected validation cases of public research organizations, as explained in Chapter 1.

The chapter is structured as follows. First we present the different models of spin-off activity in terms of their goals and objectives, resources and strategies and outcomes, and how the different models have harmony between their objectives and resources and how they link to their local environment. Second, we consider performance indicators using a larger sample of public research organizations. Finally we conclude and draw out implications for practice and public policy.

4.2   MODELS OF SPIN-OFF ACTIVITY

Although the term 'incubation' has traditionally been narrowly focused on property-based initiatives, such a definition excludes what are arguably the most important elements of facilitating support and resources required by spin-off companies (Clarysse and Moray, 2004; Lockett et al., 2003a). We employ the UK Business Incubator (UKBI; www.ukbi.co.uk) definition of business incubation, being a dynamic business development process encompassing one or more of the following functions: (1) encouraging faster growth and greater survival rates of new companies, (2) helping to identify investment opportunities, (3) facilitating the commercialization of university or corporate research and new ideas and (4) helping to create jobs and wealth and to tackle specific urban or rural economic development problems. Hence, we adopt a broad definition of incubation. We follow Degroof (2002), who has defined the different activities of a proactive spin-off management process, and the bundle of resources of Brush et al. (2001) which seem crucial in organizing the spin-off process.

We identified five distinct incubation models of managing the spin-off process. Each model differs in terms of the goals and objectives of the PRO and the resources they have with which they can implement their strategies. Three of these models we term reference models as they engage in activities and have resources that meet their objectives. These were labelled as: Low Selective, Supportive and Incubator models. Two models we term suboptimal as they have deficiencies either in terms of their resources or in terms of their competencies which create problems in their ability to meet their objectives. The following section outlines these models, distinguishing in turn the activities undertaken and resources required. At the time of performing the research, all the cases only had one centrally organized mechanism for spinning off companies.

4.2.1 Reference Models

The characteristics of the reference model public research organizations are summarized in Table 4.1. The public research organizations had different objectives and the outcome of their activities may reflect these objectives. Public research organizations with an objective of stimulating self-employment orientated spin-offs were aiming to create employment and enhance development in a depressed region, without a focus on profitable growth or creating a realizable financial return for investors.

Table 4.1 Characteristics of reference models

Name of Scientific Regions of Excellence in Europe	Name of public research organization that met the selection criteria	Public research organization's objectives in creating spin-off ventures	Number of spin-off companies (period 1995–2002)	Trigger
Vlaams Gewest	Leuven R&D	Stimulating economically profit-orientated spin-offs	27	Flexibility, financial return
Vlaams Gewest	IMEC	Stimulating exit-orientated spin-offs	12	Central decision
Bayern	BioM	Stimulating economically profit-orientated spin-offs	30	Financial return
Centre-Est (Rhône-Alpes)	Crealys	Stimulating self-employment orientated spin-offs	31	Entrepreneurial spirit
Oost-Nederland	Twente	Stimulating self-employment orientated spin-offs	60	Entrepreneurial spirit
Eastern (East Anglia)	Scientific Generics	Stimulating exit-orientated spin-offs	9	Cultural issue
Eastern (East Anglia)	TTP	Stimulating exit-orientated spin-offs	7	Central decision

Those public research organizations with an objective to stimulate economically profitable spin-offs were aiming to create economically profitable businesses but with no envisaged exit to generate a financial return for investors. Public research organizations stimulating exit-orientated spin-offs were aiming to create businesses that would generate a realizable financial return to investors, and all their spin-offs received private venture capital funding. In this section we examine, in turn, their activities, their resources, strategies and outcomes, the complementarity of the models and the role of the local environment.

Activities

The activities we focus on are opportunity search and awareness creation; intellectual property assessment and protection; strategic choice of how to commercialize R&D; (property-based) incubation and business plan development; the funding process; and control of the spin-off process after start-up of the spin-off company. The essential activities of each model are summarized in Table 4.2.

Low Selective model   In terms of objectives, the Low Selective model has a mission orientated towards maximizing the number of entrepreneurial ventures in line with the entrepreneurial mission of the research institute(s) to which the unit is attached. These ventures tend to be self-employment orientated start-ups which only rarely grow beyond a critical size of employees. This model is based on a natural selection process. The University of Twente (TOP case) in the Netherlands and Crealys in France are prime examples of this model. The region surrounding the University of Twente was confronted in the mid 1980s with relatively high levels of unemployment. The university deliberately chose to play a major role in the rejuvenation of the region by engendering an entrepreneurial climate and promoting itself as the 'entrepreneurial' university. The TOP (Tijdelijke Ondernemers Plantsen, that is, temporary position for entrepreneurs) initiative was created with money from the European Regional Development Fund. In contrast, Crealys is located near to Grenoble in the Rhône Alpes region. Both initiatives are discussed in detail below.

Opportunity search and awareness creation: the 'opportunity-seeking' activities mainly orientated towards raising entrepreneurship awareness among researchers and/or students at the PRO. Twente refers to the entrepreneurial mission of its parent university as a main driver of spin-off activity (Karnebeek, 2001). Spin-offs present an alternative to employment at an established firm.

Strategic choice how to commercialize R&D: the selection criteria are limited and projects eligible for funding are at an extremely early stage in the

Table 4.2 Activities undertaken by the different models

Activities	Low Selective model	Supportive model	Technology Incubator model
	Based upon Crealys and Twente	Based upon Leuven R&D and BioM	Based upon the IMEC, TTP and Scientific Generics
Opportunity search and awareness creation	Rather passive, relies on entrepreneurial university	Passive; might organize a business plan competition; attracting business plans rather than ideas; relies on the reputation of the fund	Active opportunity-seeking worldwide
Strategic choice how to commercialize R&D	Selection criteria are extremely low. Maximize the number of spin-offs	Among the selection criteria, growth orientation is important. But remain lower than in private VCs	Selection criteria resemble those of the VCs
Intellectual property assessment and protection	Emphasis on commercializing technology through patents	Support in patent and licence negotiation with the industry	TTO will acquire an IPR platform (not limited to one patent) at an early stage
Incubation and business plan development	Projects are offered space at the research centre or university	Incubation centre and science park; specialized support available out-house at market prices	'In-house' incubation and support at all stages of the spin-off process and to a high level
Funding process	Small amounts, ranging from €15 000 to €100 000, under the form of public grants	Public private equity fund, ranging from €250 000 to €350 000	VC money, ranging from €1 million to €4 million
Control over the spin-off process after spin-off of the spin-off company	Project is started at a pre-founding stage. All types of spin-off are selected	Spin-off company is start-up at a very early stage	Spin-off company is start-up in a late stage and with an experienced management team

spin-off funnel. In both model cases this approach results in a high selection rate. In the past two years, Crealys received 160 projects of which the selection committee approved 60. Over the past two years Twente selected approximately 60 projects out of 130 applications (Karnebeek, 2001). No economic or financial criteria are included in the selection process.

IPR assessment and protection: proprietary technology is unlikely to be the key trigger to spin-off a company. In Twente, there was a patent owned by the university in only 7 per cent of spin-offs founded after 1980. This percentage might be higher for more recent spin-offs since active patenting among university institutes is quite new.

Incubation and business plan development: spin-off support focuses mainly on the validation phase of the project when there is no need for a large infrastructure or business space. In both Crealys and Twente, space is available within the university or research laboratory facilities.

Funding process: Crealys and Twente grant public money to these early stage projects. The Twente funds are derived from the European Social Fund and are granted in the form of loans (15 000 euros) which are typically regarded as a means of subsistence rather than as spin-off capital (Karnebeek, 2001). Crealys invests in spin-off companies during the phase of validation of the project, up to a maximum of 100 000 euros per project.

Control of the spin-off process after start-up: spin-off companies are selected at a very early stage and coaching is focused upon this stage. The consequences of this model are that a variety of businesses are selected, many of which will be small with low levels of capitalization. In Twente, the average number of jobs per company after ten years was six, with only 4 per cent of all spin-offs having received venture capital. In France, the Crealys initiative is too recent to analyse growth figures, but of all projects started, about 10 per cent resulted in a growth-orientated venture capital backed company.

Supportive model   The Supportive model is orientated towards generating spin-offs as an alternative to licensing out its IP. This model tends to generate 'profit orientated' spin-offs with potential growth opportunity and takes its name from the extensive support given to the entrepreneurial team during the pre-start up phase. The TTO views the spin-off as an alternative to licensing as a vehicle to commercialize technology. The Leuven R&D and BioM cases represent prime examples of the Supportive model. Although the Leuven R&D spin-off service was formally created in the early 1970s, it was only professionalized in the mid-1990s. By that time, Leuven was one of the high-tech poles in the region. The nearby university and the presence of the Inter-university Institute for Micro-electronics (IMEC, see below) had resulted in several high-tech spin-offs and had attracted several technology intensive companies in the science park, some of which were highly successful (Moray and Clarysse, 2005). BioM is located in the Munich area of Germany. Like Leuven, this area already had a history of high technology and spin-offs. The presence of the Max Planck Institute and several universities stimulated the creation of spin-outs, especially in biotechnology. In the mid-1990s, Germany wanted to create a structure to enhance and successfully support the creation of spin-outs in biotechnology. BioM was one of the five institutes that received financing from this Bioregion competition. Although today the financing constitutes only a very small part of the budget, the competition induced the creation of BioM.

Opportunity search and awareness creation: Leuven R&D hosts the contract research activities, the IPR activities and the spin-off support of the University of Leuven. Most opportunity recognition happens in an indirect way. Usually, a professor seeks support for his/her contract research activities and is made aware of IP possibilities by the contract research department. Once the IP is applied for, a trade-off is made between licensing and the creation of a new spin-off. BioM deploys a less formal model since it does not manage contract research or IPR activities. This shortcoming, however, appears to overcome through a specialization on biotechnology and its attraction of highly esteemed scientific advisers in biotechnology whom the professors respect.

Strategic choice how to commercialize R&D: spinning off usually results from a trade-off between licensing out the technology or creating a company based on the technology, for which there are clear selection criteria. Typically, the researchers have to prepare a business plan to be selected by the spin-off service. If the research team is interested in creating a spin-off, this option to commercialize the technology might be favoured over licensing out the technology even if the benefits of a spin-out are not so clear. BioM received 130 project plans in the past five years but only invested directly in 28 spin-off companies. This results in an acceptance rate of about 25 per cent, which is ten times the acceptance rate of a typical VC.

IPR assessment and protection: the IP department is the heart of the technology transfer service. Leuven R&D has a professional IP support staff. In BioM, no specific IPR support is foreseen, but close contacts are established with patent experts who might help the spin-off. In both cases, no technology platform is built through licensing in pieces of technology to complement the existing technology.

Incubation and business plan development: incubation and business plan advice are key activities in this model. The researchers are assisted in writing a preliminary business plan that can be defended in front of a semi-public seed capital fund. The business plan is more artificial in comparison to the business case usually asked for by VCs or corporates before investing. Incubation facilities also include space and access to equipment. Support includes business advice and coaching. BioM does not have its own incubation centre, but has developed a close relationship with IZB (the CEO of BioM is the scientific CEO of IZB), which owns two incubation centres in the Munich area. The incubation centre, I&I, located in Leuven, is a separate legal entity, with its own independent management structure. Leuven R&D is represented on its board of directors, which serves as the main mechanism for providing informal specialized support and advice. Because it takes place through the board of directors, all advice is essentially free.

Funding process: this model makes greater use of public-private partnership funds, which are usually organized as a VC fund. The amount of money invested ranges from 350 000 to 600 000 euros per business plan. The typical level of investment is beyond the scope of either public funds and/or business angel support alone, but is often too low for a VC. There is real financial screening and business plans must be complete, comprehensive and validated. The fund tends to invest in earlier stages and in lower amounts than a typical VC. The evaluation and monitoring approach adopted in this model is closer to a VC than to a business angel. The spin-out service will hold equity in the company after separation, with the percentage of equity taken varying but seldom comprising a majority. For example, BioM takes on average 7 per cent of the shares of a spin-off company.

Control over the spin-off process after start-up: under this model, the amount of money available is limited and is usually only sufficient for a year. Most companies founded through this process are likely to seek complementary revenues through short-term contract research or consulting. In BioM, 35 per cent of the spin-off companies have already received venture capital financing.

Incubator model   The Incubator model makes a trade-off between the use of a body of research to generate contract research versus spinning off this research in a separate company. We term the spin-offs resulting from this Incubator model 'exit orientated' since the exit possibilities provide the financial opportunity. The Incubator model is labelled after the incubators that emerged in the early 1990s with the specific objective to create financially attractive spin-offs. IMEC, The Technology Partnership (TTP) in Cambridge, UK, and Scientific Generics are prime examples of this model. IMEC is located in the Leuven area. The IMEC was created in the early 1980s. The commercialization of research results was among the goals of the institute and has become one of its key activities. Today, 80 per cent of IMEC's revenues are generated by contract research activities. Both TTP and Scientific Generics are located in the Cambridge (UK) region (Segall, Quince, Wicksteed, 2002). Scientific Generics was founded in 1986 with four main objectives: top-level technology consulting; creating and licensing out IP; investing in the creation of spin-offs; investing in other high-tech start-ups. Being located in a known high-tech region, it is able to attract European top researchers to its base in Cambridge. In both cases the motivation for creating spin-offs is purely a financial one.

Opportunity search and awareness creation: opportunity-seeking activities are more proactively undertaken and managed under this model. In TTP this is rather informal whereas in Scientific Generics and IMEC there are formal mechanisms for assessing all contract work for spin-off potential that extend to universities outside the UK. The IMEC is a leading-edge PRO in micro-electronics and looks for projects at a very early research stage in the different universities in Flanders. In the Incubator model, creating a spin-off is a decision made by the top management of the PRO. Although it is desirable to have an entrepreneurial research team, they usually do not expect it to comprise real business entrepreneurs. Instead, some spin-offs of the IMEC do not employ the researchers that invented the technology on which the spin-off is based. Rather, they tend to recruit external top management for each spin-off. The key researchers can eventually choose to have a joint position.

Strategic choice how to commercialize R&D: in terms of project selection the decision to spin off is based on financial and strategic arguments. As contract research with or without some form of licensing is the main source of income for these PROs, they are very careful about spinning off parts of their core technology unless (1) they have sufficient reason to believe the spin-off will be able to generate more money than the potential revenue stream generated by the contract research based upon the technology or (2) the technology is so specific and/or peripheral to the core mission of the PRO that a contract research group based upon it would be difficult to sustain. Once the development of the project becomes more advanced, the criteria for receiving spin-off support are the same as those used by venture capitalists.

IPR assessment and protection: once a project is chosen to have spin-off possibilities, the IPR policy aims to build a technology platform through licensing-in other technology and cross-licensing some parts. Usually, these PROs have complex models of exclusive and non-exclusive licensing. These models need to optimize both the potential revenues for the PRO (so that contract research can be continued) and to maximize the survival chances of the spin-off (that is, VCs need to find the technology valuable enough). It is clear that these spin-offs are not one-patent companies.

Incubation and business plan development: the spin-off service provides support ranging from management and housing of the research projects to provision of offices, business plan development, recruitment of external management and the composition of their technology platform. The incubation process has both a long time horizon and aims to offer a fully in-house support service.

Funding process: both the timescale and the nature of the project mean that funding requirements are greater than under the other two models. Typically spin-offs from this model start with a capital of 1–4 million euros. Scientific Generics and the IMEC maintain good contacts with the wider venture capital community. Through their preferred partnerships and informal networks they attract financing for their spin-offs at founding. TTP has its own fund which (co)-invests at spin-off. Of course, before a company is formally founded and spun out, many investments have already been made to bring the project to this stage.

Control over the spin-off process after start-up: the stage and process of separation of the spin-off and the PRO varies. At TTP the 'demerging' of the spin-off occurs late in the process and the spin-off may go straight to IPO. Separation in Scientific Generics and the IMEC is earlier, often with a trade sale in Scientific Generics and always through VC involvement in the IMEC. In all cases, the spin-off will have a well-developed professional management team, probably involving outsiders.

Resources

The essential resource features of each model are summarized in Table 4.3. Following Brush et al. (2001), we examined six types of resources as being key to the spin-off process: human, social, financial, physical, technology and organizational.

Low Selective model   The Low Selective model needs the lowest number of resources in terms of quantity. The critical size is only a few persons and no organizational structure has to be created separate from the university. However, ideally some public money and incubation facilities should be available to support the new start-ups.

Organizational resources: the spin-off activity is a unit within the PRO or university, which is independent from the technology transfer unit. Instead, the unit has a particular mission to increase entrepreneurial awareness.

Human resources: the spin-off units employ a small team of people familiar with existing government grant programs. Their human capital is thus more public than private orientated. However, the presence of a well known and respected entrepreneur helps to achieve credibility.

Table 4.3   *Resources required by the different models*

Resources	Low Selective model	Supportive model	Incubator model
	Based upon Crealys and Twente	Based upon Leuven R&D and BioM	Based upon IMEC, TTP and Scientific Generics
Organizational resources	Public organizations, linked with universities	Private organizations linked with universities	Centre of excellence, close link with industry
Human resources	Small team, familiar with public sector	Larger (5–7 persons) multidisciplinary team, with links to the financial world to be able to evaluate the business plans	Experienced professional staff. Able to draw upon 'in-house' specialists
Technological resources	No technological focus or specialisms	Focus on the best performing departments of the universities. Mainly applied research	Relatively narrowly focused on particular specialisms in which it has a wealth of experience
Physical resources	Offer office space and infrastructure within the universities	Offer office space and infrastructure within an incubation centre, at market prices	Internal research space and infrastructure is offered for free
Financial resources	Need a large amount of public money to offer at the spin-offs	Need to set up an associated fund with public/private partners	Invested money is private money, the TTO may have its own VC fund
Networking resources	Entrepreneurial climate within university or research centre is very important	Entrepreneurial context is very important	Entrepreneurial context is scarcely important

Technological resources: the spin-off service has no technological focus since the mission is to support as many projects as possible, irrespective of technological area.

Physical resources: office space and infrastructure are organized within the universities and do not play a determining role.

Financial resources: the spin-off service should have control over a public fund, which can distribute grants or at least have close contacts with other public sector initiatives. Crealys received 1.5 million euros from the Ministère de la recherche because it was selected as a public incubator. Crealys also receives each year 200 000 euros from the City of Lyon, 1 million euros from the Rhône-Alpes region and 500 000 euros from the associated universities.

Networking resources: the success of this model depends upon the social network which the spin-off service has developed with various public agencies and the teaching curriculums of the university. Its mission lies in stimulating entrepreneurial orientation.

Supportive model   In the Supportive model, a well-functioning IP department and contract research unit tend to be key. The technology transfer unit can only use the leverage afforded by the contract research if it is able to support it in such a way that academics feel they are helped in organizing this activity. The IP and spin-off activity are then the next step in the technology transfer process. To organize all this, a minimum critical mass of at least 20 persons is needed. In addition, the spin-offs tend to need external capital at a very early stage. Therefore, public–private partnerships are set up to invest in these seed or, even, pre-seed ventures.

Organizational resources: BioM operates as a private company. Leuven R&D is the fully integrated technology transfer office of the University of Leuven operating within matrix organizational structure (Debackere, 2000) that provides budgetary and human resource management autonomy within the university. The operational autonomy allows the technology transfer to create an environment that is beneficial for researchers to undertake contract research activities and other forms of research commercialization, while the financial autonomy makes the technology transfer service less dependent upon the PRO's budgetary decisions on a year by year basis. The spin-out support service is embedded in the technology transfer services.

Human resources: the technology transfer units employ a heterogeneous team of over 15 people. Three to four team members are only focused on spin-off activity. They usually have some form of business experience or at least a business degree. Other team members have legal, human resources (HR) and various technical backgrounds, needed to engage in patenting activity.

Technological resources: the technological resources, whether provided directly or not, are likely to be more focused towards particular specific technologies. BioM has a sectored focus on biotechnology. Leuven R&D tends to be focused on information technology (IT) and biomedical ventures. The technology transfer services and the spin-off unit in particular tend to cover a number of broad technological domains. Usually the research groups in each subdomain tend to be quite small.

Physical resources: as suggested earlier, physical resources will be more developed under this model. In both BioM and Leuven R&D, the availability of an incubation centre and a science park is very important to the functioning of the service, although space is offered at market prices. The spin-off companies are in the business plan validation phase when they receive support.

Financial resources: BioM, is financed by three parties: Technologie Beteilungsgesellschaft (Tbg) together with VC companies, the State of Bavaria, and the local pharmaceutical and chemical industry. BioM has no real fund but uses a part of the financing provided by the three parties to invest in spin-off companies. Approximately 8 million euros have already been invested in spin-off companies. The Gemma Frisius Fond was created in 1997 as a joint venture between the Katholieke Universiteit Leuven – represented by Leuven R&D (20 per cent), KBC Investment (40 per cent) and Fortis Private Equity (40 per cent) – and is a 12.5 million euro fund.

Networking resources: since this model uses boards of directors as the principal advisory mechanism for the spin-offs, a well-established network and close links with local industry, specialized advisers and the VC community are important. Further, since the value added to equity investment will essentially come from second-round financing by VCs, this model is quite dependent upon the 'entrepreneurial context' of the regions. In the previous model, as the mission was the stimulation of spin-offs, regardless of growth prospects, the entrepreneurial climate within the university and the degree to which the government is willing to sponsor entrepreneurial initiatives were important in determining efficiency of the service. The Supportive model, however, is more dependent upon networks of specialized advisers in the region, which they use to perform ad hoc services within these spin-offs.

Incubator model   Finally, in the Incubator model, spin-offs are seen as an option where the technology is really cutting edge and a financial participation might generate more revenues for the research institute than might future contract research. The spin-off formation usually takes a very long time (up to three years) since all assumptions are tested before valuable IP is given to a separate venture. In addition, the venture tends to be created with formal, usually specialized, venture capital funds as shareholders at start. The Incubator model will carefully prepare this type of venture using a number of milestones before final approval is given.

Organizational resources: the PROs in the Incubator model are focused upon contract research. The spin-off support services are part of the business development department, which is usually a key department in these PROs.

Human resources: since business development and commercializing research is a core activity for these PROs, the business development department is quite well developed. Usually we find more than 30 people working in such a department, which is an interdisciplinary team of experienced persons.

Technological resources: the centres of excellence are relatively narrowly focused on particular specialisms, in which they have a wealth of experience. The distinction between fundamental and applied research is not important, but breadth is. For example, Scientific Generics is more involved in 'development' than fundamental research but is a recognized specialist in its particular narrow field. The IMEC claims to be the leading institute in micro-electronics.

Physical resources: as the origin of each spin-off company lies within the laboratory, internal office space is offered for free and infrastructure is available. This model keeps its spin-offs within the physical incubator environment of the 'parent'. TTP has extensive physical resources on site at its location on the Melbourne Science Park to the south of Cambridge.

Financial resources: the Incubator model requires substantial financial resources. First, a large investment is needed to create a centre of scientific excellence in order to generate the IP. In the case of the IMEC, the Flemish government has invested each year about 30 million euros in the institute since inception in 1984. Scientific Generics involved no public money; the money came from the personal wealth and network of its founder. In 2001, the IMEC had a budget of 115 million euros: 88 million euros came from contract research and 27 million euros came from the Flemish government. In TTP and Scientific Generics these 'investments' are subsidized by other mainstream commercial activities such as contract research and manufacturing.

Networking resources: because the spin-off services effectively manage and support all stages and processes in research-based spin-off creation, the potential for the entrepreneurial context to add to the support is quite low. The spin-off services are self-contained and self-sufficient. Scientific Generics is one of a small number of technical consultancy firms which have become a notable feature of the Cambridge high-tech environment. Scientific Generics, and especially its founder, have a very high profile in the local Cambridge business environment.

Models, strategies and outcomes

The three reference models tend to be harmonious in terms of the activities they undertake and their resource profiles. In this section, we discuss this issue in more detail and analyse how the combination of resources and activities deployed in our reference models serve specific objectives. The three reference types characterize the typology of successful strategies employed by public research organizations to create and spin off new ventures as there is harmony between activities and resources.

Low Selective model Low Selective interfaces are mainly concerned with creating as many start-ups as possible. Since self-employment orientated spin-offs include all kinds of service or consulting companies, these usually do not generate high financial returns at the beginning. As these projects are not attractive to private capital, public money is an important resource in this model. The amounts invested per company remain small (see Crealys and Twente) as most do not need substantial starting capital. The human resources needed stay limited in quantity, but are very specific in nature. The Low Selective service is typically run by a few people with the skills to enhance the entrepreneurial climate at the university (on average there was a ratio of 452:1 researchers to each technology transfer officer). The critical evaluation dimension is the number of spin-offs that surround the university. For instance, by the end of 2001, Crealys had created an average of 20 spin-offs per year. Twente came close to 30 spin-offs each year in 2001 and 2002.

The economic and financial attractiveness of each firm is less important. The businesses supported are commonly characterized by: (1) low levels of capitalization, (2) locally or nationally market focused, (3) lifestyle rather than significant wealth creation and (4) less developed management structures and processes. In both PROs examined here, the spin-offs received only a small amount of capital (minimum legal capital) and seem to have established a very small growth pattern that yields few jobs and financial returns to the entrepreneur and the regional economy. Owing to the large number of companies established, however, the total number of jobs created in the regions is considerable. For example, in the Twente area over 3000 jobs were created in total and 1500 in the Leuven area. Owing to the possibilities offered by the PRO environment, graduates stay around the campus instead of returning to their home environment. We suggest, therefore, that the imprinting effect is important in the first years after start-up, however, this does not automatically preclude some start-ups eventually turning into growth-orientated companies as well (Heirman and Clarysse, 2004).

Supportive model The Supportive model originates from the general idea of commercializing technology developed at the public research organization through means other than licensing. Hence, the spin-offs are an alternative option to create value from the technology. This aim is very different from the Low Selective model, where all students, researchers and professors are encouraged to start their own business as part of the RI's mission to stimulate entrepreneurship. By focusing on spin-offs as an alternative to licensing or contract research, the Supportive model limits the number of spin-offs in comparison to the Low Selective model.

As spin-offs are alternatives to licensing, the returns focused upon are based upon economic profitability factors rather than financial gains to be obtained for investors upon exit. The activities and resources needed to stimulate spin-offs are also very different. As discussed above, the Supportive model requires substantial resources for IP assistance and support is provided in terms of patent and licence negotiation with industry (on average there was a ratio of 184:1 researchers to technology transfer officers). These resources are less necessary in the Low Selective case where most spin-offs lack IP developed at the university. Rather than raising awareness across the university, a project-orientated approach is adopted. Initially, the technology transfer office usually tries to intensify trust-based relationships to develop partnerships with professors, both for consulting and patenting. Only when a potentially interesting technology is identified is the entrepreneurship idea promoted. Once the decision is made to commercialize the technology through a spin-off, the team of researchers is intensively coached to start-up the company, including help with looking for money.

To realize these activities, the technology transfer office needs very different resources than in the Low Selective model. First, it usually employs a larger multidisciplinary team with commercial experience and links to the financial community. The critical mass of this team seems to be around 20 people. Second, it has close contacts or even manages a public/private fund willing to invest small to medium-sized amounts (250 000–750 000 euros) in projects that are very early and uncertain (so-called pre-seed). Third, the PRO needs to have a critical mass of at least 2000–3000 researchers, specialized in a limited number of technological domains (for example two or three). Fourth, the organization needs to be organized as a separate entity with control over triggers to motivate professors to work with them. Fifth, the interface service needs to have sufficient contacts with local experts, business entrepreneurs and specialized consultants in order to support the research team during the spin-off process.

The ultimate objective of this model is to create economically viable companies that stay in the region, make the environment attractive and create contract research spillovers with their parent PRO. Interestingly, in terms of total employment, the spin-offs in the Leuven region lag behind those in the Twente region.

Incubator model   The Incubator model arose from growing interest among many organizations that had developed proprietary technology, including PROs, to analyse the specific circumstances under which spin-offs could become more financially attractive (in terms of exit opportunities that would create capital gains for VCs) than licensing or contract research with established industry. In doing so, these PROs follow closely the due diligence process adapted by a typical early stage venture capital firm.

Opportunity-seeking is proactive and orientated towards the early detection of promising technology platforms. Instead of making the trade-off between licensing out a patent or building a venture, technology is usually assessed from a freedom to operate perspective. This means that pieces of technology may be licensed in (or cross-licensed) before the company is started. Significant in-house support is provided at all stages of the spin-out process (on average there was a ratio of only 44:1 researchers to each technology transfer officer). The venture remains inside the parent PRO until all resources are in place and the venture is deemed ready to look for private VC and to hire a proven management team.

The resources needed to stimulate this kind of spin-off differ substantially from the previous two models. First, the technology transfer office usually coincides with the 'business development' division of the PRO. Second, the technology transfer activity may manage its own early stage venture capital fund or have close contacts with one or more early stage VC funds. Third, the interface office often has contacts with international advisers. Fourth, the PRO tends to be specialized in one technology and has built the physical infrastructure to develop research in this technological domain.

Our research shows that the Incubator model results in fewer spin-offs but the businesses supported will likely be VC-backed growth-orientated businesses, achieving higher levels of innovative activity at the leading edge of technology and operating in global markets. When spin-off companies leave the PRO, they are likely to be highly product/market focused, have a balanced and experienced team and be more adequately funded than ventures spun out using other models.

Complementarity of the models and objectives
The three models may be complementary or substitutable means of reaching the same objectives. Our data suggest that they are complementary and that it is difficult to achieve the aim of stimulating the three kinds of start-ups, that is, self-employment orientated, economic-profit orientated, and exit orientated, in parallel *in an efficient way* using just one model. Of course, some spin-offs in the Low Selective model, will eventually become growth orientated but this is not as a direct result of the spin-off policy of

the PRO. Similarly, start-ups with low growth opportunities, as generated by the Low Selectivity model, will have difficulties receiving support in the Incubator and, even, the Supportive model. In the Incubator model, project selection is competitive and the best projects, in terms of their investment attractiveness to venture capitalists, receive support.

The three objectives regarding the type of spin-off created are also not necessarily orthogonal. Hence, if a PRO wants efficiently to support the three kinds of spin-off activity, it might be more appropriate to adopt the three models in parallel. For instance, a central unit can be set up to stimulate entrepreneurial activity in a broad sense and support students, researchers and professors to set up a company. In parallel the technology transfer unit might develop a path to create value from technological opportunities through spin-offs. Finally, the PRO might create a specific spin-offs support group which focuses only on the creation of VC-backed spin-offs in technological domains where it is a leader. This could be pursued while referring the less mature projects to the interface unit, as in the universities of Twente in our reference sample and Oxford and Warwick in the UK in our validation sample (see below).

Role of the local environment

In Chapters 1 and 2 we discussed the potential importance of variations in the local environment. Our research shows that the drivers behind the Low Selective model are related to regional development and regional job creation. Most prior US work focusing on the link between university and spin-offs has largely overlooked this employment argument. The reason seems to be that US spin-off studies usually depart from the premise that spin-offs commercialize patented research results developed at the PRO (Colyvas et al., 2002; Shane and Stuart, 2002). European country-specific studies such as Autio and Yli-Renko (1998) have suggested a relation between the unemployment ratio and the number of spin-offs in a region. Starting a company is a way to (1) get into employment as a graduate and (2) stay in the region as a highly skilled person. Since most of these companies tend to be service orientated and have a local market (Karnebeck, 2001), there needs to be a local demand for knowledge-intensive services. Hence, this model can only exist if the local market of established firms is large enough. The Twente region in particular fits this unemployment idea. Although the region needed economic help and was classified as an Objective 5 region by the European Fund for Regional Development, it is within a one-hour drive of major commercial districts in the Netherlands. Service companies tend to be well located next to the campus and quite close to their customers. The Rhône-Alpes (Crealys) region can also be viewed in this context.

The Low Selective model seems only loosely related to the trend in many European countries to change legislation on IP issues (in line with the US Bayh–Dole Act, stipulating that universities own the IP of research developed by its employees). In contrast, the Supportive model is likely to benefit from these changes in legislation (Colyvas et al., 2002) since it is based upon IP developed within the RI. However, the two role models selected in this chapter have not directly obtained such benefits. Leuven R&D already had an active patenting policy and internal regulation before the legislation was changed. BioM is located in one of the only countries in Europe where the IP *does not* belong to the university. Therefore, it appears that legislation has not had an impact here. Instead, creating the right culture and structure to trigger the faculty seems to be the first step.

The Supportive model seems to rely very much on the regional dynamic to function effectively. The technology transfer officers, who set up the companies with a local public/private seed capital fund make use of the local knowledge network to incubate the spin-offs in a marketplace. This is in line with previous evidence emphasizing the role of personal networks in the search for venture capital (Shane et al., 2002). Suchman (1994) points to knowledge-intensive business service providers as drivers of innovation in Route 128 and Silicon Valley. Hence, this kind of spin-off service might be dependent upon the local high-tech environment. Both the Munich and Leuven areas are very dynamic high-tech regions in which Leuven R&D and BioM are only one actor. Next to them, we observe important public involvement (for example, Bayern Kapital, State of Bavaria, Tbg and KUL), presence of R&D-intensive, more established companies (for example, BMW, Siemens, HP/Agilent, LMS and ICOS) and networking initiatives (for example, Leuven Inc.).

Finally, the incubator is a local actor in a much broader worldwide environment. Typically the research team of this organization is specialized in a narrow technological field and is well-known and respected in this field. For example, the IMEC has a worldwide reputation in terms of micro-electronic research. The organization is not only respected in the field but it also attracts highly talented researchers to join the organization. Scientific Generics encourages research teams all over the world, specialized in biotechnology or electronics, to join the organization. Also in terms of outflow, these organizations tend to be less dependent upon the local environment. Most spin-offs are started with professional venture capital, often syndicated at an international level. Hence, it is not the local social network that seems to be important here but the international contacts with professional early stage VC funds. In the period between inflow and outflow, the project is managed internally. Again, contacts are made at an international rather than a local level (for example, by licensing in from international partners).

The origin of these institutes also plays a role. Scientific Generics was created by Gordon Edge, who had built up his experience in this Cambridge environment before starting Scientific Generics. The IMEC on the other hand was the result of a political decision to create better value from research on micro-electronics at the Flemish universities. It thus seems that 'research excellence' often lies at the origin of these institutes, but the local environment interacts less with them downstream in the value chain. Of course, the critical mass of research graduates in the universities surrounding them remains an important factor.

4.2.2 Departures from the Reference Models

Approaches to spin-off development may depart from our three reference models by virtue of their resources and activities. We identify two principal suboptimal types: resource deficient and competence deficient. Their characteristics in terms of number of researchers, number of technology transfer employees, technological focus and age are compared with the three reference models in Table 4.4.

Resource deficient
We labelled as resource deficient those spin-off support services with high ambitions in terms of objectives but which lack the resources to realize these ambitions. The deficiency in resources has a number of implications for PROs. First, they do not have the financial resources to make decisions autonomously from the university and invest in spin-off generation over a sufficient period of time. Second, they do not have the right mix of competencies or people in terms of experience and networking to deploy these activities. Third, they are not supported by a university board with an entrepreneurial orientation and/or they cannot rely on a strong regional network that supports enterprise. These factors produce structural shortcomings that lead these spin-off services to be positioned as weakly supportive models, and therefore unable to generate the type of returns that were initially sought. The objectives in terms of spin-offs of these resource-deficient models are usually not clear and tend to follow the visibly successful examples in their immediate region. For instance, the Flemish universities tend to look at the Leuven R&D model and mimic its ambition, even without having the key success elements of this model. These key success elements lie in its structure/culture (trigger for the professors/researchers) and its broader regional environment as well as in its unique resource base built up over a long period of time. Imitation of such a strategy without these relevant resources tends to be unsuccessful. It seems that the lack of clarity about the kind of outcome possible within the

Table 4.4 *Key figures on 43 validation cases*

Number of cases		Number of researchers	People employed at the technology transfer service	Technological focus	Age
Low Selective	10				
	Average	1462.6	5.3	No	7.2
	Median	1737	3		8
	Maximum	3000	15		15
	Minimum	46	1		2
	Standard deviation	1060.54	4.58		4.99
	Researchers/TTS people		274.2		
Supportive	7				
	Average	1808.1	6.9	No	5.3
	Median	745	4.5		4
	Maximum	11 700	25		20
	Minimum	120	1		1
	Standard deviation	2902.19	6.59		5.01
	Researchers/TTS people		262.3		
Incubator	2				
	Average	1928.3	10.6	No	12.2
	Median	1720.5	10		8
	Maximum	3000	16		30
	Minimum	1024	2		3
	Standard deviation	817.81	4.89		10.0
	Researchers/TTS people		182.4		

				No	
Resource deficient	18	Average	1678.3	4.2	6.3
		Median	1175	3	5.5
		Maximum	4950	10	15
		Minimum	70	1	2
		Standard deviation	1836.79	3.56	4.63
		Researchers/TTS people	399.6		
				Yes	
Competence deficient	6	Average	550	12.5	5
		Maximum	750	15	8
		Minimum	350	10	2
		Researchers/TTS people	44.0		

culture/structure of the PRO and the characteristics of the broader environment is the first reason why this hybrid type of organization exists.

Competence deficient
We labelled those interface services which *have* the resources to implement one of the above models, but which do not have sufficient ability to perform the activities needed to build up a successful interface service, as 'competence deficient'. There was a lack of knowledge in the form of competencies that have been developed to employ resources productively in activities that will eventually result in the economic and social returns desired. These cases show what can happen if a PRO is supplied with a large amount of resources to create what the Supportive and Incubator PRO models. Even with a desire to create the economically and financially attractive spin-offs these models produce, without the requisite knowledge to acquire and integrate resources to create the required competencies it is impossible to fulfil this ambition.

Performance of these activities requires specialized competencies that can only be developed over time. For example, at Scientific Generics, over time, teams have learnt to develop these competencies which include creating technology platforms, performing business development and raising rounds of venture capital. Some of the competence-deficient PROs tried to shortcut this learning phase by acquiring specialists from other organizations who could supply the knowledge to build competencies. These PROs continued to depart from the behaviour seen in the reference models because they lacked the ability to integrate and coordinate these competencies efficiently enough to produce results reflecting their desired objectives. Some PROs in this category can best be described as being 'in transition' from one normative model to another. Having already decided to make this shift, their current state of evolution has left them in a position somewhere between the two and resulted in an inability to deliver returns characterized by either model.

We did not find any indication that the prevalence of any model is higher in one specific region or country under study. The observed frequencies of incidence of each model are equally spread over the different regions. Further, the resource-deficient models tend to be associated with public research organizations that might be just below critical mass in number of researchers (Table 4.4). The public research organizations tend to spread their resources too thinly to achieve a critical mass in any one domain, which tends to be the starting point of a successful interface model.

Taken together, the public research organizations falling into each of the two categories that departed from the reference models failed to achieve their intended objectives. Typically, inexperienced practitioners and ill-informed policy-makers set out with the objective of creating economic growth and development by producing large numbers of 'high-value' spin-outs. These high-value spin-offs are characterized as high-tech ventures expected to generate high levels of financial returns for investors and entrepreneurs plus highly skilled employment growth for the region. In reality, the spin-offs emerging from these public research organizations tended to be under-capitalized with little or no growth. This emphasizes our earlier observation concerning the orthogonality of the different models that there is an inherent conflict in trying to create 'self-employment', 'economically profitable' and 'exit' orientated spin-offs through one business model.

Public research organizations creating high value or financially attractive spin-offs have over time acquired specialized resources and developed competencies focused on creating a small number of ventures with the capacity to become established corporations. They have built up an international social network to attract top-level researchers and to team up with venture capitalists downstream. In this process, a lot of economically viable projects are not supported because it is financially more attractive to license out the technology to an established partner. Self-employment orientated projects are deliberately not considered. The Supportive model is less selective, but still looks for economic-profitability orientated companies with a reasonable growth potential and time to break even. They support projects at a point when other financial investors are unlikely to be interested. This approach might be too slow for exit-orientated projects requiring more resources and a speed-up of the time to market from spin-off. Incubator models are not well suited to evaluate these projects since they typically do not find VCs to syndicate with. This means that often these companies have difficulties finding follow-up money if the initial starting capital is not sufficient to cover the time to breakeven.

4.3 PERFORMANCE INDICATORS

We used our validation sample of 43 public research institutes described in Chapter 1 to examine the performance of different incubation processes. Indicators of performance were available in terms of cumulative number of spinouts and number of spinouts per 1000 researchers in 2002, amount of capital raised and new jobs created per 1000 researchers. Table 4.5 shows that, while most groups perform as expected on the basis of the reference groups, indicators of the Low Selective group in the validation sample are lower than expected based upon the reference cases of Crealys and Twente. On closer inspection we note that although the PROs in the validation sample have resources and activities in line with their objectives the extent

Table 4.5   Performance metrics in validation cases

Variable	Low Selective N = 10	Supportive N = 7	Incubator N = 2	Resource deficient N = 18	Competence deficient N = 6
Spin-off 2002 (per 1000 researchers)	5.8 (3.9)	6.0 (6.1)	2.6 (0.0)	3.6 (5.9)	0.9 (0.4)
New jobs created (per 1000 researchers)	132.9 (36.8)	308.7 (299.3)	346.0 (112.2)	95.9 (133.6)	16.3 (14.0)
Total capital raised (in millions)	2.5 (1.8)	20.6 (44.5)	20.5 (2.4)	1.3 (0.7)	0.6 (0.5)
Total spin-off since proactive spin-off policy implemented per RI	43.7 (39.6)	54.0 (18.8)	3.0 (0.0)	14.7 (18.2)	11.3 (16.2)

of public funding to facilitate spin-offs varied between PROs in this group and tended to be less than in Crealys and Twente. The availability of public money invested directly in start-ups and without expectations of financial returns seems to be key to realizing maximum results in the Low Selective model. Hence, although several Irish spin-off services in the validation sample in particular clearly adopted a Low Selective model, they tended to be less effective in terms of performance than Crealys and Twente. In line with the Twente model, adding a small public grant to individual entrepreneurs might double their performance and achieve a more ambitious objective. As suggested in the discussion of the reference model cases, we find that PROs applying the Supportive model score very well in terms of number of spin-offs per year and new jobs created. They have, however, a lower track record than the Incubator model cases, which create the same amount of jobs per year and raise more capital with far fewer spin-offs.

The resource-deficient model cases have fewer spin-offs, create fewer jobs and raise only a limited amount of capital, reflecting the problem arising from their aim to create a Supportive model but their not having the resources to do this successfully. The result is that the performance of this large group of spin-off services is far below the performance of the Low Selective group, which needs less resources. Increasing critical size through collaboration between PROs might be an option to increase performance. Alternatively, individual PROs can change their strategy and adopt a Low Selective model, which is less resource demanding.

Reflecting the problem that the competence-deficient model cases lack knowledge in the form of competencies to employ resources productively, these cases have a low number of new jobs created and raise only a limited amount of capital.

4.4 SUMMARY AND CONCLUSIONS

In this chapter we have identified three types of spin-off models that have proven their efficiency and two suboptimal categories. The Low Selective model supports the creation of self-employment orientated spin-offs. These companies are predominantly service orientated. The Supportive model stimulates the creation of economic-profitability orientated spin-outs. These spin-offs might be growth orientated, but usually start with some kind of service or consulting model to limit the time to breakeven. Because of broader societal reasons or because it is incentivized by the local political environment, a public research organization might prefer to create a local spin-off over licensing the technology to a foreign multinational. Usually, the question as to whether a spin-off can survive in an economic way is central in the decision to create a spin-off. The Incubator model is based on financial gain from an eventual exit of the spin-off. A spin-off might be, potentially, a profitable company but initially it may be unattractive to a venture capital investor because the amount of money needed is too small to be efficient or the market is too small to generate the multiples expected by a financial investor. For these kinds of companies, the Incubator model may be appropriate as it provides for intensive support of the venture to get it to a stage where it meets a venture capital firm's investment criteria. We return to consider the investment criteria of venture capital firms in Chapter 7.

The models differ not only in terms of the amount of resources but also in the kind of resources required. This means that *if* a university or public research organization has relatively few resources to deploy, it should deploy them in a different way. For example, in a relatively poor resource environment, the Low Selective model might be the most feasible. However, it appears to be inappropriate to acquire/generate the resources required to perform a Supportive model and then try to perform activities associated with a Low Selective model, or vice versa. This helps explain why we observe many resource-deficient interface services in the random validation sample. They appear to be trying to emulate one pure type of model, but without the necessary resources to do so successfully. Hence it is important for universities and public research organizations to be very clear about their objectives and specify clearly the resources that are needed/activities performed to meet these objectives. Our data suggests that lack of clarity about the objectives results in hybrid types that can be either resource or competence deficient.

Our research suggests that the growing body of accounts of 'successful' technology transfer models may be mis-specified for three main reasons. First, many accounts fail to consider initial goals, strategies employed and eventual outcomes, which limits our understanding of the processes. It is only when a public research organization's technology transfer strategy is analysed in relation to its intended goals and environmental factors that we can fully judge its success. If a public research organization wants to stimulate the three different types of spin-offs identified here, it will probably need to have three different mechanisms among which there will be relatively little overlap. This implies that these three models can coexist in one public research organization but that the trajectory of a project will have to be managed from the beginning. If a public research organization has an objective to create significant numbers of spin-offs a year and is organized as an Incubator model, then we can predict that this will not work. If it is only interested in financially attractive spin-offs and is organized as a Low Selective model, again the model is unlikely to lead to the achievement of objectives. Future research should give us a better insight into how these models can coexist in one or a few public research organizations in the same regional environment. Second, a focus solely on improving the technology transfer function fails to take into account the importance of changing the organizational culture within public research organizations and establishing local environments that are supportive of entrepreneurship. Changing these last two aspects are monumental tasks compared with developing support mechanisms. Third, there is a failure to appreciate that schemes which are successful in one environment, region or context cannot be merely imitated in another. The environments found in and around Boston (USA), Cambridge (UK) and Southern California are atypical, and can be argued to act as 'regional incubators'. While these are often cited as models to emulate, in this chapter we have suggested there may be major insurmountable barriers to their successful adoption in different environments.

Our evidence suggests that those designing, running and evaluating schemes need to consider several issues. First, the size, experience and professionalism of those undertaking the technology transfer function will determine the scope and intensity of the support activities that are possible. Second, the degree of interaction and the nature of the relationship between those undertaking the technology transfer function with departments will influence the likely pool of ideas. Third, there is a need to consider the type(s) of spin-off companies to be catered for and those that will be excluded. Fourth, the organizational culture both within the technology transfer function and individual departments will influence how much the TTO needs to do in creating awareness and encouraging entrepreneurship.

NOTE

1. This chapter draws extensively on Clarysse et al. (2005b).

5. Processes at the firm level: phases and models of development[1]

5.1 INTRODUCTION

In new high-tech ventures, the novelty of the venture and inexperience of the entrepreneur, create a barrier that constrains the ability of the new venture during the early stages of growth to become an established firm. There is a need to overcome this challenge to achieve a succession of transitions from one phase of growth to the next. The problems faced by new high-tech ventures are particularly acute in university spin-offs since universities typically lack resources and academic entrepreneurs may lack commercial skills to create ventures in an attempt to commercialize technological assets. These problems may be compounded by conflicting objectives among key stakeholders such as the university, the academic entrepreneur, the venture's management team and suppliers of finance (such as venture capitalists).

This chapter examines the phases that spin-offs go through in their development, and analyses the key challenges these ventures face in their development. Stage-based models identify the organizational characteristics exhibited within each stage of development and suggest the changes required in the behaviour and practices of entrepreneurs if their business is to progress to the next stage. A resource-based perspective of the firm (Barney et al., 2001; Penrose, 1959) suggests that in order to progress through different phases of development, spin-offs need to develop both resources and internal capabilities over time. In addition, there has been increasing recognition of the role of feedback and the potential for non-linear development.

To examine the process of development across the phases of spin-off growth, we utilize evidence from in-depth face-to-face and telephone interviews with nine spin-offs from seven different UK. The spin-offs selected were all created to commercialize intellectual property (IP) initially generated from among the top-ten research elite universities in the UK actively involved in technology transfer. The spin-offs selected were all ventures that were explicitly seeking, or had secured, external equity finance. We intentionally selected the cases from a range of fundamentally different technology platforms covering biological, chemical, physical, computer sciences and engineering that were at a different stage of development.

Data were collected from the university technology transfer office (TTO) (or equivalent), a range of business development managers (BDMs), the academic entrepreneur (inventor) and the externally introduced 'surrogate' entrepreneur (Franklin et al., 2001) where applicable, seed stage investors, and the head of each department from which the spin-off originated. Triangulation was also aided by the collection of archival data from the university, the companies and the business press.

The next section examines the different phases that spin-offs pass through in their development. The subsequent section examines the junctures between the different phases of development that spin-offs must overcome as they seek to move to the next phase of development. The fourth section presents an extension of the analysis to different types of spin-offs and technology sectors. Finally, we conclude with a summary of the insights from the analysis. We illustrate the discussion with examples from the case studies. In order to protect confidentiality, the names used are pseudonyms.

5.2   PHASES OF DEVELOPMENT

In this section we discuss the different phases in spin-off development, drawing on evidence from the nine cases. These phases we identify as the: (1) research phase, (2) opportunity-framing phase, (3) pre-organization phase, (4) reorientation stage and, finally, (5) sustainable returns phase. Each phase is intended to characterize a specific group of activities as well as strategic focus that the firm must accomplish before it can move to the next phase of development. The analysis indicates that spin-offs move through a number of successive phases in their development in an iterative non-linear way. However, for expositional purposes, we analyse each phase along the development continuum in turn.

5.2.1   Research Phase

The main focus for all the academic entrepreneurs (or academic innovators) interviewed, prior to the commercial opportunity being recognized, was on perfecting academic research and publication of their work towards a particular scientific community. Within this research phase valuable intellectual property (IP) is created, which then generates the potential opportunity for commercialization. Consistent with existing research (Shane, 2004), the academic inventors involved with the cases we studied were at the forefront of research in their chosen fields and had created valuable know-how and technological assets.

5.2.2   Opportunity-Framing Phase

During this phase, the academic and the TTO worked independently or together towards examining whether the recognized opportunity had sufficient underlying value to warrant further effort in pursuing commercialization. This process involves evaluating whether the technology works and shows sufficient promise for applications outside the laboratory. If the result of this exercise was positive, attempts were made to 'frame' the technology within a commercial opportunity.

This process poses considerable challenges, with opportunities being defined imprecisely, targeted ambiguously or proving to be impracticable. There was a lack of understanding and experience regarding how best to maximize returns from commercial exploitation. Problems in identifying suitable applications of the technology, how these would perform commercially and the routes available for accessing those markets raise major barriers for the commercialization of university technology. There is a need to acquire relevant experience and capabilities in framing opportunities in order to overcome these problems.

Evidence from the cases indicates that the initial opportunities were not the best means of exploiting the potential commercial value of the technology. These opportunities did not identify which complementary resources would be required as the venture developed or where and how to acquire them. Those entrepreneurs who made more progress were those who spent significant amounts of time scrutinizing the potential risks of opportunities alongside potential investors, customers and others in their industry. This analysis may lead to the reframing of the opportunity in response to factors such as industry's lack of desire to license or co-develop early stage technologies but a preference to market later stage technologies with a higher probability of generating commercial returns. This may indicate that the best route to market may be for the academic entrepreneur to acquire the necessary resources and capabilities to exploit the IP through a spin-off venture.

5.2.3   Pre-organization Phase

The pre-organization phase represents the stage where the management of the spin-off venture can develop and start to implement strategic plans. This involves taking decisions about which resources and capabilities to develop and acquire, and when and how to do so. Decisions taken at this early stage had an important influence on the development trajectory and on the future alternatives available to the firm. For example, failure to select engineers with sufficient experience for the product development team and not relocating to premises away from the university campus may slow progress (Silicon Microchip). The importance of these early decisions emphasizes the importance of having access to prior entrepreneurial experience, human capital and networks of expertise.

Among our cases, the entrepreneurs in Optical, Biomedical, 3G Wireless and Stem Cell used their own networks and those of the university and investors to gain the commitment of key individuals who would supply the initial capital and knowledge to enable the venture to commence business operations. For example, the TTO's venturing experience and social capital helped the entrepreneur in Optical to secure resources and expertise. This activity was absent in the other cases that attempted to launch their spin-off ventures with inadequate levels of relevant resources.

5.2.4 Reorientation Phase

During the reorientation phase, when the ventures were attempting to generate returns, the entrepreneurial teams faced the challenges of continuously identifying, acquiring and integrating resources and then subsequently reconfiguring them. Reconfiguration was especially evident where the business had little capital and inexperienced management at formation. However, a learning process was evident in those ventures that had reached the reorientation stage of development. The academic entrepreneurs identified how to develop resources, information and knowledge and assemble new capabilities.

Interactions with customers, competitors, suppliers and potential investors were central in generating the information and knowledge required. In some cases, this learning process may mean changes to previous key decisions regarding how the value is to be created from the opportunity in terms of the nature of the product offering and the likely customers. For example, Human Genome came to realize after a year that they were focusing on a market that was too small and that they were marketing their technology in the wrong way. They subsequently completely transformed their business with the continued financial backing of a business angel and the acquisition of a new chairman and CEO to help commercialize the technology in the newer, larger, markets they had identified.

In other cases, entrepreneurs and TTOs either placed too much emphasis during the opportunity-framing phase on developing the technology rather than on identifying key customers, or were less competent in accessing the right resources, information and knowledge during the pre-organization phase. The result was numerous adaptations concerning how the technology was applied to meet previously unrecognized customer needs, how to gain access to markets and how to access and acquire further resources. This process of learning from previous mistakes enabled the entrepreneurial teams to reassemble stocks of resources and internal capabilities, and to develop the technology. These changes had the beneficial effect of enabling the ventures to keep ahead of alternative technologies and competitors.

Where spin-offs appeared to be more successful in making adaptations to internal resource constraints and external environmental changes, the requisite resources, social capital and capabilities related back to the opportunity framing and pre-organization phases. This suggests that the success of spin-offs in progressing from this phase of development into the next is largely dependent upon the preparatory work done during these earlier phases by the entrepreneur and the TTO.

5.2.5   Sustainable Returns Phase

In arriving at this phase of development, the spin-off will have overcome numerous obstacles to demonstrate that sufficient returns can be generated from productive activities. From the cases, key dimensions were the need for professionally managed development of the technology platform and new IP being created, the development of a management team with solid commercial experience and the development of an identity for the business that is separate from the university, which may be emphasized by relocation away from the university campus. This may be within a university-affiliated science park or incubator, emphasizing the need to retain close links with the university.

5.3   THE CRITICAL JUNCTURES

To make the transition between the different development phases, the spin-off needs to overcome the critical junctures that constrain its continued development. Critical junctures occur because of the conflict between a spin-off's existing level and type of resources, capabilities and social capital, and those required to perform in the subsequent phase of development. Unless each critical juncture is overcome, the venture cannot move to the next phase of development and hence will stagnate. The successful transition through these discontinuities in the spin-off's development demonstrates that weaknesses in the spin-off's resources, capabilities and social capital have been reconfigured, replaced or developed. The nature of the required stocks of resources, social capital and internal capabilities differs across each phase of development. The critical junctures are identified as: (1) opportunity recognition, (2) entrepreneurial commitment, (3) venture credibility and (4) venture sustainability. This section explains the nature of each critical juncture using evidence from case studies. The main reasons that critical junctures arise are summarized in Table 5.1.

5.3.1 Opportunity Recognition

The critical juncture of opportunity recognition lies at the interface of the research phase and opportunity-framing phase. Opportunity recognition is the match between an unfulfilled market need and a solution that satisfies the need that most others have overlooked (Ucbasaran et al., 2003b). The possession of idiosyncratic information allows people to see particular opportunities that others cannot, even if they are not actively searching for such opportunities (Shane, 2001). The co-founding academic entrepreneur of Stem Cell, for example, reported that his discovery was a chance insight based on research being done in a different field which benefited from his previous experience in industry from which he expected there were potential commercial products because it solved a major medical problem more effectively than current treatments. In Optical, the surrogate entrepreneur recognized the opportunity almost by accident while engaged with academics in the design of applications of their technology. Analysis of our case evidence suggested that to overcome the critical juncture of opportunity recognition required the ability to synthesize scientific knowledge with an understanding of markets that was enhanced significantly by higher levels of social capital in the form of partnerships, linkages and other network interactions. However, a tension existed in that universities and academics possessed significant technological know-how yet had insufficient knowledge of how to serve markets and unrealistic expectations of the profits that could be derived from the technologies they had discovered.

5.3.2 Entrepreneurial Commitment

In order to move from the opportunity phase to the pre-organization phase the critical juncture of entrepreneurial commitment must be overcome. Entrepreneurial commitment involves acts which bind the venture champion to a certain course of events. The academic entrepreneur may need to make an important choice about whether to remain as an academic or become involved full time in the venture. For example, the senior academics on the research team in Optical did not want to leave their posts. In Software, the academic had no business experience, but was dissatisfied with a career in academia and decided to take the risk. In Materials, both

Table 5.1 Development phases and critical junctures

Growth phase:	Research phase	Opportunity-framing phase	Pre-organization phase	Reorientation phase
Nature of phase:	Creation of valuable IP which generates potential opportunity for commercialization	Screening to evaluate for technological validity and performance and framing within a commercial opportunity through identification of potential markets	Steps to decide what resources and capabilities to develop, what to acquire now and in future and timing	Continuous process of identifying, acquiring and reconfiguring as nature of market needs became clearer in order for sustainable returns to be subsequently achieved
Factors initiating critical junctures:	*Moving through opportunity recognition critical juncture between research phase and opportunity-framing:* Lack of prior knowledge about how markets and industries operate Inability to understand and focus upon how a technical discovery can be applied to serve a residual customer need Inability to research, define and articulate a clear route to market for the technology	*Moving through entrepreneurial critical juncture between opportunity-framing and pre-organization:* Reluctance or inability to act against convention Inability to accept risks, and tolerate uncertainty Little prior business management experience and responsibilities Inability to attract surrogate entrepreneurs and experienced managers	*Moving through credibility critical juncture between pre-organization and reorientation:* Inability to attract and secure initial seed finance from investors Unable to secure suitable facilities outside of the university department to locate the new venture Inability to secure quality human resources to form a well-balanced managerial and scientific team	*Moving through sustainability critical juncture between reorientation and sustainability:* Inability to manage growth through the identification, acquisition and integration of resources and capabilities Inability to attract and secure next round finance from existing and new investors

Lack of incentive to think commercially and behave entrepreneurially	Lack of self-awareness over personal limitations Inability to obtain and leverage social capital through social, academic, commercial and industrial networks	Inability to achieve proof of concept and evolve the technology to a state of market readiness Inability to generate or show a clear route to revenues and profitability in order to attract financial resources Lack of depth and breadth in the technology portfolio to provide sufficient long-term options for commercialization Lack of receptivity for the technology by supply chain distributors and customers in the market	Inability to employ resources and develop capabilities to acquire speed to market Inability to recognize opportunities and threats and make strategic decisions under pervasive uncertainty Inability to gain traction and build momentum in the market through generating sufficient sales and capturing market share Inability to integrate knowledge and learning into the venture
Resulting critical juncture: Opportunity recognition	Entrepreneurial commitment	Threshold of credibility	Threshold of sustainability

academics could not fulfil the role of the venture champion and recruited a surrogate entrepreneur from industry who had the product development experience necessary to manage the growth of the company. The presence of someone who is committed full-time to the venture may be central to accessing external finance. The critical juncture of entrepreneurial commitment appears to arise for four main reasons.

First, a lack of networks to access successful entrepreneurial role models led to reluctance by the academic entrepreneurs we surveyed to commit to taking their idea forward commercially as this would be contrary to accepted conventions in their institutions. Second, an absence of prior business experience and lack of confidence about surviving in an environment that was outside their expertise also featured as a major reason for a reluctance to commit full-time to developing the project. Third, an absence of awareness of personal limitations affected the extent to which academic entrepreneurs were involved in the venture, with some not recognizing that their value-adding ability was more likely to be with respect to the science whereas it may be better to delegate to others the process of developing a marketing plan or negotiating terms with a venture capitalist. This may be difficult for academics who are experienced as directors of large research groups. Finally, academic inventors and TTOs may find it extremely challenging to access the services of a surrogate entrepreneur because of their limited social capital, their inability to offer sufficient incentives and their reluctance to relinquish control of their company.

Those spin-offs we interviewed that were not able to resolve these conflicts and where the academic entrepreneur worked part time in the spin-off, experienced inherent weaknesses that restricted their ability to develop further.

5.3.3   Credibility

The critical juncture facing all cases was the entrepreneur's ability to acquire the initial stock of resources to enable the business to begin to function. Finance was the key resource enabling the transition of the venture from a pre-organization phase to an operational business. Frequently the difficulty that entrepreneurs encountered with developing fundable investment propositions was that, apart from intangible technological assets in the form of know-how and IP, there was often very little else they had to demonstrate their commercial credibility. The finance constraint meant that the resources required to form the venture could not be acquired. In the case of Optical, the academic and surrogate entrepreneur realized they needed to form a strong team and put the building blocks to develop the business in position before approaching a venture capitalist. In Software, without adequate funding and having a small team it was not possible to penetrate the market, so sales growth was very slow. In Biomedical, the team realized that it needed to assemble resources quickly and create a professional image in order to attract customers.

This credibility threshold is characterized by an inability to acquire key resources. Failure to demonstrate sufficient credibility in recruiting key personnel and other resources as well as identifying potential customers may severely weaken the entrepreneur's ability to secure financial investment. These problems may have remained unresolved from earlier phases despite advice from potential investors and TTOs.

A further dimension of overcoming the credibility threshold was to relocate outside the university departments to project a distinctive corporate identity to customers, suppliers and certain investors who would not otherwise value the products and services on offer.

The evolution of resource stocks, capabilities and the level of social capital up to this critical juncture may provide the ability to access the right resources, information and knowledge to secure significant resource endowments or lucrative contracts from new clients. For less successful cases, these entrepreneurial capabilities were not available or took considerable time to develop. It took the learning from several attempts for these spin-off ventures to access, acquire and assemble the building blocks required to be sufficiently credible with customers, financial intermediaries and other resource providers.

Our evidence suggests that external financiers and customers may be suspicious of the influence of universities' non-commercial cultures on spin-offs so that some ties with the university may be seen as a liability. In Materials, the team invested considerable effort to create the perception with potential customers that they were not linked to the university or that they were academics. Rather, they presented themselves as having industrial and commercial experience plus technical expertise.

5.3.4 Sustainable Returns

At the sustainable returns juncture, the ability continuously to reconfigure existing resources, capabilities and social capital with new information, knowledge and resources was required. This ability enabled the more successful cases we interviewed to continue creating value from existing technological resources and capabilities as well as from new opportunities recognized.

At this critical juncture, spin-offs may need to transform their existing configurations of resources, capabilities and social capital. Some of the resources acquired, capabilities developed and relationships formed during previous development phases may now cease to be valuable in terms of generating sustainable returns.

Entrepreneurial teams were identified as needing to acquire the ability to continuously reconfigure existing resource weaknesses, inadequate capabilities and social liabilities into resources strengths, distinct capabilities and social capital that will enable the spin-off to generate returns. It may be easier to develop physical, human, technological and social capital resources than capabilities.

In the spin-offs we studied, the entrepreneur (and team) had to introduce and frequently adapt over the development of the venture an organizational structure and routines that enable the allocation and consumption of scarce stocks of resources to be coordinated. Informal structures also need to be developed in order to facilitate communication within the organization. The need to reconfigure the venture's resources in order to overcome this critical juncture was common across the cases. Without developing internal systems to manage a larger operation and competences to survive in a competitive marketplace, the spin-off may not be able to obtain further rounds of venture capital financing. In 3G Wireless, the entrepreneurial team raised too little seed finance to support their growth plans and the venture stagnated in a period where the venture capital market for high-tech investments had become difficult. In Stem Cell, in contrast, by ensuring a large first round of funding, the team acquired almost 50 scientists, over 200 patents and an experienced management team, and developed organizational structures and processes to enable the firm to grow.

The more successful spin-offs in transforming their existing resources, capabilities and social capital achieved a clear route to market that enabled profitability to be achieved. Acquiring key customers helped to legitimize spin-offs by acting as a signal to investors that the venture is capable of achieving sustainable growth under the current management team. The sustainability juncture was more problematic for those spin-offs unable to resolve deficient levels of social capital, resource weaknesses and inadequate internal capabilities. Where resources became depleted before sustainable returns are achieved the problems inherited from earlier development phases may be too difficult to resolve, making it unlikely that the spin-off will progress.

5.4   VENTURE-BACKED AND JOINT VENTURE USOS

The previous section considered spin-offs that were developed with backing by business angel or venture capital investors. In some cases, commercialization may take place through a joint venture with an industrial partner. Comparing the evolution of spin-offs that involve joint ventures with industrial partners with venture capital backed spin-offs, based on evidence from two joint venture spin-offs (JVSOs) and two venture capital (VC) backed spin-offs, shows that spin-offs typically lack the financial and human capital (managerial) resources and capabilities they need in order to fully exploit the commercial potential of their technologies. Table 5.2 provides illustrations from the companies. Creating a spin-off company as a joint venture with an industrial partner, may be a means of overcoming some of the potential problems associated with managing resource weaknesses and inadequate capabilities that may be difficult to achieve as a free-standing spin-off company with or without venture capital backing.

Specifically, we identify four areas where joint ventures with industrial partners may be beneficial. First, given their prior knowledge of their industries and the superior market intelligence of the industrial partner, JVSOs may be better able to develop opportunities from scientific discoveries which better serve unmet customer needs. Second, in a JVSO the industrial partner and the university may be better able to cooperate in assembling a well-balanced team with the necessary background successfully to commercially exploit the technology. Third, the credibility acquired from both parent organizations may enable the JVSOs to access and acquire resources more readily and gain organizational momentum and access to markets. Finally, JVSOs may lead to a more rapid process of professionalization and capability-building that better equips them than spin-offs to enter dynamic markets and emerge as resilient firms able effectively to compete with incumbents. We would caution, however, that a potential downside is the need to put mechanisms in place to control the joint venture partner and to select a partner with compatible objectives and expertise.

5.5 TECHNOLOGICAL SECTORS AND DEVELOPMENT

The nature of the development process may be associated with the type of technology involved. Druilhe and Garnsey (2004) distinguish three types of spin-off, each of which they see as evolving through a range of business models. First, development companies are based on some novel scientific breakthrough where resource creation and opportunity recognition are interdependent. Second, product companies involve opportunity recognition that builds directly on the scientist's knowledge and connections. Third are software companies which appear distinct as they benefit from lower scale-up costs and the relative ease of switching from service to

Table 5.2 JVSOs versus VC-backed spin-offs and critical junctures

Spin-off firm	Partner/investor description	Opportunity recognition	Entrepreneurial commitment	Threshold of credibility	Threshold of sustainability
Therapeutics To develop treatments for skin ailments and tissue damage including burns and scarring [Lead VC 40%; co-investor 15%; university 20%; academic 25%]	Large international early-stage venture capital firm specializing in growing high-technology based firms in different industries 150 technology companies currently in its portfolio Vast international network of business contacts	The research group worked on an extensive research programme. The findings led to the recognition that the results may be applicable to humans The scientist knew that potential commercial products could result, because it solved a major medical problem After discussing the discovery with physicians, feedback indicated that the discovery fulfilled a sizeable unmet need for millions of patients worldwide	Commercial partners and industry were not interested in commercializing the technology because it was too early stage The academic resolved to set up a spin-off and commercialize the intellectual property himself The academic was supported and encouraged by friends, family, colleagues and investors to take the lead in starting the venture himself while retaining his post at the university He hoped that raising venture capital would allow him to bring in commercial management	The academic/CEO was careful in signalling credibility to investors by hiring headhunters to independently recruit a management team and benchmark existing team members He carried out extensive due diligence and patent protection over the IP and secured laboratory facilities on the university science park The academic/CEO turned down seed investment because early investors lacked depth of experience and knowledge to add sufficient value	Through ensuring a large first round of funding from experienced investors, the team has acquired 48 scientists, over 200 patents, a management team of seasoned industry experts Both investors and the management team assembled organizational structures and routines to enable the spin-off to manage rapid growth The VC investors facilitated introductions to partners in specific markets that would enable Therapeutics to get its products to suffering patients
RF Devices To design low power	Small UK private equity firm Only 2 years	The scientist had been working for nearly 10 years on science that	The scientist lacked business experience and managerial expertise to	Taken together, the research results, market analysis and due diligence	The entrepreneurial team raised too little seed finance to support their

consumption micro-processors and license the IP to manufactur-ers world-wide in the mobile telephone market [VC 15: university 15%; surrogate entrepreneur 33%, academic 37%]	investing experience in high-tech with one fund raised RF Devices was the fourth investment. 11 technology companies currently in its portfolio Limited network of business contacts restricted to the UK	did not have an obvious market application. The technology provided a solution to a market need that the surrogate identified based on knowledge gained in industry	grow a technology business. He did not want to give up his research post at the university because it provided him with the infrastructure to create new technologies After attending several networking events and meetings with business angels, the academic met with a surrogate entrepreneur who was enthusiastic about starting a venture to commercialize the technology This allowed the academic to continue with his research	were not enough to convince large investors that the entrepreneurs and their technology had the potential to create a substantial business The scientist and surrogate entrepreneur found it challenging to raise initial seed funding from experienced investors to start the venture The VC investors that did offer terms were not experienced in building high-tech ventures and did not understand the technology	growth plans and the venture stagnated in a period when the venture capital market for high-tech investments had gone flat Without adequate funding, the team could not penetrate the market Sales growth was very slow during the first year as product development had to be downscaled and adapted to account for lower than expected demand
Green Power Systems To design, manufacture and sell products and services to power the generation	PowerGen UK is a part of The PowerGen Group Inc based in Washington, PA, USA PowerGen UK specializes in providing services,	While working on industry sponsored research the academic spotted a need for novel applications of the technology in an alternative market sector Further investigation and discussions with	The academic had no business experience and did not want to leave his job at the university He decided to take the risk following encouragement from colleagues, friends and family and work part-time on the venture. However he realized that	The PowerGen brand was recognized by customers in the sector and Green Power Systems fitted well alongside other portfolio of companies in the PowerGen Group PowerGen had a large network of contacts	Trading profitably Awarded a contract to supply industry's leading manufacturer Planning to expand to overseas markets Working with industrial partner on developing new products for other markets

Table 5.2 (continued)

Spin-off firm	Partner/investor description	Opportunity recognition	Entrepreneurial commitment	Threshold of credibility	Threshold of sustainability
sector to improve efficiency and reduce harmful emissions PowerGen (Industry Partner): 42% University: 17% Academic entrepreneur: 28% Management team: Share of 13%	products and technologies which improve and enhance the performance of their customers' power plants and equipment 40-year history of supplying products and services including the design, manufacture, supply and installation for heavy industrial applications	PowerGen revealed that the same engineering principles applied across a number of industry sectors and that the technology could be adapted easily in most cases to solve customer's problems	this approach would take years to develop into a profitable business With the support of the UTTO, an industry partner was identified that had the market experience and capabilities to help create a substantial business venture Working with PowerGen allows the academic to continue with his research at the university and retain equity in the joint venture	in the industry giving relatively easy access to customers, suppliers and intermediaries through introductions PowerGen contributed human resources, premises and equipment to get the business operational quickly A prototype was installed and tested at a client site to validate the product and demonstrate value to other customers	Looking to hire 5 new engineers to support expansion
Telecom To design, and manufacture specialized fibre optic	Broadband is a UK-based telecoms firm with sales offices in Europe, North America	The academics recognized potential opportunities for the commercialization of their research discoveries while	The senior academics on the research team did not want to leave their posts. An enthusiastic post-doctoral student was	Broadband and Telecom combined managerial and scientific expertise to form a strong team to develop the joint venture. Broadband had proven	Awarded several new contracts by US and Canadian customers and is now trading profitably Successfully raised

components for use in telecommunication networks to be sold worldwide to device manufactures

Broadband (Industry Partner): 40%

University: 12%

Academic entrepreneurs: 21% shared between 3 scientists

Management team: Share of 27%

and Asia. Broadband specializes in the design, manufacture and distribution of technology solutions that satisfy customer requirements in the communications sector

Broadband has a large global network of customers and suppliers and an industry respected brand name

attending an industry trade show in the US

They got ideas from other start-ups and spin-off companies were exhibiting new products, technologies and devices targeting the telecommunications sector

Early meetings with Broadband lead to recognition of what problem the technology could solve for customers if it was applied in the right way

strongly committed to leading the commercialization of the technology, and had the support of the research team

Through the Head of School's network, the post-doc student was introduced to Broadband who agreed to collaborate and take the technology to market

commercial capabilities, an established brand and a large network of contacts with which to gain access to market

Telecom operated from Broadband's offices in a prime location yet close to the university

$6 million first-round venture capital to accelerate growth and market the technology worldwide

Relocated to own premises on science park

Second new product released in spring 2003

20 new employees recruited

Sponsoring more university research to supply future innovations

Note: Company names are pseudonyms to protect anonymity.

product business models. Druilhe and Garnsey use longitudinal case studies to show how the business models of new ventures are modified as entrepreneurs improve their knowledge of resources and opportunities. This modification may imply that the ventures shift from a research contract company to a licensing company, or that the entrepreneurs reconsider starting a product company and develop a technical consultancy instead. Through engagement with others and involvement in entrepreneurial activities, academic entrepreneurs develop relevant knowledge and experience. This allows them to improve their perception of opportunities, while gaining a better understanding of the resource configurations required to pursue the refined or newly perceived opportunities. Development companies may initially be set up to commercialize a technology for licensing but may later aim at downstream services and production. A reverse mutation may occur as the objectives of the business model change from production to licensing, thereby offering a plausible alternative to the transitional type identified in the previous chapter. Academics who provide research-orientated services benefit from a ready-made productive base from which to operate and can secure returns more easily than those with generic technologies far from market. Academic entrepreneurs who are sufficiently motivated, skilled and market focused can create a productive base in-house that delivers products of high value to customers and secures them a very high level of returns.

5.6 CONCLUSIONS

Our analysis indicates that spin-offs go through a number of distinct phases of activity in their development and that between the different phases of development, ventures face critical junctures that need to be addressed before they can progress to the next phase of development.

Each phase of spin-off development can be characterized as an iterative process of development. In the opportunity-framing phase there is iteration to find the appropriate commercial proposition and iteration to identify the appropriate commercial resources that will be needed later. In the pre-organization phases there is an iterative search process to develop and acquire the necessary resources. The reorientation phase is characterized by a reconfiguration of resources as previous decisions need to be altered in the light of new information and knowledge. At the sustainability phase, there is a need for further iteration of activities to achieve the critical mass to serve the market in order to obtain further rounds of funding resources. In reaching each successive phase there may be a need to revisit and resolve issues that arose at previous phases of development. Revisiting earlier decisions is made using the resource and capabilities base developed to this point, which may itself need to be augmented.

In the opportunity-framing phase, academics are likely to return to their research programmes and refine them to meet the needs of furthering the opportunity in the marketplace. In the pre-organization phase, academics are likely to revisit the definition and scope of the opportunity as new information provides insights into the feasibility of the proposed venture's business plan. In the reorientation phase, the entrepreneurial team recognizes the resources, capabilities and networks that will enable sustainable returns to be achieved. Existing configurations that are identified as not likely to achieve sustainable returns may need to be developed or replaced. In the sustainability phase, the ability to access, acquire and reconfigure resources, capabilities and networks enables the venture to establish resilience.

With respect to the opportunity recognition juncture, there is a need to acquire the capability to synthesize scientific knowledge with an understanding of the market to which it may apply, notably through developing high levels of social capital resource outside the traditional scientific research environment.

At the opportunity phase, the intense uncertainty surrounding the technology and the application of that technology in a particular market suggests a need for a champion who is committed full time to resolving this uncertainty and intense complexity beyond the start-up phase. The commitment of the academic may be especially important to ensure a continued flow of innovations to enable the venture's product portfolio to develop, but the scientist may not be the best candidate for the role of venture champion.

The critical juncture of entrepreneurial commitment appears to develop through a combination of human capital deficiencies in the academic scientist and an institutional culture that discriminates against those with an entrepreneurial orientation and which prevent the academic scientist or surrogate entrepreneur from championing a new venture.

Credibility was identified as a key issue in obtaining seed finance to establish the venture. It may be particularly important to access surrogate entrepreneurs and acquire initial resource endowments including seed finance, space and human resources. In order to attract a potential surrogate entrepreneur, it may be necessary for the spin-off at the pre-organization stage to develop some credibility with the surrogate. Credibility of spin-offs to the market can be achieved by presenting IP as a potential portfolio of products, demonstrating proof of concept of technological assets, clarifying the route to market and profitability, and being able to locate the venture off the university campus in order to demonstrate clear intentions to develop the technology commercially. Differences between the universities examined in the existence and quality of the formalized systems and mechanisms through which spin-offs were formed and created, and the level of external social capital, appeared to play an important role in creating credibility.

The spin-offs that had moved beyond the sustainable returns critical juncture had developed the ability to continuously reconfigure existing resource weaknesses, inadequate capabilities and social liabilities into resources strengths, distinctive capabilities and social capital. Achieving this transformation depended on the ability of the entrepreneurial team to develop entrepreneurial capabilities to reconfigure weaknesses inherited from decisions and commitments made during earlier development phases, as well as organizational capabilities to coordinate productive activities.

NOTE

1. Parts of this chapter are an edited version of Vohora et al. (2004).

6. Entrepreneurial teams in spin-offs

6.1 INTRODUCTION

In the entrepreneurship literature, an increasing number of authors have highlighted founding team characteristics as potential key success factors. Heirman and Clarysse (2006) have shown that founding teams with a high degree of commercial (sector-specific) experience show significantly higher growth rates in employment and revenues than those with low levels of such experience. Zahra and Wiklund (2000) on the other hand show that the team 'behavioural integration' (among others, the ability to work together) to be found in start-up teams leads to a significantly higher rate of new product introduction in comparison with those founding teams that do not show high levels of integration. According to them, this also explains the comparative advantage which certain start-ups have *vis-à-vis* incumbent companies without such teams. Further, MacMillan et al. (1987) and Muzyka et al. (1996) show that the quality of entrepreneurial teams are an important factor in decisive entrepreneurial events such as raising venture capital.

Among the high-tech start-ups, spin-offs are probably the start-up ventures in which team formation is the most crucial aspect: most of the spin-off ventures need to develop a product and therefore are in need of external forms of capital. As mentioned previously, the quality of the team is an important decision factor for external equity providers. Moreover, spin-offs usually have at least the expectancy to grow after start-up and are situated at the innovative edge of their industry segment. Again, this is exactly where the behavioural integration of the team and its sector relevant business experience are considered as very important. In contrast to the perceived importance of balanced teams with considerable business experience lies the fact that researchers in universities might experience difficulties in meeting potential co-founders with relevant experience. Franklin et al. (2001) observe that the attraction of such so-called 'surrogate entrepreneurs' in spin-off teams is a crucial step in the formation of a spin-off. This means that founding teams in spin-offs are not necessarily complete at the moment of idea conception, but are formed in the process of spin-off formation, as described in Chapter 4.

In this chapter, we specifically focus on the role of teams in spin-offs. The chapter proceeds along the following lines. First, we outline the theoretical perspectives which have been used in the literature to study teams. Second, we discuss how the composition of spin-off teams differs from founding teams in other spin-offs. Third, we analyse the dynamics of team formation in spin-offs. Finally, we conclude and discuss our findings.

6.2   THEORETICAL PERSPECTIVES

6.2.1   Defining Entrepreneurial Teams in Spin-offs

There has been considerable debate as to what exactly is meant by an 'entre-preneurial team'. Kamm et al. define entrepreneurial teams as 'two or more individuals who jointly establish a firm in which they have a financial inter-est' (Kamm et al., 1990, p. 7). Gartner et al. (1994) broadened this definition to cover those individuals who have direct influence on strategic choice. Ensley et al. (1998) combine both delineations by stating that an individual has to fulfil three criteria in order to be considered a member of the entrepreneurial team: (1) jointly establish a firm, (2) have a financial interest and (3) have a direct influence on the strategic choice of the firm. Other researchers have made the equity stake condition stricter and impose a minimum equity stake before someone can be considered a member of the entrepreneurial team (Ucbasaran et al., 2003a).

A definitional flaw in the aforementioned studies is based upon the fact that entrepreneurial teams are conceptualized as a homogeneous group of indi-viduals at the moment of start-up. They therefore often implicitly neglect the evolutionary aspects of entrepreneurial team formation and the hierarchical nature of the relations. Recent research has attempted to tackle this problem and has studied team entry and exit (Ucbasaran et al., 2003a; Vanaelst et al., 2006). Vanaelst et al. (2006) show that entrepreneurial teams in spin-offs are quite dynamic and subject to many changes in the first years before and after formal legislation. In addition to the researchers, Vanaelst et al. (2006) argue that representatives of the parent institute are involved in the creation of the spin-off. In most cases, this role is performed by the technology transfer officers, who act as 'privileged witnesses' and, during a certain period of time, also belong to the 'extended' founding team. Privileged witnesses are often the driving forces behind new team formation in spin-offs and actively look for new team members such as 'surrogate entrepreneurs' (Franklin et al., 2001; Lockett et al., 2003b). According to these authors, a surrogate entrepreneur is an outsider with commercial experience, who might be attracted to work together with the researchers to develop the venture.

Drawing on the literature, we introduce in this chapter the notion of 'core founding team' and 'extended founding team'. The core team involves the members of the entrepreneurial team consistent with the definition introduced by Ensley et al. (1998): they played an active role in the founding of the start-up, have a financial interest and are involved in the strategic decision-making. The extended team consists of those persons who do not match the three criteria, but only one of the three. For instance, the TTO officers defined as privileged witnesses by Vanaelst et al. (2006) are actively involved in the founding of the spin-off, but do not have a financial interest nor are they necessarily involved in the strategic decision-making after start-up. Their role of privileged witness might be fulfilled by neutral directors in the board of directors afterwards.

6.2.2   Structure of the Founding Team

The structure of teams and the impact of team structure on performance has been extensively studied by a stream of researchers, which is called the upper echelon perspective. Researchers in this tradition assume that top management team characteristics such as psychological characteristics, cognitive base, and observable characteristics such as age and functional expertise, determine strategic choices. The environmental factors surrounding the firm, upper echelon characteristics and the strategic choices made by the top management team interact to determine organizational performance levels (Hambrick and Mason, 1984). Translated to entrepreneurial teams, these findings suggest that changes in the composition, and hence characteristics, of the team may have an impact on the strategic choices made by the entrepreneurial team and ultimately on the venture performance. As mentioned previously, the upper echelon theory posits that entrepreneurial team characteristics significantly influence the new venture performance. The team characteristics that are studied by the upper echelon theory are reviewed in the next paragraphs.

Cognitive diversity
Cognitive diversity means the existence of multiple and different styles among the team members of a new venture (Zahra and Wiklund, 2000). This diversity arises from the founding team members' (1) individual characteristics, (2) varied educational backgrounds and (3) different business experiences (Hambrick and Mason, 1984). The main underlying hypothesis put forward by the upper echelon perspective is that cognitive diversity has a positive effect on team performance and, therefore, on the performance of the venture.

Individual characteristics   Vanaelst et al. (2005) used the framework developed by Van Muijen et al. (1999) to distinguish between four extreme types of individual job orientation (Figure 6.1). The sum of each team member's individual orientation can be seen as the 'team culture', which is in itself

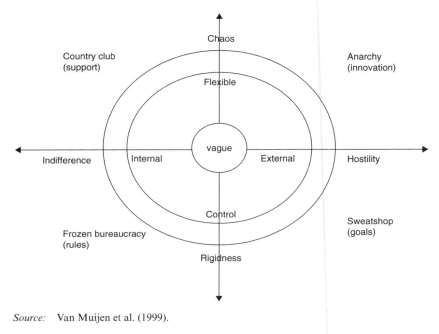

Source: Van Muijen et al. (1999).

Figure 6.1   Individual cognitive differences

a predictor of team performance. The four different extremes are based upon two underlying dimensions: the opposite poles of flexibility versus control form the first dimension. The second dimension represents the internal versus external focus of the team members (Van Muijen et al., 1999).

A combination of these two dimensions results in four different types of orientation. Team members who are internal orientated but very flexible are identified as mainly *support orientated.* They find concepts such as participation, cooperation, being people based, mutual trust, team spirit and individual growth very important. Communication is often verbal and informal. Employees are encouraged to bring ideas about their work and feelings about each other forward. Decisions are often made through informal contacts. Team loyalty is very much appreciated by these team members. On the other hand, team members who are internal orientated, but tend to focus on control, are *rules orientated.* They find respect for authority, rationality of procedures and division of work important. Communication is often written and top down. The structure is hierarchical and power is based on formal authority. Team members who tend to focus on control, but are external orientated are mainly *goals orientated.* They find concepts as rationality, performance indicators, accomplishment, accountability and contingent reward very important. Team members who are external orientated but flexible are considered to be mainly *innovation orientated*. Searching for new information in the environment, creativity, openness to change, experimentation and anticipation are much appreciated by these team members. Control from above is neither possible nor required, and management expects commitment and involvement of employees.

Functional and experiential heterogeneity The upper echelon perspective assumes that functional and experiential heterogeneity introduce complementary skills into top management teams. These complementary skills allow teams to recognize a more diverse set of opportunities and to fulfil a diverse set of tasks in a more efficient way than they would if they did not have this background.

Behavioural integration
Cognitive diversity, as discussed in the previous section, leads into a task-orientated disagreement arising from differences in perspective and is supposed to have a positive impact on venture performance. However, affective conflict is individual-orientated disagreement arising from personal disaffection and may be detrimental to the development of the venture. Ensley and Pearce (2001) examine cognitive conflict and introduce the term 'affective conflict' in entrepreneurial teams. According to these authors, both cognitive and affective conflict are very predictive in explaining venture performance. The underlying hypothesis is that cognitive conflict is positive as long as it does not lead to affective conflict.

Zahra and Wiklund (2000) introduce the term 'behavioural integration' into the entrepreneurship literature as an intermediating concept which is useful to explain the chances that cognitive conflict results into affective conflict. Behavioural integration is defined as the ability of the venture team to work in unison in order to build a collective outlook among its members and benefit from their different skills. Venture teams that are behaviourally integrated deal in a much better way with the cognitive conflicts that emerge because of functional and experiential heterogeneity and differences in the individual characteristics as explained above. According to Zahra and Wiklund (forthcoming), behaviourally integrated venture teams usually interact, share information and discuss strategic issues. This creates a culture that rapidly integrates different decision-making styles, transcending individual differences.

6.2.3 Founding Team Dynamics

Recent research underlined that founding teams can not be considered as a static concept (Ucbasaran et al., 2003a; Vanaelst et al., 2006). Over the life of the organization the team's composition is likely to change: some members are added to the team while others leave the team. Boeker (1989) posits that changes in the composition of the team are the result of challenges that teams face in the different stages of the venture's life cycle. The stage of development of the new venture creates different demands of the team in terms of capabilities and competences, and often are translated in changes to the team. But the causality goes in both ways. Team turnover of a new venture team in its turn influences strategic direction and performance. According to Chandler et al. (2005), even in the initial stages of a team, adding members can be disruptive. The disruptive effect of adding a team member increases as the team and organization develops.

Chandler et al. (2005) argue that the dynamism and uncertainty of the task environment is likely to influence teams. Spin-offs operate in unstable and unpredictable task environments. Therefore, we expect that they will try to address unforeseen and unforeseeable contingencies by adding members to the team.

6.3   FINDINGS

We subsequently discuss the main findings in our research with regards to team definition, team structure involving the cognitive heterogeneity, behavioural integration and, finally, team evolution. The findings are drawn from previous papers and also contain some new research calculation.

6.3.1   Team Definition

As discussed in the literature review, a team can be defined as a two-layer concept. At the core of the team, the members have a financial interest in the company *and* are actively involved in founding (or growing) the company *and* are in power to take strategic decisions. As shown in Table 6.1, the core team of spin-offs tends to be larger than that of their high-tech counterparts.

However, the core team is only one aspect of the total team. The *enlarged* team also includes those people that have *either* a financial stake in the company, *or* are involved in the founding *or* are in power to make strategic decisions. In spin-offs these stakeholders are usually business angels who are involved financially, one or more privileged witnesses such as members of the TTO staff who are supportive during the founding and early growth phase and, finally, different representatives on the board of directors.

A particularly interesting team member is the *surrogate entrepreneur*. Often this surrogate entrepreneur does not belong to the core team of the spin-off, meaning that he/she either is not involved in the founding process

Table 6.1 Team characteristics

Team variable	Spin-off	High-tech start-ups
No. of founders	2.56 (1.57)	1.82 (1.13)
No. of members enlarged team	3.16 (1.47)	2.60 (1.07)
No. of average years R&D experience	6.95 (5.80)	4.22 (5.62)
No. of average years commercial experience	0.61 (1.34)	3.01 (5.13)
Functional heterogeneity	0.86 (0.22)	0.81 (0.24)
Experiential heterogeneity	0.62 (0.34)	0.41 (0.45)

Note: N = 188.

Source: Own calculations.

or has no financial stake (and risk) in the venture. This occurs especially in spin-offs which in Chapter 3 we called the prospector type. Prospectors usually do not have the credibility and financial attractiveness for surrogate entrepreneurs to take a risk. Hence, instead of taking a risk and investing in this type of company, they become hired managers that work in the start-up for a fixed salary.

In the remainder of this chapter we consistently make a distinction between the description of the core team and the enlarged team.

6.3.2 Structure of the Founding Team

Experiential heterogeneity
Core founding teams of spin-offs appear to be unbalanced in terms of experience. Their experience is highly concentrated in research and development, while sectoral experience in commercial functions such as product management or business development is completely lacking. This might turn out to be one of the major weaknesses for later success. Figure 6.2 shows the structural differences between the core founding teams of the 20 top growers and those of the 20 bottom growers. It is clear that those founding teams in which the experience is highly technical are not the top growers. Moreover, those core founding teams in which the commercial, sector-relevant experience is lacking appear to be the worst-performing teams. Heirman and Clarysse (2006) have shown that the degree of commercial experience in a founding team is the single most important predictor, after controlling for venture capital availability, of growth during the first five years after start-up.

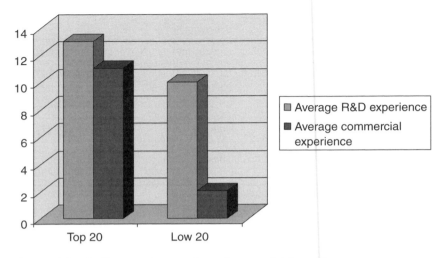

Figure 6.2   Differences in experience between high and low growers

The lack of commercial experience in the core founding team is often resolved by including surrogate entrepreneurs in the founding team. However, it does not seem to be so straightforward that these artificially created teams will actually be successful. In the literature, we find two common ways of attracting new team members. A first decision criterion for attracting new team members is the use of *instrumental* or economic arguments. This means that new team formation is a rational process driven by economic, instrumental considerations. A second way is the use of *non-instrumental* or affective contacts (Forbes et al., 2006). Using non-instrumental contacts, team formation is a process driven by interpersonal attraction and social networks. This is what Francis and Sandberg (2000) refer to as *gemeinschaft*.

It is never the case that new team members are *only* attracted using non-instrumental or instrumental contacts. In other words, there is always a combination of both. However, in most of the spin-off teams we studied, there is some prevalence in one way or the other. When we simplify the relations into a two by two matrix, we observe four kinds of teams (Figure 6.3).

The first kind of team is called the 'kinship team', in the upper left corner of the quadrant (strong non-instrumental and weak instrumental relations). In this team, newcomers are attracted as founders, mainly based upon non-instrumental relations. This means that co-founders are recruited within family or friendship circles. When this is the case, social network theory predicts that those recruited will have a very similar opinion to themselves. This means that the newcomers will not bring about a lot of

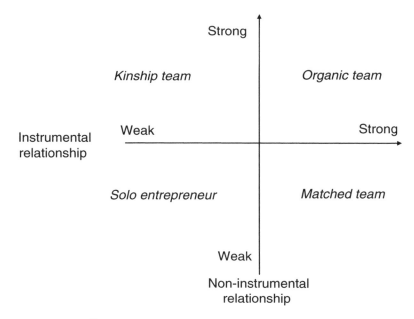

Figure 6.3   Different team structures

cognitive diversity nor challenge the original founder about the strategy to follow.

The second quadrant includes 'solo entrepreneurs' who did not want to attract newcomers due to weak instrumental and weak non-instrumental contacts (lower left quadrant). These solo entrepreneurs do not like to have others in the founding team who challenge them and who are different from them. Hence, they develop both weak non-instrumental and weak instrumental contacts, and stay alone.

The third quadrant is situated in the lower right part of Figure 6.3 and consists of the 'matched teams'. As mentioned before, matched teams imply that an outsider such as a privileged witness attracts potential new team members based on *instrumental contacts*. This witness might conclude that the team is unbalanced and needs commercial skills to match the technical skills of the researchers. In this case, extra team members are attracted to the team to develop the business. Usually, these extra team members are surrogate entrepreneurs who themselves liaise with the TTOs in order to promote the extra skills they can contribute to the team. These kind of matched teams have lots of cognitive diversity, but lack affective relationships.

Finally, we distinguish 'organic teams' in the upper right quadrant of Figure 6.3. These teams are formed based upon non-instrumental *and* instrumental contacts. In other words, the team members are bringing complementary skills and cognitive diversity to the team, but already have some shared history as well.

In a second step, we matched the growing and non-growing companies on Figure 6.3. First, we came to the conclusion that not all of our growing companies were so-called sustainable growers. Seven of the growing companies were non-sustainable. This means that they were growing at a fast rate, on average, but at a certain point in time they either went bankrupt or had to restructure their venture. So, eventually we had three groups left: the non-growers, the not-sustainable growers and the sustainable growers.

The results in Figure 6.4 are intriguing. First, we find that 70 per cent of the solo entrepreneurs are non-growers. This means that most of the solo entrepreneurs who are not able to build a team because of weak instrumental and equally weak non-instrumental relations do not grow at all. Second, one could only identify one team that had weak instrumental but very strong non-instrumental relations. Apparently, most of these teams are not even able to start up and fail before founding. The one team that we could identify that was able to start did have access to family money with which they started their business. Third, 75 per cent of all the non-sustainable growers were

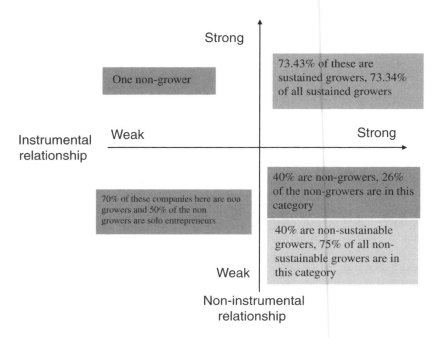

Figure 6.4   Teams related to growth

started with strong instrumental but very weak non-instrumental relations. Their growth proved to be non-sustainable because the cognitive diversity in the team led quickly to affective conflict about the strategy to be pursued. Affective conflict in turn was detrimental for the organization. Finally, we found that 75 per cent of the businesses that were sustainable growers were founded by teams that were organically grown through instrumental and non-instrumental contacts. The non-instrumental contacts implied that there was enough affective appreciation among the members to counterbalance the arguments arising from the cognitive diversity in the team.

Entrepreneurial experience heterogeneity

Teams in the first phase of the spin-off process, who are still deciding how to commercialize their knowledge, show a lack of entrepreneurial experience. Once the decision is taken to create a spin-off, team members with a high degree of entrepreneurial experience are attracted to the team. After the legal establishment of the firm, no clear finding on the nature of entrepreneurial experience was identified. Both extreme situations, of highly experienced and complete novice teams, were found. It is perhaps counter-intuitive that complete novice teams do not attract entrepreneurially experienced people. Fully experienced start-ups teams more often make the choice to attract a manager, who does not necessarily have entrepreneurial experience. However, the results remain inconclusive.

Cognitive heterogeneity

We assumed that the further along the spin-off process a firm is, the larger would be cognitive heterogeneity of the team in terms of the perceived necessary strategic orientation.[1] Our assumption was that start-up teams would be homogeneous, but new members would introduce another perspective on how to do business. For instance, researchers tend to be supportive and innovation orientated, often lacking goal orientation and avoiding bureaucracy (rules orientation). We supposed, therefore, that when teams were formed further along in the process, the newly attracted members would bring in these different values. We did not, however, find that the team became more heterogeneous. Instead, post-start-up teams seem to show significantly less cognitive heterogeneity than pre-start-up teams, in contrast to what might be expected.

Looking at the individual orientation of the new members in the team after the legal start-up of the new venture, we observe that the newcomers are also significantly innovation orientated and therefore reinforce the cognitive homogeneity of the team. This might be related to the fact that researchers usually prefer to recruit those people whose way of looking at a business is very close to theirs. As they are often leading people in their own domains, they may find it difficult to appreciate the values of people looking at the business in a totally different way. Another explanation for the reinforcement of the cognitive homogeneity of the team might be found in the involvement of the TTO in the attraction of new members to the team. These newcomers are often recruited from the TTO's personal network of people whose way of looking at a business is likely very close to his own.

When looking in detail at the strategic orientation of the additions to the team at the different stages of the spin-off process, we expected that these people, who were mostly business developers, would show a more pronounced goals orientation for their strategic orientation than the other team members. This was not supported by our cases. In most cases their goals orientation was similar to that of the other team members. Indeed, in one case the business developed had even less goals orientation. We find that it is visionary people in particular who are attracted that get along well with the researchers at a cognitive and strategic level. However, cognitive conflict is assumed to have a positive effect on strategic decisions and performance (Amason and Sapienza, 1997; Ensley et al., 2002). The lack of cognitive conflict in spin-off teams might explain their long incubation time and the difficulties experienced in changing their business model to obtain sustainable growth levels.

To conclude, our cases show that people attracted to the teams had different experience from the original team members, but they showed a comparable strategic orientation, leading to more cognitive homogeneity in the team.

Drivers of team turnover

Our research shows that, irrespective of the specific phase considered, there is a clear distinction between the drivers leading to team exit and entry. The reasons why people leave the team are related to conflict. A distinction can be made between intrapersonal and interpersonal conflict as drivers leading to team exit. Intrapersonal conflict concerns one individual person. Interpersonal conflict implies different persons, in our cases the different team members. A team exit caused by the fact that the personal ambition of a team member cannot be reconciled with the ambition of the venture is an example of an intrapersonal conflict. Conversely, a team exit caused by conflict over the strategy regarding how the firm should realize its ambition and the implementation of the strategy, is an example of interpersonal conflict. Interpersonal conflict in its turn comprises cognitive and affective conflict. Although previous research (Amason and Sapienza, 1997; Ensley et al., 2002) found cognitive and affective conflict to be positively related to one another, our case analysis suggests that affective conflict outweighed cognitive conflict and led to the decision to leave the team. Moreover, our case analysis indicated that when people left the team, negative aspects of conflict were a common denominator. However, we do not suggest that the people remaining in the teams are free of any kind of conflict. Moreover, as indicated by Eisenhardt et al. (1997), conflict can be beneficial if effectively handled. For instance, in a particular example, beneficial conflict in the team, expressed in several discussion rounds and disagreements as a result of differences in perspectives, has led to a major change in the firm's strategy. The original product was the delivery of tools that facilitate the research process in the pharmaceutical and biotechnology industries. However, the entrepreneurs learned that some pharmaceutical companies do not want to outsource their screening so they decided to also sell the tool thereby enabling companies to design their own experimental designs. Currently, the firm has adjusted its business plan, since it became clear that the food industry and the chemical market also can use their tool. A detailed analysis of conflict in entrepreneurial teams is an interesting research path; however, it lies beyond the scope of this study.

The drivers leading to team entry have a need for resources in common. Team entry can be the result of the attraction of additional human, technological or financial resources. The ambition to reach the next step in a firm's life cycle might call for a reallocation of existing resources. However, the need to attract supplementary resources is far more common. For instance, when technological know-how is brought into the firm through a patent owned by the university, the technology transfer officer can become part of the team. The attraction of specific human resources, for instance a surrogate entrepreneur, will lead to addition to the team. Additional financial resources might be found internally in the firm. However, mostly they call upon external financing. This is often found by attracting venture capital. Attracting venture capital has implications for the team, since the venture capitalist takes a seat on the board of directors and often appoints a new member of the management team, for instance a CEO.

Changes in the composition of the team have an impact on the different roles performed by the team members. When people are added to the team, existing roles can be split up, refined and performed by more people or new roles can be identified and filled in by the additional team member. On the other hand, when people leave the team their role is transferred to one or more of the remaining team members.

6.4 CONCLUSIONS AND DISCUSSION

Using novel, hand-collected data comprising all venture team members, this chapter has built on the upper echelon perspective to analyse the effects of team dynamics on new venture performance of academic spin-offs. In the literature under the upper echelon perspective the relationship between teams and firm performance has been studied. Ensley and Pearce (2001) also build on this upper echelon perspective to develop a theoretical framework that links shared strategic cognition in top management teams to group process and new venture performance. Another stream of research positioned within the literature on organizational culture has in a parallel way analysed the underlying dimensions of what Ensley and Pearce (2001) referred to as shared strategic cognition. Based on Quinn's (1988) competing values model, Van Muijen et al. (1999) identify extreme types of orientation towards how a team should ideally work. Four different types of orientation were identified: the support, innovation, rules and goals orientations. We use Van Muijen et al.'s. (1999) four orientations to measure heterogeneity in the perceived strategic orientation needed for new venture success.

We built upon these insights to perform an in-depth analysis of different spin-off teams. This analysis has led to several new insights on *how* entrepreneurship is infused into ventures through the evolution of teams as they take the spin-off from research to an independent venture. At the start of the venture formation, we propose that a new team role, which we describe as the 'privileged witness', is important in affecting the successful development of the venture. This role might be specific for spin-offs, which are coached by dedicated persons at their parent organization. In line with previous studies, our research shows that not all researchers involved in the original research activities, and identification of the market opportunity, are actively involved in the spin-off today. Indeed, the members of the team change as the spin-off evolves. Our findings lead us to propose that some researchers who are actively involved in the first phase of the spin-out process, where the market opportunity is identified, do not show the entrepreneurial commitment to create the spin-off and leave the process before the formal creation of the spin-off. That is, they make a career choice to stay with the parent organization. The decision to stay with the parent organization may be the result of the philosophy of the parent institute, since the combination of full academic tenure and a position in a venture are restricted by the parent institute. Alternatively, our findings also lead us to propose that researchers may leave the spin-off during the phase in which the spin-off has to prove its viability, since they found it was taking too long. Based on our cases, we are able to propose that once the spin-off has survived this third phase, the researchers stay and take the spin-off to maturity. In other cases, surrogate entrepreneurs are attracted to set up the venture.

Second, we provide an important extension to previous research, which used to view team development in a static framework, in that different teams are considered in a certain moment in time, whereas we take into consideration the same teams at different moments in time, and by doing so we take a dynamic perspective that covers different phases in the venture's development. Next to teams, success is not a static concept. We describe success in terms of reaching well-defined entrepreneurial events in the spin-off process. In particular, we analyse the team structure before and after formal start-up of the venture. In line with expectations, we found that new team members brought in different kinds of experience. Recruits with commercial background are especially appreciated. However, contrary to our expectations, these newcomers did not have a different view on doing business from that of the initial founders of the new venture. Hence, these findings lead us to propose that new entrants to spin-offs will reinforce shared cognition. This is surprising since the degree of shared cognition has been shown elsewhere in the literature to have mixed effects on performance. In other words, cognitive conflict is sometimes necessary to make strategic decisions and increase venture performance.

This study suggests a number of areas for further research which derive from some of its limitations. The selection of the cases included in our study was based on the stage in which they are active in the spin-off process. Druilhe and Garnsey (2004) identify three types of spin-offs that may evolve through a range of business models: companies based on novel scientific breakthroughs where resource creation and opportunity recognition are interdependent, product companies involving opportunity recognition that builds on the scientist's knowledge and connections, and software companies. These different configurations and evolutionary paths may have implications for the evolution of the entrepreneurial teams involved. As we have noted, this study focused on the first category. Given the nature of the firms in our sample, our cases represent a continuum. The micro-electronic firms and the technological test equipment firm, which represent the two ends of this continuum, lead us to conclude that the lead time is determined by the technology transfer officers. They have a tendency to speed up the spin-off trajectory for complex projects. On the other hand, they seem to slow down the spin-off trajectory of less complex projects since they impose the same procedures as for complex projects. Further research might usefully perform a cross-sectoral analysis using both qualitative data and statistical analysis in a large sample of spin-offs. A further potential feature of spin-off development concerns regression resulting from the 'reinvention' or reorientation of the venture along the way, or the possibility of merger of two ventures into one organization. These aspects were not covered in this chapter but offer a further avenue for in-depth analysis.

We have focused on spin-off development in one geographical area. Different institutional environments, which may be more or less munificent in terms of both the university context and the area surrounding a particular university, may have different impacts on the availability of potential incoming team members as well as the alternative options available for academics. For example, Clarysse et al. (2005b) identify different incubator models that may be applied in different contexts and may be associated with different types of spin-off. Team dynamics differ between these incubator models. There is, therefore, a need for further research that examines the development of teams in different institutional contexts. With the small number of cases examined and the focus on a limited set of issues, we were also unable to examine the relationship between financial aspects and expertise and team size. Further case studies might be used to address this issue. By examining a small number of cases, we have emphasized conceptual development rather than general empirical testing. There would appear to be scope for more large-scale testing of the insights generated in this chapter.

The study examined different aspects of the spin-off development process, but the spin-offs involved were at different stages in their development. Although we adopted an approach that addressed this issue, there is a need for longitudinal studies that trace the development of teams over time. However, obtaining access in such cases may present major barriers for research.

Finally, in terms of further research, our study has focused solely on academic spin-offs. There is, therefore, a need for studies that compare directly the development of academic spin-offs with the trajectory of similar non-academic spin-offs. To what extent do differences in heterogeneity occur in such cases? To what extent does the availability of different networks and social capital affect the changing nature of heterogeneity in the team?

With respect to managerial implications, the study provides a number of insights into optimizing the management of the spin-off process and the spin-off ventures themselves. First, we have shown the existence of a 'privileged' witness. This person is involved in the start-up process of the company and has a very important stake in the subsequent composition of the founding team. He/she is often a substitute for the founder/entrepreneur and plays an important role as a sounding board for the entrepreneurs involved in the start-up process. The presence and impact of this person in the early stage of company development has both good and bad consequences. The good thing is that he/she makes sure things happen. The bad thing is that by definition he/she is involved in starting venture capital backed start-ups. The privileged witness tends to look for a manager or business developer to introduce into the start-up. However, this kind of top-down approach usually requires some form of starting capital to enable these individuals to be recruited. Moreover, the privileged witness also regulates the IP involvement of the university, which again makes a valuation and external capital injection necessary. The emerging question is whether bottom-up stimulation of entrepreneurship associated with organizational and cultural changes may be a more appropriate alternative way of creating spin-offs.

We also observe that in the early stages of spin-off formation, the composition of the founding team tends to undergo drastic changes. Surprisingly, while it might be expected that the changes will embody team diversity, they do not. In terms of 'attitude' in particular, the team newcomers tend to be similar to the surrogate entrepreneurs–practitioners that are already in place. This recruitment of similar personalities might be inspired by the consensus-building that takes place between the surrogate entrepreneur who usually has some power over the technology which he/she developed and the privileged witness who wants to bring the technology onto the market. The privileged witness has to legitimize his/her own position and can seldom realistically propose somebody who the entrepreneur does not like. The entrepreneur, however, does not evaluate the proposed person based upon purely economic arguments, but also takes more interpersonal aspects into account, such as their ability to get along with the person, or that person's personality. The latter seem to weigh more heavily than the economic arguments.

NOTE

1. We examined the strategic orientation of individual team members versus the teams' strategic orientation but no clear differences emerged; the results are therefore not reported here.

7. Financial constraints and access to finance[1]

7.1 INTRODUCTION

A key constraint for spin-offs is finding access to finance. Our survey of TTOs in the UK identifies access to finance as the major constraint facing university spin-offs (USOs) (Table 7.1). The existence of a financing gap for new and small ventures has long been recognized in policy initiatives to help fill that gap both at the European level (European Commission, 2000a) and in individual countries (Bank of England, 2003). The pecking-order hypothesis assumes that internal funding is preferred over external sources and where these are insufficient then debt is preferred over equity (Roberts, 1991; Watson and Wilson, 2002). Debt is preferred over equity in order to avoid ownership dilution. In line with the pecking-order hypothesis, we would expect that university spin-offs, which are innovative start-ups facing severe financing constraints (Westhead and Storey, 1997), look for different forms of internal financing complemented with debt financing before they seek venture capital. Alternatively, we would expect that policy-makers first make internal and debt financing easier to obtain before they introduce mechanisms to encourage venture capital as a way to stimulate spin-offs.

Issues surrounding both demand and supply side aspects of the search for finance for USOs may create market failure problems that could be more significant than for other ventures. On the demand side, shortfalls in human capital in terms of the knowledge and understanding required to develop the case for investment in a way that is persuasive and meaningful to external funds providers might be particularly problematical. The very early stage nature of these developments would also make the case more difficult to construct even if the requisite expertise were available within the university. Academic and university staff responsible for the preparation of such cases may find it difficult to predict the amount of funding required. They may have unrealistic or impractical expectations in terms of the distribution of equity between participants and a poor understanding of investment readiness from a funder's perspective. Understanding and developing the business model of the spin-off, that is, the way in which the resources are to be deployed to capture value, may be important in

Table 7.1   TTOs' views on factors impeding the creation of university spin-off companies

Rank	Impediments	Mean value
1	Ability to obtain finance from venture capital firms	2.4
2	Availability of proof-of-concept funding for developing prototypes of the technology	2.5
3	The number of staff to manage the IP identification, assessment and exploitation process	2.5
4	Availability of proof-of-concept funding for conducting market research/analysis	2.6
5	Availability of proof-of-concept funding for conducting IPR due diligence	2.6
6	Incentives and rewards to attract commercial management to spin-offs	2.8
7	Availability of proof-of-concept funding for business plan development	2.8
8	Availability of resources to maintain patent applications	2.9
9	Ability to obtain finance from industrial partners	2.9
10	Ability to obtain finance from business angels	3.0

Note: Institutions were asked to indicate the factors impeding or promoting the creation and development of spinout companies during financial year 2002 on a scale from 1 to 5 where 1 = Strongly Impeded; 2 = Impeded; 3 = No Effect; 4 = Promoted; and 5 = Strongly Promoted.

Source: Authors' survey of TTOs.

positioning ventures to attract outside funding. This suggests a need to undertake activities to establish the appropriate market positioning of the spin-off. The institutional context may also influence demand side factors as universities' objectives and support processes may affect the kind of spin-offs emanating from universities that may be attractive to venture capitalists as well as the resources and incentives made available to develop spin-offs (see Chapter 4).

On the supply side, information asymmetries relating to the proposed venture may raise issues for funds providers. Shortcomings in the management team and the early stage and unpredictable nature of the technologies emerging in USOs may be especially problematical. The academic scientist may not be the most appropriate CEO and there may be problems in finding suitable alternatives (Franklin et al., 2001). Risk assessment may be more difficult due to high levels of uncertainty surrounding the technology and its marketability. The IP may be owned by the university rather than the academic inventor. The nature of individual universities' objectives, strategies and support for commercialization may affect the ability of external funders to negotiate an appropriate deal that would enable them to achieve their target rates of return (Chapter 4).

This chapter examines these issues. Section 7.2 provides evidence on the importance of different sources of finance for USOs and the extent to which they are used. Section 7.3 examines each funding source in turn in the context of USOs. The final section provides some conclusions.

7.2   ACCESS TO FINANCE

The most important sources of funding for USOs are seen to be government grants, university challenge funds, venture capital and joint ventures between the university and an outside firm (Table 7.2). Those universities most active in spinning off ventures are significantly more likely to recognize the

Table 7.2   TTOs' views on importance of sources of finance for spin-off companies

Source of finance	Combined mean	Top performers mean	Non-top performers mean
Venture capital	2.8**	2.2	3.1
	(2.7)**	(1.8)	(3.2)
Government grant (e.g.	2.2	2.2	2.1
SMART awards)	(3.0)	(3.2)	(2.9)
University's own funds	3.2	3.2	3.3
	(3.3)	(3.3)	(3.3)
Joint ventures between the university	2.8	3.2	2.6
and an outside firm	(3.3)	(3.1)	(3.4)
University Challenge Fund money	2.8**	1.8	3.3
	(3.5)**	(2.1)	(4.2)
Business angels	3.0	2.9	3.0
	(3.5)	(3.1)	(3.7)
Licensing deals	3.0	3.2	2.9
	(3.8)	(3.7)	(3.9)
Founder's own savings or capital	3.9***	4.6	3.5
	(4.1)	(4.2)	(4.0)
Bank debt	4.1	4.5	3.9
	(4.4)	(4.4)	(4.3)

Note: Significance levels: ** $p < 0.01$; *** $p < 0.001$.

Source: Authors' survey of TTOs.

importance of access to venture capital (VC). Indeed, for these universities, after university challenge fund (UCF) finance, venture capital is seen as the second most important source of finance ahead of business angels and industrial partners.

Evidence from the UK on the actual sources of equity finance for investments in new and established spin-offs is presented in Table 7.3. In terms of *new* companies attracting equity finance, notwithstanding the fact that UCFs may not be accessible to all institutions, this is the most popular source of finance. In total 50 investments were made in spin-offs across the 113 universities providing data. The second most popular source of finance was VC with 20, followed by industrial partner (14) and business angel (12) investments made respectively. In terms of *existing* spin-offs, that is companies established prior to financial year 2002, VC finance was the most popular source of funds with 42 investments made, followed by UCF (32), business angel (21) and industrial partner (5).

Using the same questionnaire in continental European universities, we find consistent evidence with our UK results. In continental European universities UCF equivalent finance is mainly a substitute for internal funds of universities or public research institutes. In those countries where no UCF type of programme exists, such as Germany, the *pre-seed* capital is invested by the university itself.

These findings are not in line with the pecking-order theory, which seems to suggest that the founders' own savings would be the most important source, followed by debt financing. In fact, technology transfer offices (TTOs) view these two sources as not important at all, albeit the top universities find the investment of personal funds to be significantly less important than those universities without a track record in spinning off companies. In those universities, it seems that challenge fund instruments are substituting for the lack of internal funding.

Table 7.3   Sources of external finance for new and existing spin-offs, financial year 2002

Source of investment	New spin-offs	Existing spin-offs
Venture capital firms	20	42
Business angels	12	21
Industrial partners	14	5
University Challenge Funds	50	32
Other external providers	31	24
University	33	37

Source: Authors' survey.

University spin-offs that attract external equity investments tend to be skewed across a small number of universities. In particular, for new spin-offs only, 16 universities had companies that attracted VC investment, 11 business angel investments and 12 industrial partner investment. Investment in existing spin-offs is also skewed, with only 17 universities attracting UCF finance investments, 25 attracting VC investments, 12 accessing business angel investments and 3 finding industrial partner investments for these ventures.

The following sections seek to shed light on the reasons for this level of activity.

7.3   DIFFERENT FUNDING SOURCES

7.3.1   Internal Funding

Internal financing is generated by the founding entrepreneurs themselves or by the university's own funds, which may include mixed private and public funds. Smilor et al. (1990) reported that over 70 per cent of the spin-offs from the University of Austin were financed by internal funds. However, in Europe many university researchers may not possess enough financial sources to cover the start-up cost of such a venture. Universities may provide small amounts of funding to cover the costs of IP protection and very early stage developments, but their finances would not normally accommodate large investments in commercialization. In the financial year 2002, 33 universities in the UK funded the development of USOs in this way (Wright et al., 2003).

Some universities channel funds from public sources to USOs, while others are beginning to establish their own venture capital funds. The extent and nature of these funds typically relate to the incubation model adopted by the university. For example, Twente University, which traditionally has a Low Selective approach (see Chapter 4), use funds from the European Social Fund to grant loans of up to 15 000 euros. Crealys received 1.5 million euros from the government, 200 000 euros per annum from the City of Lyon, 1 million euros from the Rhône-Alpes region and 500 000 euros from the associated universities. Universities adopting a Supportive model are likely to use public/private partnership funds organized as a VC fund but investing in earlier stages and lower amounts than a traditional VC. The funds provided are generally in the range of 250 000–350 000 euros. The 12.5 million euros Gemma Frisius Fond was created in 1997 as a joint venture between the Katholieke Universiteit Leuven (20 per cent), KBC Investment (40 per cent) and Fortis Private Equity (40 per cent).

Universities adopting an Incubator model, which requires considerably larger funds, may be more likely to make use of significant government funding (for example, the IMEC in Belgium) or private sector funds from wealthy individuals or private VC firms.

7.3.2   Debt Finance

The majority of smaller businesses tend to rely on bank debt as their major source of external funds (Keasey and Watson, 1992; Scherr et al., 1993). Information asymmetries between the bank and the entrepreneurs may have negative consequences for the provision of bank finance and result in credit rationing. However, some bank lending decisions reflect evaluations of human capital rather than implicit information-based credit rationing and collateral provision can be used to ameliorate the negative impact of information asymmetries (Cressy, 1996).

Universities may be relatively well placed to provide collateral for debt finance but this poses problems where it involves the use of public funds. An alternative is the use of the university's reputation or network as a quality guarantee, as well as visible indicators of technology quality such as patents and the founding team's track record. Generally though, apart from overdraft facilities, the cash flow profile of USOs and the lack of collateral mean that bank finance is problematical. Supporting our direct findings, there is evidence from elsewhere of the limited role played by bank finance for spin-offs in both UK and US studies (Roberts, 1991; Moore, 1994; EC, 2000a; 2000b).

7.3.3   Government Financing Schemes

As discussed in Chapter 2, UCFs have been introduced to help improve the entrepreneurial culture of universities. University challenge funds can provide the means for universities and investors to engage with each other to develop mutually beneficial relationships. These funds provide incentives for universities to learn how to develop the right commercial capabilities. They also provide incentives for investors to increase their exposure to USOs and hence to learn to engage with universities. University challenge funds should continue to focus solely on achieving proof of concept for technologies. However, there is a need to enhance the ability of USOs to achieve proof of concept and reach a point of investor readiness that is sufficient to access funding from early stage investors. This could be achieved by raising the limit at which UCF funds can be used to capitalize USOs, enabling them to bring in co-investors. Greater dissemination of the activities of UCFs could alert venture capital investors to new opportunities, reducing their search costs.

This could facilitate involvement in the market by more venture capital investors but may also need to involve the development of close relationships between universities and venture capitalists for deals to be consummated. Mechanisms might also be developed to enable UCFs to decrease the complexity involved in negotiating terms with several existing stakeholders when USOs reach the stage where they require larger amounts of venture capital funding.

7.3.4 Industrial Partners

Corporations may invest directly or indirectly as finance providers to new ventures. Indirect investment involves investing in venture capital funds which then make the investment in new ventures, some of which may be USOs (McNally, 1997). Indirect corporate investment in venture capital is relatively uncommon. Corporate investors generally account for around 5–10 per cent of finance raised by VC funds (EVCA, 2004). Corporate venture capital activity has been variable over time but there has been a move to more direct investment in the search for early access to new products and exposure to new technologies (McNally, 1997).

Spin-offs involving joint ventures between universities and corporations may in some circumstances be better placed to overcome the critical junctures faced by developing ventures, discussed in Chapter 5. Spin-offs involving joint ventures with corporations derived resource benefits from the prior knowledge of their industries and the superior market intelligence held by the corporate partner. As such they may be better positioned to develop opportunities from scientific discoveries, which better serve unmet customer needs. In these cases, the corporate partner and the university may be better able to cooperate in assembling a well-balanced team with the necessary background successfully to exploit commercially the technology, for example, by seconding staff. The corporate partner may be able to use its reputation to attract experts in product development and manufacturing to work for the new venture. Corporate partners can provide greater access in-house to critical resources such as marketing, technology, raw materials, equipment, facilities, financial assets, managerial expertise, and organizational routines and control systems. The credibility acquired from both the university and the corporation may enable these ventures more readily to acquire further resources. The transfer of knowledge from the parent corporation may also produce more rapid professionalization and capability-building that enables them to enter and compete in new markets. The stock of social capital developed by corporate partners from their long-term involvement in a sector can help expedite the development process.

Corporate partners, however, may have agendas that are incompatible with those of the entrepreneur, may have shorter-term horizons that are incompatible with the development of the technology, may have considerably greater bargaining power over the distribution of gains at later stages in the process and may also place pressure on a university to cede IP to them on disadvantageous terms. Contractual devices may be used to control for opportunistic behaviour by the corporate partner, such as narrowly defined domains of exploitation of the IP, clawbacks on licences in the event of failure of the venture, and agreement on the sale of equity stakes to other investors.

7.3.5 Business Angels

Business angels are wealthy private individuals, typically with entrepreneurial or business backgrounds, who provide modest amounts of equity finance to businesses in which they have no family connection. Business angel financing is long established for early stage businesses across Europe. Evidence indicates that investment by business angels is concentrated at the start-up and early development stages of financing, and less at the seed or later stage. Business angel and venture capital financing may be complementary. Business angels may provide finance at an earlier stage than venture capital firms or may invest alongside venture capital firms at early stages.

In contrast to venture capital firms, business angels tend to place more emphasis on agency risk than market risk. Business angels may be more experienced in the markets in which they invest but, as they generally screen fewer deals, they thus have more limited information. For business angels it becomes important to find the 'right' entrepreneur that they can trust and work with as they tend to make less use of the costly contracting devices adopted by venture capital firms to deal with agency risk (Fiet, 1995).

Business angels may be motivated by non-economic as much as economic factors but typically have a desire to make a value-added contribution. There are marked international differences between the involvement of informal investors in their investee companies, with investors in the UK seemingly devoting little attention whereas in Sweden involvement is high (Landstrom, 1993). Contrary to views that informal investors are less constrained by the need to earn returns in a specified period, their exit horizons are usually around five years. There is also evidence (Ehrlich et.al., 1994) of significant differences between formal and informal venture capitalists in respect of investee monitoring, with the former providing more difficult targets, and greater feedback and involvement in monitoring, especially when the firm is experiencing problems. These differences may arise because private investors neither have the time, expertise nor flexibility to engage in close monitoring, so that formal venture capitalists may be more appropriate for entrepreneurs with high technical but low managerial skills, and vice versa for private investors.

Informal venture capital markets tend to be inefficient in terms of the communications channels between investors and entrepreneurs. Research emphasizes that the more shrewd investors identify the most attractive deals through personal networks. Unlike venture capital firms, business angels typically do not have a high profile and in some contexts, where open displays of wealth are frowned upon, may even prefer to remain discrete in their activities. Various networks have been established and have enjoyed some success in making the market more efficient by bringing together investors and entrepreneurs either through newsletters or fora. However, there is a lingering concern that the proposals that are made public in these arenas may be those that are less attractive since they may have failed to obtain finance from other sources or through personal networks with business angels.

This discussion emphasizes the importance for universities of developing networks with potential angel investors who may also be able to offer commercial managerial input, even acting as surrogate entrepreneurs (Franklin et al., 2001). While there may be a need for universities to develop links with business angels who may have backgrounds in the technology area (Mason and Harrison, 2004), a central problem lies in finding such partners. It is debatable whether the highly successful entrepreneurs necessary as partners to stimulate high-growth ventures are to be found among the members of local business angel networks. University TTOs might envisage building up a European-level network of business angels in those technologies in which the university is strong. Alternatively, the European Association of Business Angel Networks could play a more active role in this for those universities that do not have the critical mass to build up such a network.

7.3.6   Venture Capital

Venture capital investing
In marked contrast to the US, the European venture capital industry has developed since the early 1980s as a 'hybrid' embracing both early stage investment ('classic venture capital') and later stage financing of established enterprises via management buyouts ('private equity'). The collective experience of private equity providers in the UK and continental Europe stands in marked contrast to that in the US. Compared with their US counterparts, venture capital firms in Europe have traditionally been criticized for being

reluctant to invest in early stage high-tech investment (Murray and Lott, 1995) although there are some indications that attitudes are changing (Lockett et al., 2002a). Early stage technology investments accounted for around a quarter of all BVCA investments during the period 2000–2003 (BVCA, 2004). The value of early stage VC investments in technology was 5.5 per cent of the total VC investment in the UK in 2003. A similar picture is evident at the European level. Early stage investments accounted for 34.7 per cent of the total volume and around 7 per cent of total investment value in 2003 (EVCA, 2004).

Venture capital firms make investments in private ventures where the investor trades-off short-term illiquidity in the shares held for the prospects of a greater future return. Venture capitalists seek a return on their specific and distinctive skills in identifying, investing in and monitoring new ventures where asymmetric information problems between the financier and the entrepreneur are significant. Under these circumstances it may be difficult for VCs to obtain reliable information on which to base an investment decision.

Information asymmetry problems may be particularly intractable in the case of complex high-tech/biotechnology ventures than for more straightforward ventures using existing technology, which raise issues concerning the specialist skills of both the entrepreneur and the venture capitalist. The processes adopted by venture capital firms in screening potential investments have been widely researched (Wright et al., 2003). For other than the most confident and/or informed investors, the chaos and opacity of a new technology market may create a very high barrier to investment (Von Burg and Kenney, 2000). Venture capitalists have to make trade-offs between various criteria in their screening of investments. Venture capitalists appear to prefer to select an opportunity that offers a good management team and reasonable financial and product market characteristics, even if the opportunity does not meet the overall fund and deal requirements (Muzyka et al., 1995). Early stage venture capital investors emphasize a range of product-strength and market-growth characteristics, particularly as early stage transactions are technology based with little available data on market acceptance.

Venture capital firms will put in place both contractual and relational monitoring and advisory devices to help ensure that the venture achieves target rates of return. These devices may include the staging of financial commitments over several rounds of investment according to whether initial development milestones have been met, covenants in the firm's articles of association that limit the entrepreneur's actions without the venture capital firm's permission, requirements to provide detailed and regular reporting of financial and operational progress, and board representation by the venture capital firm.

For both screening and monitoring of technology investments there is, thus, a need for venture capital firms to possess both appropriate human capital and network assets to enable them to undertake these functions effectively. These assets are expensive to acquire and to maintain. Accordingly, there exists a transaction size below which the cost of processing and subsequent governance is incommensurate with the value and potential returns from an investment. The costs of undertaking detailed scrutiny may discourage participation in smaller investments and create what has long been referred to as an 'equity gap' where formal venture capital is not available to projects below around £500 000.

Venture capital firms will set target rates of return for different types of investment. These returns are generally realized when the investment exits through stock market flotation (initial public offering – IPO) or sale to a strategic partner (trade sale). In some cases, exits may be achieved through sale to another venture capital or private equity firm or a buy-back by management. These realizations may be full or partial, the latter involving some retention of an equity stake by the original investor. Given that venture capital investments are risky, a significant proportion may fail, with the investment being written off.

Returns to VCs are typically measured in terms of internal rates of return. Alternatively, returns may be measured in terms of multiples of initial investments. Early stage technology-based investments, which typically carry the greatest risk, are likely to have the highest target rate of return. Lockett et al. (2002) report target internal rates of return (IRRs) for early stage technology investments of up to 80 per cent compared with up to 50 per cent for early stage non-technology investments. Notwithstanding the skills of the venture capital firm in selecting and monitoring investees, problems of asymmetric information and uncertainty in the market environment mean that not all venture capital backed ventures will succeed. Hence, while these target IRRs on individual deals may seem high, this is less the case in the context of a portfolio where only 10–20 per cent of investments will succeed, perhaps 20–30 per cent may fail outright and the remainder will be either 'living dead' with little prospect of growth or modest performers (Ruhnka et al., 1992).

Against these expectations, and in the light of the difficulties in identifying successful ventures at the investment stage, it is perhaps not too surprising that the returns on early stage technology venture capital portfolios are relatively low. Mean internal rates of return on technology investments fell 12.8 per cent at the height of the dotcom boom in 2000 to 7.4 per cent in 2003. Over the same period, mean internal rates of return for non-technology investments fell from 17.3 per cent to 14.5 per cent (PWC/BVCA, 2004). Across Europe, the median IRR for all venture capital investments (excluding buyouts) for funds formed over the period 1980–2003 at the end of 2003 was 0.0 per cent and the top quartile IRR was 7.4 per cent, while the corresponding figures for all later stage private equity funds were 0.0 per cent and 10.9 per cent, respectively (EVCA/Thompson Venture Economics, 2004).

The main forms of exit are trade sales, followed at some distance by IPOs. Data in the UK indicate that relatively few spin-offs have exited (Wright et al., 2003). Based on returns from the full UK higher education sector, 20 full exits were recorded in 2002; these involved one IPO, five sales to strategic partners and 14 liquidations. The total value realized was £6.8 million, with by far the largest share coming from sales to strategic partners. In addition, five partial sales were identified, which included one partial exit through IPO, two trade sales and two management buy-backs. However, reflecting the development of the sector and also improving stock market conditions, a reported ten spin-offs were floated in 2004. Eight of these floated on the London Alternative Investment Market (AIM); OHM (Southampton); Vectura (Bath); VasTox (Oxford); Synairgen (Southampton); Ceres Power (Imperial College); IDMos (Dundee/St Andrews); MicroEmissive Displays (Edinburgh/Napier) and Andor Technology (Belfast). At the end of 2005, it was reported that in the previous two years, 20 spin-offs from UK universities had floated with a combined IPO value of over £1 billion.

Examples of exits through stock market flotation include Proximagen Neuroscience which in March 2005 obtained a listing on the London Alternative Investment Market (AIM). The company was formed in 2003 as a spin-off from King's College London to discover and develop new treatments for neurodegenerative diseases. Kings College received a reported £1 million from its share in the company. The commercial development of the business was facilitated by seed investment from IP2IPO Limited who specialize in commercializing university technology. Proximagen's capitalization on listing was £29.7 million, with the flotation raising £13.5 million for the company. In October 2004, the University of Southampton spin-off Synairgen also obtained a listing on AIM with a valuation of £28.2 million, with new capital of £10.5 million being raised. The university sold 10 per cent of its shareholding and retains 16.6 per cent of the shares of the company. IP2IPO also funded the company. Synairgen was founded in 2003 and is a drug discovery company focusing on identifying and out-licensing pharmaceutical products, which address the underlying causes of asthma and chronic obstructive pulmonary disease (COPD). Earlier in the year, the university also floated the spin-off company, OHM. Although these two companies floated very quickly after formation, there can be a long time lag. For example, Wolfson Electronics, a spin-off from Edinburgh University obtained a stock market flotation in 2003, 19 years after formation.

Preliminary pilot evidence suggests that the survival rates among university spin-offs in the UK may be better than the average for new technology companies (Minshall and Wicksteed, 2005). The failure rate from ten universities studied was less than 10 per cent, compared with the average of 60–70 per cent. However, these figures need to be treated with some caution given the small sample.

Table 7.4 shows the valuation of portfolio of spin-offs created by the Inter-University Institute for Microelectronics (IMEC) in Belgium, which were primarily venture capital backed from proprietary and external sources. As described in Chapter 1, this institute employs over 1000 researchers in a focused domain, namely, micro-electronics. Because the IMEC has professionalized its technology transfer activities, we have split up the portfolio in three subsequent periods (Moray and Clarysse, 2005): 1984–94 characterizes period 1. In this period, spin-offs were not really supported. During period 2, 1995–98, the IMEC developed a supportive environment for spin-offs. It actively assisted their business plan development, helped form the teams and had close relations with a professional VC fund. From 1999 onwards the research institute had become involved in straight incubation activities. From that moment on, ventures were nurtured and pre-financed by the institute itself.

As of 2003, the institute had spun off 18 companies. Five of these had experienced a trade sale, on average nine years after the initial spin-off of the company. It is important to note that the trade sale happened only nine years

Table 7.4   IMEC: an example of valuation of a portfolio of spin-offs

	2003	1998	1994
Number of spin-offs (in portfolio)	18	12	7
Total capital invested in the spin-offs in portfolio (in thousand euros)	123 656	32 373	7 035
Number of trade sales	5	1	–
Bankruptcy	3	–	–
Total fair market value of the portfolio (in thousand euros)*	215 808	78 674	10 937
Average percentage shares of IMEC (first round of funding, in the portfolio)	18% (13%)	24% (16%)	25% (12%)

Note: * Fair market value is calculated as the capital at start-up minus the depreciations in capital and bankruptcies according to the EVCA accounting rules plus the value added realized on trade sales.

after the initial founding of this company. Only three of the companies had resulted in a bankruptcy. The research institute had an average of 18 per cent shares in the start-up capital of the companies founded in the period 1999–2003. This share is lower than the percentage of shares in the companies founded in the initial period. However, the average capital at start-up of the spin-offs had increased significantly from 500 000 euros on average in the first period, to 3.2 million euros in the third period. The portfolio of spin-offs around this institute represented a fair market value of 215 million euros in 2003, which is about twice the investment they represent in the same period. The case clearly shows that a focused spin-off policy *can* be profitable.

Lockett et al. (2002) found that venture capitalists believed that high-tech proposals generally display greater shortcomings than non-technology projects regarding management quality, intellectual property protection and potential market size. The emergence of new ventures from universities that have not traditionally been commercial environments may introduce differences in the approaches adopted by venture capital firms to screen these ventures. Similarly, there has been growing recognition of the notion that ventures need to be investor-ready, that is, in a pre-prepared state that enable venture capital firms to evaluate them more easily. As such, new ventures from universities, where the skills to prepare for venture capital investment are lacking, may face problems in attracting investment. The following sections examine these issues.

Proposals and investments
Venture capitalist interest in USOs is quite skewed even among those VCs that invest in high-tech ventures. According to data provided by VC firm respondents, they received investment proposals from six different universities on average. The same respondents reported spending time actively engaged in developing business plans with an average of 3.8 different universities. Of the 27 responding VC firms, during calendar year 2002, only eight made spin-off investments with at least four different universities. Only three VC investors funded more than one spin-off from the same university.

In our face-to-face interviews with the 65 VC firms, located in six different European countries noted above, 41 explicitly mentioned their willingness to invest in spin-offs, while only 15 do not consider such an investment and eight were undecided.

Investors preferred to invest in both spin-offs and high-tech companies at their start-up stage where there is a lower level of risk than at the seed stage at which proof-of-concept work occurs. At all stages of investment, more VC firms were willing to invest in high-tech companies than in spin-offs. This is in line with the pecking-order theory.

Table 7.5   Venture capitalists investment proposals and investments

	Seed stage		Start-up stage		Late stage	
	High-tech	USO	High-tech	USO	High-tech	USO
Panel A: proposals						
Total number of proposals	815	369	4599	135	201	69
Percentage of total number of proposals	13.1%	6.0%	74.3%	2.2%	3.2%	1.1%
Panel B: investments						
Total number of investments	15	24	41	18	4	1
Percentage of total number of investments	14.6%	23.3%	39.8%	17.5%	3.9%	0.9%
Panel C: investments to proposals						
Ratio of investments to investment proposals	0.018	0.065	0.001	0.13	0.02	0.014

Source: Authors' survey of venture capital firms.

Proposals for start-up stage high-tech investments accounted for almost three quarters (74.3 per cent) of all investment proposals received (Table 7.5, panel A). Across all stages, 90.2 per cent of investment proposals received were for high-tech ventures and only 9.2 per cent were for spin-offs, suggesting that VC firms have comparatively little exposure to or experience of this type of investment.

The 27 respondents made a total of 60 investments in high-tech companies and 43 investments in spin-offs in calendar year 2002 (Table 7.5, panel B). Start-up stage high-tech investments accounted for almost 40 per cent of all investments by number. This category of investment also received the greatest number of investment proposals.

The figures, however, reveal that a higher proportion of seed stage investment proposals may be attractive to spin-off investors than start-up stage investment proposals. We find that the ratio of investments to proposals is highest in respect of seed stage spin-off ventures (Table 7.5, panel C). For spin-offs, the ratios of investments made to proposal ratios are higher at both seed and start-up stages. Interestingly, these figures indicate that at both these stages, spin-off investment proposals stand a reasonable chance of leading to investment alongside similar investment proposals. These ratios also show that investment proposals for spin-offs stand a better chance of receiving funding at the start-up stage than at the seed stage from VC firms. The relatively high acceptance rate for spin-off proposals compared with high-tech proposals may be indicative of screening and preparation being undertaken by technology transfer offices.

Venture capital firms have invested significantly smaller average amounts in spin-off investments at each stage. However, it is evident that the average amounts invested in USOs are smaller than for other high-tech investments. Our UK evidence indicates that the mean early seed stage investment in a USO is £0.28 million whereas the average for a non-USO high-tech venture at this stage is £0.86 million. The comparable figures for early start-up stage investments are £0.44 million and £0.60 million, respectively. Spin-offs may be seeking lower amounts than non-spin-off high-tech companies but if these results are an indication that spin-offs are raising too little finance at this early stage, they may be under-capitalized, which may have adverse implications for their ability to grow.

Screening of proposals

Spin-offs compete for venture capital with other private sector projects. Differences in screening processes leading to proposal rejection between those VCs who are interested in spin-offs and those who are not highlights the issues that TTOs and spin-offs may need to address if they are to persuade venture capitalists to invest in their ventures. The significant differences between VC firms who are willing to invest in spin-offs and those who are not in terms of the criteria they use to reject an investment proposal are ranked in order of importance in Table 7.6.

Non-spin-off investors place greater emphasis on the size of the potential market when considering investment proposals. The difficulty many universities have in commercializing disruptive technologies emerging from basic research is that of identifying markets in which to apply the technology and estimating the level of demand. This result is confirmed in the findings from the 65 VC firms spread over different European regions. Non-spin-off investors are significantly more concerned about market size, which can provide them with a significant exit opportunity. Spin-off investors, on the contrary, seem to go more for economic viability of the venture and find the estimated time to breakeven a major point of importance.

Joint ownership of IPR with a university is significantly more important to non-spin-off investors. Investors feel uncomfortable about investing in spin-offs when IP is licensed as opposed to being assigned in return for an equity share in the company. Universities often prefer to retain control over

Table 7.6   Venture capitalists' views on factors leading to rejection of investment proposals: main significant differences between spin-off investors and non-spin-off investors

Factors of significant differences between spin-off investors and non-spin-off investors	Combined score	Non-spin-off investors	Spin-off investors
Size of potential market for applications of the technology	4.2***	4.6	3.9
Stage of development of the product/service	4.1**	4.7	3.6
Availability of a prototype/test data to demonstrate proof of concept	3.5**	4.6	2.8
Difficulty in identifying key decision-makers	3.4#	4.1	3.0
Lack of formalized university technology transfer procedures	3.3*	3.9	2.8
Requirement for service development to support customers who will use the product/service	3.0*	3.7	2.4
Concerns over co-investing with public sector funds	2.9*	3.7	2.4
Concerns over co-investing with universities	2.8*	3.4	2.3
Joint ownership of the IPR with universities	2.6**	4.0	1.9

Note: Respondents scored each factor as: 1 = Unimportant; 2 = Not Very Important; 3 = Quite Important; 4 = Important; and 5 = Very Important. A Mann-Whitney test was performed to analyse the differences between spin-off and non-spin-off investors: # = 10% significance level; *5% significance level; **1% significance level; *** 0.1 significance level.

Source: Authors' survey of venture capital firms.

IP to spin-offs as they wish to retain some control over IPRs as well as expecting an equity stake in lieu of royalty payments. In this way, non-spin-off investors may perceive universities as wishing to retain ownership and control without sharing the risk involved.

Non-spin-off investors place more emphasis upon the need to see a prototype, in order to assess the viability of the technology concerned. This finding is also in line with our European sample of 65 VC firms. Spin-off investors in this sample departed from the idea that a good contact with the entrepreneur and a protected technology are good starting points for an investment. Both the development of the technology into a product and the development of a viable management team is, in their view, something

Table 7.7 *Venture capitalists' attitudes and perception of risks associated with investment in USOs*

Rank	Compared to high-tech companies, USOs are more likely to:	Mean
1	require building a management team	4.4
2	require a longer investment time horizon	4.3
3	require close monitoring	4.2
4	require several rounds of funding	4.2
5	have higher variability of return	3.6
6	fail	3.6
7	involve protracted pre-deal negotiations	3.5
8	be small niche market companies	3.3
9	pose valuation difficulties	3.2
10	have financial structuring problems	3.1

Note: Respondents ranked each factor as: 1 = Strongly disagree; 2 = Disagree; 3 = Neither agree or disagree; 4 = Agree; and 5 = Strongly Agree.

Source: Authors' survey of venture capital firms.

that could be accomplished afterwards. In contrast, non-spin-off investors put much more emphasis on a working prototype and a professional management team being in place before the investment is made.

Difficulties in identifying key decision-makers in universities and a lack of formalized university technology transfer procedures are also a significant source of discouragement for non-spin-off investors. Negotiation procedures with universities and the possibility of their future participation as co-investors are also problematic issues.

A second dimension of screening that TTOs and spin-offs need to address relates to VC investors' perceptions of risk and reward when considering investments in spin-offs as compared to other high-tech companies. The most important issue where potential investors considered there were greater risks in spin-offs involved having to build management teams (see Table 7.7).

The length of time taken to realize substantial returns, and the prospect of multiple funding rounds before an exit can be achieved, make investment in spin-offs less attractive. Problems of early and efficient exit are a reflection of the early stage of development of most university technologies and the lengthy product development cycles in sectors such as life sciences.

Frequently the difficulty encountered by entrepreneurs in developing fundable investment propositions is that, apart from intangible technological assets in the form of know-how and IP, they had difficulty in showing that a team was in place that could demonstrate it was committed *and* able to create and deliver value.

Investor readiness

Spin-offs need to be matched up to acceptance criteria expected by investors. As shown in Table 7.8, those universities that were most active in spinning-off ventures were significantly more likely to identify the importance of various processes in meeting these criteria when promoting spin-offs.

Our interviews with TTOs also indicated a number of procedures that were undertaken to render ventures investor-ready. These included the provision of help with business planning, finding managers and assisting with

Table 7.8   TTOs views on factors promoting the creation of university spinout companies

Impediments	Combined mean	Top performers mean	Non-top performers mean
Incentives and rewards for institution staff to spend time on IP exploitation activities	3.2	3.5	3.0
Internal processes for conducting business development	3.2**	3.7	2.9
Internal processes for spinning off new companies	3.3	3.7	3.1
Internal processes for conducting IPR due diligence	3.3**	3.7	3.1
The level of marketing, technical, negotiating skills of staff involved in IP exploitation activities	3.4***	3.9	3.2
Incentives and rewards for academics to exploit the IP generated from their research	3.5**	4.00	3.3

Note: Institutions were asked to indicate the factors impeding or promoting the creation and development of spin-off companies during financial year 2002 on a scale from 1 to 5 where 1 = Strongly Impeded; 2 = Impeded; 3 = No Effect; 4 = Promoted; and 5 = Strongly Promoted. A Mann-Whitney test was performed to analyse the differences between the top performers and the non-top performers. The most significant results are highlighted in the table as follows: * 5% significance level; ** 1% significance level; *** 0.1 significance level.

Source: Authors' survey of TTOs.

fund-raising. More active TTOs had informal networks to find managers and budgets to pay for consultancy, academic secondments and the purchase of specialist equipment.

Most TTOs were involved with IP assessment and due diligence. Some universities made use of patent attorneys while others had the expertise in house. There were some indications that sufficient due diligence was not being undertaken and that too much reliance was being placed on the motivation of the academic.

Venture capitalists' experience

An important constraint on VCs' ability and willingness to invest in USOs is the skills of VC executives to screen and manage investments. In our survey (see Table 7.9) the most common form of experience for VC executives was in the financial services sector (47 per cent). This was followed by chartered accountancy (31 per cent), non-executive or executive director of a technology firm (30 per cent), graduate qualification in a technology subject (29 per cent), managerial experience in a technology firm (28 per cent), a PhD in a technology-related subject (14 per cent) and law (12 per cent). The low proportion of executives with a technology background raises issues relating to how well VC executives are able to understand the science on which the spin-off companies are formed.

Again, this problem is evident across continental Europe. The experiences of the investment managers in the 65 European VC firms interviewed were very similar to the ones reported by the British VC firms. Moreover, only in the VC firms with an explicit biotechnology focus were PhDs found.

Table 7.9   High-tech venture capital executives' experience and backgrounds

VC experience/background	Mean percentage of a firm's executives	SD
Graduate qualification in a technology subject	29	37.21
PhD in a technology subject	14	25.31
Managerial experience in a technology firm	28	39.07
Managerial experience of financial sector	47	36.39
Non-executive director or director of a technology firm experience	30	40.79
Chartered accountancy	31	34.48
Law	12	23.07

Source: Authors' survey of high-tech VC firms.

Venture capital funds with an explicit ICT focus, employed a disproportionate percentage of managers with a financial background.

7.4 CONCLUSIONS

Our analysis indicates that in contrast to the pecking-order hypothesis, TTOs and spin-offs see venture capital rather than internal funds as more important early in the process. Our evidence also shows that venture capitalists do invest smaller sums, reflecting both a willingness to invest in promising early seed stage ventures and to provide further follow-on financing when certain milestones have been reached.

However, our findings also indicate that the majority of VC investors surveyed prefer to invest in spin-offs *after* the seed stage, particularly once proof of concept has been achieved; this is in line with the pecking-order hypothesis. The finding does not seem to be unique to the UK. Moray and Clarysse (2005) came to a similar finding in an in-depth study of a Belgian public research organization, while Heirman and Clarysse (2004) reported that less than one out of ten spin-offs could attract VC, other than that from the Belgian UCF programme in the seed stage. Surprisingly, although universities point to the difficulties in attracting VC and business angel money, they seldom develop mechanisms to increase the possibility of internal funding and debt financing as an intermediate step towards VC investment. This is no doubt due to the financial constraints which universities face. It is only among the top universities in the UK that the almost 100 per cent public challenge funds can be seen as a real substitute. Furthermore, the lack of debt financing as an intermediate step is notable. Moreover, most countries have developed guarantee schemes so that the need for collateral is backed by public money. We suggest that it is important for TTOs to invest much more effort to develop these sorts of finance.

NOTE

1. This chapter draws extensively on Wright et al. (2006b).

8. Conclusions and policy implications

8.1 INTRODUCTION

The purpose of this concluding chapter is threefold. First, we summarize the main findings as presented in each of the chapters, covering the different levels at which the spin-offs can be examined. Second, we discuss the implications of the findings from each chapter for the different actors that deal with spin-offs. These actors include the policy-makers, the individuals involved in the process of spin-off formation and the technology transfer office. We demonstrate the importance of multi-level change in an innovation system if spin-offs are to become a central feature of wealth creation in European economies. Third, we develop an agenda for future research. This chapter is structured as follows. First, we give an overview of the main chapters and discuss the implications of the findings in each of the chapters for the relevant stakeholders. Second, we develop future areas for research. Finally, we conclude the chapter with the main highlights.

8.2 CONCLUSIONS AND MAIN FINDINGS

In this section we summarize the conclusions and main findings on a chapter by chapter basis.

Chapter 2: Various Policy Mechanisms Have Been Developed to Bridge the So-called Knowledge and Financial Gap. However, Their Efficiency and Effectiveness Need Further Evaluation

Our review in Chapter 2 showed that European countries have developed various framework conditions to facilitate the process of start-up creation in general. These countries' experiences have shown that neither these frameworks, nor money alone (VC funds) were enough to create a dynamic spin-off sector. It was necessary to create diverse micro (or meso) schemes or instruments. These measures concern (1) the ownership of IP, (2) the change of researcher status so that academics, who are public servants in many countries, are able to create a company, (3) the support for a project or firm, and (4) the development of TTOs, incubators and seed capital funds in or around universities and public research institutions.

Although there is debate about the aims of national-level initiatives and the growth of regional and European initiatives, the national level was generally the engine of policy to encourage spin-offs. In the UK and France, for example, the ministry or the department in charge of research launched the programmes: the office for Science and Technology (OST) in the UK, and the Ministry of Research in France. In contrast, in Germany, support from the *Länder* has played a more important political role (Audretsch and Beckman, 2005). For example, the biotechnology spin-off located in BioM receives 75 per cent of its support from the state and city of Bayern and only 25 per cent from the federal government.

The ownership of IP and the legislative changes, which make it possible for an academic to take equity, are so-called facilitators. However, each European country also developed stimulators for spin-off policy. At first, the general opinion was that researchers were facing a so-called 'finance gap'. This gap implied that there was not sufficient friends, family and fools (3F) money to cover the pre-seed and even the seed phase, which researchers faced at the moment they had an idea. It is common knowledge that in the US, so-called 3Fs provide the first financial resources to start-ups (Roberts, 1991). In Europe, the various Global Enterprise Monitor (GEM) reports have clearly shown that 3F money lags behind in comparison with the US. This immobility of capital has inspired national governments to develop a range of initiatives financially to support innovative start-ups and spin-offs in particular. We have classified these initiatives into six categories, ranging from loan guarantee schemes to 100 per cent public funds. The countries included in this book have launched initiatives in each of the categories described in Chapter 2.

There is little doubt about the fact that the various public forms of finance have boosted the number of spin-offs created in the mid and late 1990s. However, it remains questionable whether these spin-offs will become sustainable companies. There exist very few evaluations of the various sorts of financing schemes and those that do exist are not disclosed to the public. Heirman and Clarysse (2006) have shown that in the Belgian population of young technology-based firms, spin-offs are the fastest-growing subpopulation. Although promising, a true evaluation is too early. Most of the spin-offs have been founded since the mid-1990s and were therefore less than ten years old at the time of our data collection. The rapid growth might just be a reflection of the larger amounts of capital these companies can dispose of.

After the boost in the number of VSOs created following the development of various financing schemes, the average number of companies created gradually began to fall. Universities complained about the lack of projects among their researchers and the low level of entrepreneurial initiative among their academics. So, business plan competitions and various forms of entrepreneurship training were developed to bridge the so-called 'knowledge gap'. This knowledge gap refers both to the lack of awareness among the researchers to engage in entrepreneurial activities and the lack of knowledge among them about how to develop a business plan.

Along these lines, various sorts of business incubation initiatives were stimulated. Although these business incubators have theoretically a very clear role, they apparently lack in-depth knowledge about the sector or the technology in order to be really useful. The tenant companies included in our analysis were not impressed with the services offered to them by the incubator in which they were located. Only Chalmers incubator, which clearly focuses on the commercialization of research results from Chalmers University, delivers services that match expectations to a large degree. This finding suggests that incubators are most useful when they are really focused on a certain technology, sector or at least the main departments of a technological university. If not, the services that are offered tend to be of marginal importance only and remain limited to the facility management offer.

Since incubators have been a subject of policy attention in many countries for several years, the finding of their relatively low value-added to the tenant companies is very intriguing. If they have so little value added, why do policy-makers then repeatedly use incubators as an instrument to leverage business plans. One explanation might be the legitimacy which these organizations have developed. Legitimacy of an organizational form leads to institutional isomorphism. This means that policy-makers use benchmarks from the initiatives taken in other countries upon which to base their own policy actions. Incubators are clearly such a benchmark result. Despite their low value added, they continue to receive large amounts of public money.

Next to the analysis of the different policy initiatives independently. An important policy concern relates to the complementarity between the diverse initiatives taken to promote spin-offs. The SQW (2005) evaluation report shows that in July 2003, fewer than 50 per cent of the funded higher education institutions (HEIs) in the UK received funding from more than one programme. On the other hand, 51 HEIs received only HEIF funding, seven only SEC funding and three only UCF funding. However, SQW (2005) note that the activity additionality of all programmes is high in terms of the recruitment of extra staff, which the institutions would not have funded on a similar scale from their own budgets, and the generation of additional commercialization of research ideas and company formation.

In the French case, there appears to be a degree of complementary, with 32 per cent of the creators being involved in more than one of the four incentive measures. The most important overlap is observed between the competition and the incubators. Of the total companies resulting from the competition and the incubators, 23 per cent are common to both measures, the 315 companies concerned accounting respectively for 47 per cent of the companies created from the incubators and for 45 per cent of the companies resulting from the competition.

However, our analysis of the available data and our discussion with the managers of the incubators and the public seed capital funds show that there is a significant gap between these two instruments. The government intervention model in its present form functions only partially. The linear model adopted by governments is limited as only a very small percentage of the start-ups financed by seed capital funds are from public-sector incubators. Although the French government perceived there to be complementarity in its measures concerning incubators and start-up funds, this complementarity did not materialize, since only eight of the 344 firms created from incubators by the end of 2001 had benefited from seed capital funds. Indeed, 77 per cent of the firms supported by the seed capital funds (that is, 27 out of 35) were not created from incubators. Conversely, only 2 per cent of the firms created in incubators (eight out of 344) benefited from seed capital. Even by the end of 2005, companies funded by public seed funds represented only 6 per cent of the total companies generated by the incubators. This result would seem to undermine the main premise of French policy towards spin-offs.

Chapter 3: Spin-offs Are Not a Homogeneous Group of Companies. Policy Actions Should Take into Account the Different Business Models and Not Concentrate on the Most Visible Ones

In Chapter 3, we addressed the diversity in the spin-off population. More specifically, we suggested that three very different types exist, which we have labelled respectively the 'venture capital backed type', the 'prospector type' and the 'lifestyle type'. Each of these types is significantly distinct from each other in terms of institutional link, resource base and business model.

The venture capital backed type is probably the most visible and attractive one from a policy perspective. It is the kind of company that primarily plays a role in the market for ideas, builds up credibility and visibility in a fast manner and looks for continuous media attention. This means that its business model is orientated towards convincing different stakeholders, among which investors are an important party, about its technology. In the market for ideas, the strength of the technology is not the most important factor. Rather, the social acceptance of the technology by the different stakeholders is central. Therefore, the ability to build up this credibility is a key determinant of performance. However, this credibility can only be built if the parent group from which the technology is spun off is widely recognized as an important and leading research group. Only then, will other important stakeholders such as financial and corporate investors be interested in taking a risk in the company and accelerating the growth path. This growth path can result in an incumbent company which plays a significant role in the market for products. However, it is much more likely that the path leads to a trade sale to an incumbent company. Tellis et al. (2003) have shown that probably only 6 per cent of the companies that play a leading role in the market for ideas also play such a role in the market for products, and in the latter market they represent only 4 per cent of market share. Hence, it is quite likely that a trade sale will be the destiny of this kind of company.

Although the venture capital backed academic spin-off is attractive through its growth process, it implies a number of risks which have to be recognized by both the university and the policy-maker. First, few research groups have the potential to start up such a company. As mentioned in Chapters 5 and 7, this company requires a balanced portfolio of technology, which is carefully constructed through the licensing or buy- in of IP developed by others and protected by its own IP. It also requires a research group that has received recognition in the scientific community and that plays a significant role in the market for ideas. Finally, it requires human and financial resources that underscore this reputation. In other words, it must be able to attract a significant amount of venture capital at start-up to be credible in its actions and it must be able to attract most of the researchers that were working on the technology at the university or public research institute to retain scientific credibility. However, each university is likely to have only a few research groups that are able to generate this kind of company. As a result, it is unrealistic to set quantitative targets for public research institutes and universities in terms of the number of spin-offs they should create each year. In fact, the possibility of creating such a spin-off will be rather exceptional. On top of this, the spin-off will inherently represent a risk. Most probably, the spin-off will be sold to an incumbent firm. If the incumbent firm is not located in the region or even the country in which the spin-off was founded, this probably means that it will have a foreign parent company and may become an R&D laboratory of this company. In other words, policy-makers cannot expect these companies to generate excessive amounts of employment. Only a few of these spin-offs will be able to achieve significant growth. Even then, there are a number of challenges. The market for products for this type of company is by definition international and mainstream. This means that they have to grow from a probably locally embedded and supported company into a multinational company that has the necessary human resources to be credible at the international scene. This also means that its top management has to turn into an international team. Again, the country or region in which the spin-off was founded might not be attractive enough for expatriate top managers to move into. Having no international top management experience usually results in bad experiences, as the dramatic failures of companies such as BAAN in the Netherlands and Lernout & Hauspie in Belgium have shown.

Most academic spin-offs will not belong to the happy few of the venture capital backed group. The potential of these spin-offs will be more limited because the technology base that underpins their founding is not sufficiently new or credible to play a significant role in the market for ideas. Usually, they have a patent-protected prototype or maybe a beta version to sell on the market for products. Unlike the market for ideas, the market for products follows a bootstrapping logic. This means that the company should economize on its expenses and use internal funds instead of external forms of capital. The time to breakeven is crucial and the sources of finance that are used should not interfere with the business model. In fact, in most cases the business model adopted by these companies is focused on consulting or contract research. As shown by Druihle and Garnsey (2004), academics are familiar with this kind of business model and they feel comfortable with it. On top of this, it requires few investments. In contrast, external capital is provided by equity investors, who have expectations in terms of returns that might by far exceed the market for products. Therefore, they tend to interfere with the business model of spin-offs since they are not interested in investing in companies that do not have any potential to grow in an exponential way. Consulting or contract research companies typically do not have such a growth path. So, academics who have a business model which essentially follows a contract research or a consulting logic are suggested to productize.

This results in a new kind of company which we have labelled the 'prospector' category. These companies attract external capital from public or private equity funds, which are linked to the university or public research laboratory. Usually, the amount of capital is not sufficient to play a role in the market for ideas, nor do the human or technological resources show the intrinsic quality or quantity to attract different stakeholders. So, the question arises as to why these companies will still attract a significant amount of capital at start-up. An explanation is that the capital serves to value the technology licensed or transferred from the university into the start-up. Another explanation is that the capital is used as pre-seed money to test some assumptions behind the business model. In both cases, the multiple that can be realized will not be in line with that expected by an investment manager. Policy-makers and university administrators should be aware that external capital as a pre-seed capital fund is probably not the best way to finance these prospectors. In the early phases of the start-up, especially when the business model is not clear, pre-seed sources of finance should allow the company to fail or to be free to adopt a business model that is not in line with an investor's expectation. As a result, one should carefully analyse the need for, and the management of, pre-seed capital funds.

Finally, we have identified academic spin-offs which follow a very famil-iar model such as contract research or consulting. These spin-offs start small in a market for products or services and optimize the time to breakeven, following the pecking-order theory in terms of financing. Some of these companies might become high-growth companies later on, but this is often not clear at start-up. External factors such as increasing customer demand, particular partnerships or favourable financial market conditions, might be the reason why their business model transitions from low-growth orientated towards a high-growth orientated. But even if they stay low-growth orientated companies, their value added as a population might be significant. However, technology transfer officers usually overlook these initiatives and universities show very little support for researchers or aca-demics who want to create a company that does not involve a formal trans-fer of technology. This is remarkable since these companies are less demanding in terms of human, financial and technological resources, and might increase the visibility of the university in the region. They form the heart of what is often referred to as the entrepreneurial university.

Chapter 4: The Way in Which Your TTO Is Organized Has a Direct Impact on the Kind of Spin-offs that Will Be Created

Chapter 4 gives an insight into how universities and public research orga-nizations organize their spin-off support activities. We distinguish between three sustainable models: (1) the Low Selective model; (2) the Incubator model and (3) the Supportive model. First, the Low Selective model fits very nicely into the idea of an entrepreneurial university. Its objective is to stimulate as many entrepreneurial ventures as possible. The entrepreneurs that set up these ventures do not need to belong to the university's perma-nent or contractual staff, nor do they have to be based upon technology developed at the university. The model facilitates the spin-off process through granting small amounts of money to potential entrepreneurs and the provision of office space at the university. The spin-off profile that makes up the majority of the spin-offs created is the 'lifestyle' company. As described in Chapter 3, this company focuses on contract research and consulting as its main activities. It seems perfectly normal that this lifestyle company is the most popular one in a university setting. As Druihle and Garnsey (2004) have argued, researchers or academics will have a tendency to set up a company with a business model that is familiar to their pre-start up activities and which needs little investment. Lifestyle companies fit this profile. They need little investment and the business model of consulting, contract research or – in a rare case – product sales is familiar to the researcher, academic or student who wants to set up this type of company.

Despite the attractiveness of the Low Selective model, the Incubator model has received much more attention among policy-makers and TTOs. The Incubator model focuses on the creation of spin-offs which we have labelled in Chapter 3 as venture capital backed. Because this model wants to stimulate the creation of growth-orientated ventures, it is highly selective in projects it supports. In other words, it is the quality and not the quantity of created ventures that counts. As suggested in Chapter 3, this venture capital backed model implies that the technology is innovative and can be protected. As a result, we observe that TTO officers in the Incubator model spend significant time in the protection of the technology base in the incubation or pre-start-up phase. This includes the licensing in of missing elements and a clear distinction between exclusive and non-exclusive patent rights. Further on, the VC-backed model demands a well-balanced founding team, preferably with experience in the sector. Again, during the incubation phase the TTO officer is actively searching to compose a team which can attract an investor. Finally, the VC-backed model assumes that the spin-off can attract a sufficient amount of capital at start-up. Again the TTO is actively looking for private venture capitalists who are willing to invest the capital at start-up. Because of the company's size at founding, public VCs cannot provide the capital without the help of private VCs.

Finally, universities like KUL have developed an in-between type, which we label the Supportive model. Unlike the Incubator model, the supportive model is not so selective in terms of the kind of spin-offs it wants to stimulate. Quality is traded off against quantity. So, even companies with fewer growth prospects can receive support in this model. In contrast with the Low Selective model however, the companies that receive support usually embody a formal transfer of technology from the university to the company. They also start with a larger capital base than lifestyle companies and they might attract surrogate entrepreneurs to complete the founding team. The company model that probably best fits the kind of companies targeted by this model is the 'prospector' type. These companies are started very early in the product development process and are not certain at start-up about their business model. They are not able to attract venture capital yet, but their ambition is higher than creating a lifestyle company. The public money associated with the university allows these companies to start. The development of a structure to support academics who want to create a company within the university seems to be a key success factor in the development of such a model. In such a company, academics usually perform contract research or consulting. Without having to leave the university and with a business model very familiar to them, they can experience whether creating an entrepreneurial venture is attractive to them or not.

A general university might be in need of the three models described above. The Incubation model might serve a research department which is leading in its field and which has developed a critical mass in a certain domain. The Low Selective model fits very well the idea of an entrepreneurial university and can also serve the social science departments. Finally, the Supportive model might be useful for those departments where the critical mass is lower but that have developed a specific type of technology which might be a success on the marketplace. A major difficulty at most universities is that TTOs tend to be structured following one of these models and have difficulty in allowing the existence of deviant models at the same institute. This leads to a uniform set of spin-offs. However, these spin-offs do not usually follow a VC logic.

Chapter 5: The Process of Spin-off Development Is an Iterative One Over the Different Phases of the Venture's Growth. Policy Actions Need to Be Differentiated According to the Particular Phase of Development

In Chapter 5 we examined the different phases in the development of spin-offs and showed that these could be characterized as involving an iterative process that may require issues that arose at previous phases to be revisited. In moving between phases, spin-offs needed to address specific critical junctures. The first critical juncture involving opportunity recognition typically requires the spin-off to acquire the capability to synthesize scientific knowledge with an understanding of the market to which it might apply. There may be a need for networks of market contacts outside the scientific environment of the university. The second critical juncture requires the venture to acquire an entrepreneurial champion committed to the development of the venture. Where this is a problem, it appears to arise from universities not providing sufficient resources and network contacts or not developing appropriate incentives and policies. As a result, academic scientists or surrogate entrepreneurs failed to become sufficiently committed to developing the spin-off. The third critical juncture, that of credibility, was particularly problematical because of the academic entrepreneurs' lack of a commercial track record, the often intangible nature of the spin-off's resources at this early stage, and the non-commercial environment from which the spin-off was emerging. All these elements pose barriers to the attraction of customers and financiers. The development of links with surrogate entrepreneurs at earlier phases in the development process may help the spin-off overcome this juncture. However, universities need to devise policies to attract the surrogate in the first place, such as through building network links. The demonstration of proof of concept and the potential for a portfolio of products may also help to establish credibility in relation to financiers. Relocation in commercial premises away from the university can help signal a commercial approach to prospective customers. The fourth critical juncture requires the spin-off to develop entrepreneurial capabilities that enable the venture to reconfigure deficiencies from earlier phases into resource strengths, capabilities and social capital.

In the absence of overcoming social capital deficiencies, resources weaknesses and inadequate internal capabilities, spin-offs did not have the absorptive capacity (Cohen and Levinthal, 1990; Zahra and George, 2002) to become established as rent-generating businesses. In the earlier development phases it is the individual entrepreneur who needs to acquire the requisite human capital that embodies these entrepreneurial capabilities. Over time, as growth became more turbulent and the complexity of the challenges increased, the entrepreneurial capabilities became located in the team.

Chapter 6: The Most Important Resource in Spin-offs Are the Entrepreneurial Teams. An Effective Spin-off Policy Should Start with an In-depth Understanding of Their Dynamics

In Chapter 6, we discussed the importance of founding teams in the process of creating spin-offs. In particular, we have shown how TTO officers as 'privileged witnesses' tend to match researchers with surrogate entrepreneurs who offer their services to the TTO. As such, the TTO officer plays a very important role in this team formation process. However, since various researchers (for example, Heirman and Clarysse, 2006) have shown that the quality of the founding team has a very important impact on the later performance of the spin-off, this team formation process needs to be addressed carefully. More specifically, researchers have shown that teams which are diverse in their functional background but combine this with joint working experience tend to be quite successful. This is often attributed to the positive impact of 'cognitive diversity', which stimulates members of a team to challenge each other and hence make better decisions. Cognitive diversity does not only assume a different functional background, it also implies that the team members have a different view on how the spin-off should develop.

We positioned these different perspectives within an organizational culture framework, which classifies team members according to their flexible versus control orientation and their internal versus external orientation. Team members who combine flexibility and external orientation tend to be 'innovative' individuals who embody a high degree of creativity and vision. Many high-flying academics tend to have a high degree of this orientation. In contrast, people with a high degree of external orientation but also a high degree of focus on control, tend to be 'goals orientated'. In a founding team, it is very important to have a person with such a vision since its absence is likely to be a project killer. Privileged witnesses such as TTO officers should recognize the need for these different personalities. However, our research shows that often the surrogate entrepreneurs attracted to form a founding team with the researchers have the same kind of 'innovative' orientation as the researchers themselves. This leads to homogeneity instead of heterogeneity at the founding team level. Usually, TTO officers do not want to be in conflict with the researchers on whom they are dependent for deal flow and invention disclosures.

Functional heterogeneity is related to what researchers label the 'cognitive diversity' in teams. Cognitive diversity means that founding team members challenge each other about the strategy the spin-off ideally should follow. Cognitive diversity increases the performance of a team because discussion leads to better decisions. However, this discussion should not result in affective conflict, which means that founders start to dislike each other. We have shown that teams, who know each other and who have developed non-instrumental relations before starting the spin-off have much less chance of experiencing affective conflict than those who do not know each other. Non-instrumental relations can be joint working experience or similar.

Chapter 7: There Are Important Interactions between Finance Provision for Spin-offs, Relationship-building between Venture Capital Firms and Universities, and the Development of Adequate Human Capital Expertise

Technology transfer offices and spin-offs see venture capital as more important than internal funds early in the process. While venture capitalists do invest smaller sums, their preference is to invest in spin-offs *after* the seed stage, particularly once proof of concept has been achieved. University Challenge Funds, or similar schemes, appear to have become more important in the very early stage of funding requirements but these are typically concentrated among the top universities.

Universities point to the difficulties in attracting VC and business angel finance but mechanisms to increase the possibility of internal funding and debt financing as an intermediate step towards VC investment remain underdeveloped, reflecting the financial constraints upon universities.

Our findings also indicate that venture capital firms consider that universities fail sufficiently to understand their requirements or to present proposals for the funding of spin-offs as investor ready. Few venture capital firms have developed links with universities and even fewer with more than one university.

Many venture capital firms do not possess sufficient appropriate human capital skills to screen and add value to potential spin-off investees.

8.3   POLICY ACTIONS

In this section we suggest policy actions that emerge from our empirical findings associated with the development of spin-offs.

8.3.1   Develop Compatible Entrepreneurial Teams with Diverse Commercial Skills: A Leading Role for Business Schools?

Our analysis in Chapter 6 highlighted the problems in building appropriate entrepreneurial teams to develop the spin-off. A problem often mentioned by TTO officers is the lack of balance in entrepreneurial teams. Most founding teams consist only of researchers. In developing such teams, TTO officers tend to make use of external experienced industrialists, that is, surrogate entrepreneurs, to bring specific commercial knowledge into the spin-off. The effective use of surrogate entrepreneurs might be more problematic than initially thought. First, it seems extremely difficult to fit people together who do not have any shared experience at all. By definition, the way in which the surrogate entrepreneurs look at the business will be different from the vision the researcher has. In Chapter 6, we have indicated that the lack of any form of joint experience results in very unstable teams that tend to split when difficult decisions have to be taken. This implies that successful team formation has to start *before* researchers spot an opportunity. Cross-functional training courses such as MBAs with a major in entrepreneurship might be a good way of bringing people with industry experience together with those without. Business schools associated with universities that have a technical orientation could play a major role in this by adjusting their curriculum. Universities, on the other hand, should introduce scholarships for their researchers to participate in these MBA programmes. As in a business environment, the scholarship (including tuition and time) could be part of the remuneration package for senior researchers.

These cross-functional degree programmes can also play a major role in bringing people with market opportunities together with those that spot technical solutions. Researchers very seldom have an idea about market opportunities. If they could integrate with individuals who can spot market opportunities in the industrial environment in which they work, this might be a good basis for matching skills to opportunities. Again, the need for an active awareness-raising about, and stimulation of, these degree programmes is an absolute necessity.

The discussion above does not mean that academics can be substituted by a surrogate entrepreneur. The commitment of at least part of the research group to the entrepreneurial team engaged in the commercialization process is fundamental. Without this commitment the vital knowledge necessary to make the technology function in the marketplace is likely to be missing and the chances of the spin-off becoming a sustainable venture are diminished. Our evidence suggests that a substantial number of researchers have to transfer from the university to the start-up if the latter is to be successful. Without a substantial knowledge base, it is extremely difficult, if not impossible, to retain sufficient credibility in the marketplace. In line with this, public authorities in general, and universities in particular, have launched programmes to stimulate academics and senior researchers to start a spin-off as full-time founders without losing their tenured position at university for a number of years. Despite the usefulness of these support actions, they remain limited in their scope. A basic problem lies in the structure through which most universities operate. For the majority of university researchers, career progress and, even, their job depend upon the evaluation of their output by the team or department in which they operate. This makes it extremely difficult for them to get involved in any spin-off activity without giving up their academic aspirations.

8.3.2   A Common Policy to Stimulate Spin-offs Is a Gross Underestimation of Reality and Leads to Suboptimization

Our review in Chapter 3 and analysis in Chapter 4 showed that spin-offs are a heterogeneous phenomenon and therefore important policy implications relate to the role of the incubator contexts in which development occurs. Our analysis equally identifies the different institutional linkages and resources associated with different types of incubators. In addition to providing physical resources, policy may need to focus carefully on introducing the appropriate linkages and resources required to create and develop different types of spin-offs. There may need to be a differentiated approach. On the one hand, this may facilitate large numbers of lifestyle, consulting or service start-ups that, individually, are unlikely to grow large but which collectively may have a significant impact on local economies. On the other hand, a more intensive support regime may focus on producing fewer spin-offs in areas of research excellence.

A great deal of emphasis has been placed on those spin-offs which have high growth prospects. It may be more problematical to attract outside entrepreneurs and financiers to those cases where the prospects are not so positive. In Chapter 4 we examined the different models for the development of spin-offs and their links with different types of company. This suggests an important need to develop skills within TTOs that can help develop these kinds of spin-offs.

Our findings in Chapter 4 demonstrate that TTOs need to implement very different systems to produce different forms of spin-offs. Technology transfer offices need to be clear about the type of companies they are producing and how they add value to them. This observation raises a number of issues relating to the 'fit' between the resources at the TTO level, in terms of the availability of skilled personnel and capabilities for spinning-off ventures, and the espoused strategy of the TTO. Our case evidence indicates that a mismatch frequently occurs between the strategy of the TTO or university and the resources/capabilities the university commits to achieving the strategy. The development of high-growth venture-backed type spin-offs is a much more resource-intensive strategy than one that involves the creation of service-orientated companies. It already starts with a profound IP strategy at the level of the department. Universities need to be careful not to fall short in stimulating real VC-backed companies, while overemphasizing the support for service-orientated ventures. The latter should not need external capital or incubation if they only serve to finance the lifestyle of the academic.

The heterogeneity of spin-offs requires the establishment of parallel tracks for their development. It may not be possible to manage the three different forms of spin-off companies identified, that is, self-employment orientated, economic-profit orientated and exit orientated, within one model. If a university or public research organization wishes to encourage the development of different forms of spin-off, different incubator models may need to be introduced that run separately from one another. For example, instead of involving the TTO, it may be appropriate for self-employment (lifestyle) orientated companies to be managed under a unit within the university, with a remit for stimulating entrepreneurial - activity in a broad sense, which support students, researchers and professors to set up a company. In parallel, the TTO might develop a path devoted to creating value from technological opportunities through spin-offs.

8.2.3   Spin-off Support Should Be Adjusted to the Specific Phase of Development in Which the Spin-off Is Situated

Practitioners should consider carefully *when* and *how* PROs could add most value to new spin-offs. There is a clear need to distinguish between the creation and the development of different types of spin-offs in the design and implementation of spin-off strategies. Practitioners may need to differentiate their approaches to the creation and the subsequent development of a spin-off as the latter does not simply require the continuation of activities, resources, business models, and so on utilized during the former phase. Our analysis in Chapter 5 showed that the development of spin-offs is a non-linear iterative process as ventures move across the different phases. For the successful, adaptation was typically necessary in the light of new information and knowledge. For the unsuccessful, while resources and capabilities may have been acquired at earlier phases these were of lesser quality and were only likely to enable the venture to achieve limited development. Support may need to ensure that greater nurturing is provided at the initial stage so that spin-offs are not created too early before a prototype is available.

8.3.4   Reconsider the Role of the TTO and Adjust It to Its Competences

Our analysis suggests a number of implications for TTOs. First, a major problem concerns the attraction of skilled personnel to perform the functions involved in supporting the creation and development of spin-offs. Individuals who have an understanding of both science and business are relatively scarce. In addition, university remuneration systems are not geared up to remunerating and incentivizing these individuals.

University policies to increase the size of technology transfer offices, without also focusing on the skills of those involved, will not be conducive to creating and developing spin-offs that create wealth. In the UK, a review of the business interface training provision (BITS review) (Zeitlyn and Horne, 2002) noted that this problem extended beyond the need to be able to provide legalistic skills in protecting IP to a requirement to be able to provide opportunity recognition and other commercial skills. The development of spin-offs may also be constrained by the complexity of the organizational context and skills are needed to be able to manage this.

University and public research organizations are now making changes to fill skills gaps by recruiting individuals with business experience from industry and through the provision of training courses by industry associations. A central issue, however, concerns whether the training of existing technology transfer officers will yield the desired results or whether there is a need to recruit technology transfer officers with an appropriate private sector background, including experience of starting a business. The UK government's response to the Lambert Review, while noting the development of training for TTOs by professional bodies, also emphasized the need for further developments in training and the use of individuals with industry background and experience (HM Treasury, 2004).

Many of the venture capital firms we have interviewed expressed frustration (Chapter 7) that TTOs still had some way to go in learning how to present viable investment propositions relating to spin-offs and that this behaviour compared unsatisfactorily to other early stage high-tech ventures. It was considered rare for proposals to present details of how ventures would achieve proof of market and proof of technology. This lends support to the notion of recruiting more technology transfer officer skills from the private sector. This raises implications for how public research organizations (PROs) should attract and retain technology transfer officers. If PROs are constrained to remunerate technology transfer officers in line with other elements of university bureaucracies, they may be unable to attract staff with the more entrepreneurial capabilities required to stimulate and develop successful spin-offs. To prevent experienced TTOs from being attracted by competing institutions offering improved remuneration packages, remuneration schemes may need to be devised that tie TTOs into the success of the spin-offs they are involved in creating but which they forgo if they leave. Such arrangements are widely used in the venture capital industry.

Just as there is a need to develop the skills of technology transfer officers, there is also a need for venture capital investors to acquire the specific skills and understanding required when assessing spin-off proposals; these skills *still* appear to be in short supply. The emphasis on financial expertise and the limited expertise in science and technology may have an effect on the type of early stage investment opportunity venture capitalists decide to fund. The investment executives in our respondent firms, which were those venture capital firms most focused on high-tech investments, tended to have a background in the financial sector or possess finance-orientated industry qualifications. On average, just under half the investment executives have a background in the financial sector, and a third have a chartered accountancy qualification or equivalent. In contrast, only little more than a tenth of the investment executives at each respondent firm have a PhD in a relevant scientific subject. Some executives may have both financial and technology experience, however, 46 per cent of responding venture capitalists had no one with experience of technology through either a PhD in a technological subject, a graduate qualification in technology or managerial experience in a technology area.

8.3.5 Develop a Clear IP Policy Both at the University and the Department Levels

There was widespread evidence that TTOs were not carrying out effective intellectual property (IP) due diligence prior to submitting proposals to venture capital firms (Chapter 7). The importance of intellectual property rights protection expenditure for spin-offs seeking to obtain external equity investment (Lockett and Wright, 2005) signals the need for technology transfer offices to make sure intellectual property is clean, well defined and protected before trying to raise external equity finance. This point suggests that technology transfer offices need to develop sufficient expertise in the area of intellectual property protection as well as adequate budgets to finance the cost of external advice in this area.

A related issue concerns the need for technology transfer offices and investors to resolve questions of the ownership of the IP. On the one hand, because of the amount of risk involved in commercializing inventions, venture capital firms may seek assignment rather than licensing of IP to a spin-off as a condition for investment. On the other hand, technology transfer offices may be reluctant to do this as it may reduce further economic benefit from continued scientific developments. To some extent, technology transfer offices and academics may need to be more realistic about the value of their IP at the very early stages of venture development. Of course, the problem may also reflect risk aversion on the part of venture capitalists. However, overvaluation at the initial stage may create problems in raising finance in subsequent rounds (Clarysse et al., 2006a). A way forward might be to negotiate unrestricted rights for spin-offs to use the IP to develop commercial products in a particular field but for PROs to be able to claim back ownership if the venture fails to become established.

Intellectual property based spin-offs are often successful only if they can play a role on the market for technology. This means that they need a sound technology platform, which probably includes the licensing in of pieces of technology from other companies as well. In addition, the research department from which these companies are spun off should be able to continue its research and even its contract research activities in order to keep its worldwide reputation. This implies that not all the rights on the technology should go to the spin-off. Building such a vision at the department level requires a *patent strategy*. A patent strategy includes a careful consideration about what technology is proprietary to the department, which technology is licensed on an exclusive base to spin-offs and incumbents, and which parts of the technology are licensed on a non-exclusive base so that cooperating organizations can learn from each other.

8.3.6   Develop a Regional Network of Relevant Stakeholders

Our findings indicate that TTOs need to consider developing relationships with key stakeholders in the spin-off process, including potential commercial partners, technology partners, investors, potential customers and suppliers. Relatively few universities and public research organizations have developed links investors for instance. However, given the nature of the venture capital firm's screening process, as seen in Chapter 7, there is a need for further investment in developing these relationships. In general, potential partners are extremely important for spin-offs to overcome the liability of newness and to grow. Bruneel et al. (2006) show for instance that young, technology-based firms including spin-offs build upon the skills of their customers and investors to successfully internationalize their activities. Very often, TTO officers have developed a network among the public partners in the region such as regional development agencies, public research laboratories and intermediary organizations. However, the network with private partners, such as incumbent companies that are by definition interested in the department's technology, or specialized investment funds in these technologies are completely lacking. Still, regional success must be embedded in an international network of relations.

While academic entrepreneurs may have strong scientific networks, these may contain insufficient links in relation to the finance and commercial skills required for successful commercialization. Difficulties in communicating between the networks of academic entrepreneurs and those of venture capitalists may arise because of differences in knowledge, codes, goals and assumptions. These problems create imperfections in the distribution of information between networks. There is a need to bridge this divide by identifying individuals with the appropriate skills who can perform boundary-spanning roles.

Similarly, TTOs might also do more to establish and nurture good links with private-sector companies to gain a better understanding of how to develop scientific research into commercial applications. These links may also help TTOs in deciding whether an invention is most appropriately developed as a licence or a joint venture with a private-sector corporation rather than as an independent spin-off with venture capital backing. As shown in Chapter 5, not all innovations are suitable for exploitation through independent spin-off companies. Again, there may be a need to recruit people with the skills to make the link between the university and the commercial environment.

There may also be benefits for venture capital firms to develop relationships with universities that are likely to generate a flow of possible investment opportunities. Venture capital firms need to put greater emphasis on ensuring that universities understand their requirements and present their proposals as 'investor ready'. Such developments may help reduce costs of due diligence that may contribute to the reluctance of VCs to fund spin-offs. At present, few venture capital firms are developing links with more than one university. A longer-term perspective may be required that is involved in developing potential deals from an early seed stage and which may also need to take account of the need to make follow-on investments.

8.3.7 Develop Bridge-building/Boundary-spanning Capacity

A key issue concerns the need to develop the skills required to promote academic entrepreneurship and attract venture capital finance. Government intervention has involved various initiatives to promote education regarding entrepreneurship for both students and faculty, and further efforts in this direction seem warranted.

However, one of the central issues is that spin-off development may be constrained as academics, TTOs, venture capitalists and potential customers may effectively speak different languages. There may thus be a need for individuals who can act as intermediaries or boundary-spanners between the academic scientist and the commercial environment. This suggests a requirement for the development of local policies to enable the development and recruitment of individuals who can perform boundary-spanning roles. These individuals will need to be able to transfer knowledge through building links between academics and business. These linkages might usefully involve the development of understanding of business/market concepts and the identification of customers, finance, and so on.

In the UK, for example, the Medici Fellowship Scheme was established with the specific remit to equip scientists with commercialization skills (Mosey et al., 2006). The initial focus was on the commercialization of bio-medical research in five Midlands universities. Fellows are required to have significant prior, typically post-doctoral, research experience. Local training is provided in the host institution in finance, marketing, IP and business strategy. Fellows are encouraged to develop links with practitioners from the biotechnology business community, TTOs, the legal and regulatory professions and finance providers. The aim is then that these scientists would act as agents for change in their own department by raising the visibility of the opportunities of commercialization to other scientists. An evaluation of the Medici Fellowship Scheme, carried out in 2005, showed that the scheme provided key skills and that fellows subsequently exhibited entrepreneurial behaviour in host schools (Mosey et al., 2006). The principal benefit to the departments where the scheme was introduced involved raising awareness of, and attitudes towards, commercialization. The scheme was reported as having the most important impact on spin-off activity (77 per cent of respondents) compared with other schemes. The main benefits identified by the fellows were: encouraging academics to exploit IP generated from their research, access to market information, working with other higher education or research institutes, access to potential firms, working with other departments within the university, access to potential customers and availability of proof-of-concept funding. More problematical was the ability to obtain finance from business angels and attracting commercial management to spin-offs. The scheme was identified by participants as having most impact on raising awareness of IP funding among the academic network (21 per cent), an ability to conduct early stage market research (18 per cent), identifying undiscovered/undeveloped IP and raising funding and writing business plans (14 per cent). Future policy might usefully consider the development of similar schemes that bridge the divide between academia and industry.

A further option concerns the role of business schools in universities. Business schools may be able to provide generic tools, such as courses for students and faculty on entrepreneurship and creating businesses, as well as more direct involvement as consultants and non-executive directors (Wright et al., 2004a). Master of Business Administration students and the business people with whom business schools had contacts may have valuable roles to play in developing academic entrepreneurship. Some business schools have developed links with TTOs which enable MBA students, who have business experience, to get involved in a spin-off either in terms of developing business plans or in becoming part of the spin-off team. Products of MBA programmes can also be used directly in academic entrepreneurship in a management role. Business plan competition and prizes can get students involved in spin-offs. For example, one university in the UK has developed a module where MBA students preparing a business plan link with the TTO and academic founders of businesses. Students in teams of five are assigned a piece of IP and are tasked to figure out how to exploit it. Elsewhere in universities, science and engineering student placements in spin-offs coupled with entrepreneurship modules provided by business schools may be a means of developing an awareness of the entrepreneurial process in the longer term.

The development of policy to promote the role of business schools in spin-off creation and development needs to address a number of challenges (Wright et al., 2006c). First, there is a gap between the provision of courses and what it is really like to be involved 'hands on' in the creation of a spin-off. Faculty in business schools typically have expertise relating to larger firms rather than close involvement with entrepreneurial new ventures. Second, as with academic scientists and TTOs, there are issues concerning the incentives to undertake such activities. For example, how does involvement in spin-off activities relate to promotion mechanisms that give primary emphasis to research? Third, there are questions relating to the comparative advantage of business school academics *vis-à-vis* other providers such as TTOs and outside consultants. Fourth, there are issues concerning the recruitment, career structure and integration of faculty in business schools whose role is to promote entrepreneurship. Faculty required to contribute to the development of spin-offs may need to have considerably more practical experience than typical business school academics. They are therefore less likely to be able to contribute to academic research and risk being marginalized in a business school striving to develop a world-class research profile.

8.3.8 Develop a Critical Mass in Scientific Departments

For a spin-off strategy to be successful it is important that the universities and public research organizations create areas where they have world-class research. However, it is not feasible for most institutions to develop world-class research in a wide range of areas. For example, many mid-range provincial universities may traditionally have adopted a broad base of disciplines but their resources may constrain their ability to be world class in all areas. If spin-offs are created in these institutions, this may be at the expense of further research activities within the department from which they originated. If researchers are transferred from the university to the spin-off, insufficient critical mass may remain within the department. Mid-range universities may need to take careful strategic decisions to build up those areas where they have scope to make an international impact but also to differentiate investment in those areas where they can make a more local regional contribution (Wright et al., 2006a). From the perspective of developing a spin-off strategy, these institutions may therefore need to focus on developing a critical mass of world-class research in a more focused number of areas where they can attract industrial partners. Of course, any strategic decisions taken by the university management in relation to research focus may be taken as an attack on academic freedom and integrity.

8.3.9 Develop and Implement University Strategies that Are Consistent with Espoused Aims

Achieving commitment from academic entrepreneurs to creating and developing spin-offs may be difficult because of the conflicting demands that may be placed on them by the university. There is a need for greater career support for academics who wish to participate in the commercialization of their academic research.

However, the incentive and remuneration structures in many universities actively discourage academics from becoming an entrepreneurial champion. For academic members of staff there is an opportunity cost of engaging with commercialization activities, which is their investment in the skills of research, teaching and administration and the impact on career progression. To encourage faculty to take risks and build companies, universities may need to adapt their promotion and remuneration systems so that commercialization activities are valued. They may also need to consider creating space for academics to focus on the development of a spin-off in terms of, say, a period of leave with the possibility of a return if the venture is not successful or the academic skills are no longer required to such an extent. As noted above, universities also need to be aware of the need to devise appropriate remuneration and incentive mechanisms for the TTOs and surrogate entrepreneurs they need to create and develop spin-offs and who may well have attractive alternative career opportunities both within and outside universities. This suggests a need to develop incentive packages that depart from traditional university administrators' remuneration scales.

The integration of third stream activities involving academic entrepreneurship needs to become a core component of universities' activities. Research by Wright et al. (2006a) clearly demonstrates that, to date, third stream activities have merely been a bolt-on to the traditional streams of research and teaching. Claims that a university or public research organization is active in academic entrepreneurship may be little more than rhetoric or at best an espoused aim that is not followed through with a clearly articulated implementation strategy that engenders a culture change. Changing the culture may be much more difficult than changing management systems (Leonard-Barton, 1992). However, by setting the right incentives and reward structures the culture can gradually be changed.

To enhance the attractiveness of universities to venture capital firms, there is a need to improve decision-making processes regarding venture capital investment in spin-offs. Universities may need to develop standard procedures for creating spin-off companies in order to speed up decision-making and offer greater transparency in the decision-making process. Universities also need to address the difficulties faced by venture capital firms in identifying key decision-makers and having to deal with multiple stakeholders. This may be a function of the clarity of development of universities' objectives and strategies towards spin-offs. Some universities may adopt a very conservative approach because of their concerns about accountability for public funds. It is clear, however, that those universities that are more active in spinning-off companies adopt an approach to decision-making that is more in line with commercial business practice (Lockett et al., 2003b).

8.3.10 Revisit the Existing Financing Schemes

Our analysis suggests a number of areas for future development of policy. Schemes such as University Challenge Funds (UCFs) in the UK have helped to improve the entrepreneurial culture of universities and public research organizations. These schemes provide the means for universities and investors to develop mutually beneficial relationships and incentives for universities to learn how to develop the right commercial capabilities. They also provide incentives for equity financiers to increase their exposure to spin-offs and to learn to engage with universities. However, financing schemes find their roots in the observation that the market for capital in Europe is imperfect. Researchers do not earn sufficient salaries to be able to invest in the early stages of their career so-called 3F money in their own or a friend's business. Therefore, mechanisms should be introduced which simulate as far as possible the pre-seed market as it exists in an economy such as the US where capital flows are more efficient. These mechanisms might also include attempts to stimulate further business angel investment in this early phase of spin-off development. This might involve the introduction of individuals who have both finance to invest as well as the expertise to develop very early stage high-tech businesses.

There should also be careful analysis of the timing of equity investment and the 'sunk' kind of money which needs to be invested in a project. Logically, the chances that money invested in the project phase will be lost are very high. So, money invested in such an early phase should not interfere with the business model of the potential start-up nor should it be evaluated against profitability measures. Although this sort of pre-seed funding is available in large research organizations and companies under the form of incubation money, it is absent in several universities and especially in the smaller research departments.

Most attention has been devoted to the provision of seed funding in the form of equity funding. There seems to be, even, an oversupply of this kind of funding, which has lead to the emergence of a new type of spin-off company: the 'prospector'. This type of company is looking for a business model and uses equity funding in its search.

A further gap may exist in the slightly later phase where the venture has established that there is a market but has yet to earn revenues or become of sufficient size to be attractive to mainstream venture capital firms. Government could consider the provision of incentives, such as tax breaks, that encourage investment in spin-offs that have gone beyond the initial seed phase, having achieved proof of concept, but which require funding to continue with product development and prior to accessing customers and generating revenues. Mechanisms might also be developed to enable UCFs to decrease the complexity involved in negotiating terms with several existing stakeholders when spin-offs reach the stage where they require larger amounts of venture capital funding.

8.4   AREAS FOR FURTHER RESEARCH

In this section we outline an agenda for future research relating to the different levels of the spin-off process analysed in previous chapters.

8.4.1   Academics, Surrogate Entrepreneurs and Entrepreneurial Teams

Our analysis of the spin-off development process suggested that the academics developing high-tech ventures are typically leaders in their fields. Van Looy et al. (2004) find for the University of Leuven in Belgium that engagement in entrepreneurial activities coincides with increased publication outputs, without affecting the nature of the publications involved. As resources increase, this interaction becomes more significant. Further empirical work might usefully examine the extent to which spin-offs are created by academics who are less strong as researchers and who are frustrated by lack of academic recognition. Some faculty who are not star researchers may have research contracts with companies that generate possibilities for joint venture spin-offs.

Second, and related to the issue of which academics bring forward the ideas for spin-off companies, is the effectiveness of fellowship programmes. Fellowship programmes have been introduced to encourage academics to engage with commercialization activities in order to both raise their awareness of the issues and to equip them with the basic skills to undertake the early stages of commercialization. As these programmes are relatively new we know little about their effectiveness, both in terms of the individual who undertakes the training and their wider effects on the departments into which they return after the training.

In terms of surrogate entrepreneurs, there is a need for further understanding of the process by which they can be more fully utilized in the spinning off of companies. The introduction of non-academic people into the academic world creates interesting human resource management issues in relation to the potential for conflicts of interest and remuneration.

Surrogate entrepreneurs also raise issues related to the development and management of entrepreneurial teams. A key issue arising from the research into spin-offs is the need for the skill set (or human capital) of the team to change over time as the spin-off develops. Research into the management of entrepreneurial teams has tended to focus on the issue of the need to add new team members, in order to broaden the range of skills of the team. A much neglected issue, however, is that of team member exit and the process by which a team member may be removed from the team. The academic may want to reduce his/her involvement with the spin-off over time, or it may be in the interests of the spin-off for this to occur. Surrogate entrepreneurs may be appropriate replacements for the academic entrepreneur. More research is required that analyses aspects such as at what point(s) surrogate entrepreneurs are introduced, what networks are required to identify them and whether they replace or complement the academic entrepreneur.

There is general consensus of the importance of building a balanced team of individuals who have complementary skills. The implicit assumption is that an effective team can be built by merely bringing together people with the right skills. However, making the team members work together poses major challenges, as the emerging research stream on conflict in entrepreneurial teams indicates. Chapter 6 presented some analysis of entrepreneurial teams in spin-offs, but further work is needed that examines the dynamics of the interactions between team members during the development of the spin-off.

8.4.2 Spin-offs

Further research is required to understand the heterogeneity of spin-offs. As shown in Chapter 3, typologies of spin-offs based on business models have tended to neglect aspects relating to the influence of the degree of vertical integration and outsourcing decisions on the structure of the value chain, and the influence of cost leadership and international expansion strategies on the organization of the spin-off.

The resource endowment perspectives reviewed in Chapter 3 have emphasized the importance of the human capital characteristics of founders on the diversity of spin-offs. There has been a growing emphasis on the importance of different financial resources. Spin-offs can be distinguished in terms of the relationship between the resource configuration of a spin-off and the resource base of their venture capitalist or industrial finance partner (see Wright et al., 2004b, and Chapter 5). There remains a need for further understanding of the types of business ventures that are more likely to involve industrial partners and that are more likely to involve venture capitalists. Also there is little understanding of the heterogeneity of industrial and venture capital partners (national versus multinational firms, experienced versus non-experienced firms, and so on) or of whether the timing of their involvement in the development of spin-offs is different.

There has been some examination of the technical resources of spin-offs focusing on the stage of the technology development cycle and the scope and innovativeness of the firm's technology. The conditions of knowledge transfer between the university and the spin-off and different types of technology have also been examined. However, other types of technical resources such as firms' plants and equipment, distribution channels and access to raw materials have remained unexplored in the literature.

Typologies of spin-offs based on resource endowments, business models and institutional linkages have generally been rather static in nature. Further research might usefully examine how each of these aspects differ as spin-offs evolve through their different phases of development. There is a clear need to build insights into the dynamic capabilities which these companies develop over time and which make them different from each other in terms of performance. Dynamic capabilities refer to the routines they have developed in order to become a successful player in the market for products or the market for ideas, to successfully internationalize, to grow in a sustainable way or to prepare an IPO or a trade sale. So far, research has focused on the starting conditions of these firms, not on the processes that have been developed.

Finally with respect to spin-offs, further research is required about the mechanisms relating to the development and growth of these firms. To some extent this relates to the roles of TTOs, which we consider below, but it also concerns analysis of the development by these spin-offs of their links with trading partners and the extent to which mergers and acquisitions play a role in their growth and development.

8.4.3   Technology Transfer Offices

There is a need for further analysis of the link between spin-off incubation models and the range of industries that are appropriate to each case. For example, models identified for biotechnology sectors may not be applicable for IT-related sectors or nanotechnology. In addition, most universities and public research organizations – even those that cover a broad range of disciplines – have one or two technological domains in which they excel. This spread of activities might interact with the most appropriate spin-off model for them. This raises a need for research into the costs and benefits associated with the specialization of the TTOs in particular fields with their specific business models.

Given our emphasis upon the importance of the human capital capabilities in TTOs, a major issue concerns how TTOs can build their own human capital capabilities over time. Technology transfer offices in many universities and public research organizations have traditionally not developed the resources and capabilities to spin-off companies successfully. There is a need for longitudinal studies of the development of TTOs to examine issues relating to capability-building.

The effect of performance targets on the behaviour of TTOs also requires further enquiry. The use of short-term management targets may lead TTO managers to inflate the paper valuation of their portfolios in the short run. The problem for managers in trying to manage the process is that it will normally take a substantial amount of time to realize the gains from a spin-off and, so, assessing performance in the short to medium term becomes difficult.

8.4.4 Universities and Public Research Organizations

Further research at the institutional level of analysis should examine the establishment of the broader focus of technology transfer strategies and the balance of spin-offs versus other modes of technology transfer such as licensing and contract research. Since successful spin-off performance tends to be rare, it might be that for some universities spin-offs are a poor choice by which to commercialize their research results. When forming a company means that all IP is transferred to the spin-off, this choice has important implications for further licensing and contract research possibilities of the institution.

An important issue in encouraging academics to undertake different types of spin-offs relates to both their skills and incentives. In the Supportive model identified in Chapter 4, the availability of structural and cultural mechanisms to incentivize academics to engage in contract research activities was a key element. Also, in the Low Selective model the 'entrepreneurial culture' of the university or public research organization was important. It is, however, questionable whether the entrepreneurial culture of the institution in the Low Selective model is similar to the one stimulated in the Supportive model. This is in line with the contemporary notion of entrepreneurship, and science-based entrepreneurship in particular, which is shifting from serendipitous and individual to being perceived as social and organized (Jacob et al., 2003; Moray and Clarysse, 2003). Further research may usefully examine how structural changes can be made and which cultural transitions are necessary to select and incentivize new academics towards entrepreneurial activities.

Given the nature of the sector, the spin-off process in many PROs is still evolving. Further research might examine the extent to which the three Incubation models identified in Chapter 4 are sustainable in each institution.

For example, few spin-offs from the incubator models have so far realized successful trade sales or IPOs and it will be interesting to analyse how this model adapts to failures in expected outcomes of its spin-offs. It will also be interesting to examine the extent to which the resource and capability deficient cases are able to overcome barriers to the successful development of spin-offs.

Studies that examine how parent organizations and technology transfer offices facilitate spin-off creation and development have focused their attention on direct support mechanisms, while ignoring indirect ones. Yet, universities and public research organizations can support their spin-offs indirectly through staging and contractual arrangements aimed at sharing the cost of qualified personnel between the spin-off and the parent organization, or through the signalling effect of the reputation of the universities to investors, potential partners and potential high-quality personnel. The parent institution can also be a source of network links that are key in reducing the costs of the search for partners, thus favouring the establishment of alliances (Nicolaou and Birley, 2003b; Scholten et al., 2001). Further research is required to understand these indirect links and the extent to which they are substitutes for, or complementary to, direct links. This research may also examine the extent to which these links are changing and the nature of such changes.

There is also a need for a greater understanding of the process of cultural change within universities and public research organizations. We argued above that an important implication of our findings is the need to promote change in universities and public research organizations both in terms of the management systems and the culture. Arguably, management systems are easier to change than culture, but management systems also help shape culture. As many institutions are currently attempting to undertake a programme of culture change, there is an important opportunity for researchers to investigate this process. In particular, the large differences in ethos between the public sector and the private (commercial) sector present an opportunity to study organizations' attempts to manage a large culture shift.

8.4.5 Venture Capitalists

Many seed capital funds have been established using public money in order to try and overcome the perceived equity gap that exists for early stage high-tech ventures – for example, the introduction of UCF in the UK. An interesting issue arising from the public provision of seed capital is the effect of such funding on venture capital firms' behaviour. More research is required to investigate whether or not the presence of public seed money increases the likelihood of a funded spin-off receiving more VC money later in its development.

There are two potential problems with the provision of seed capital early in the development of a spin-off. First, if the TTO wishes to attract significant amounts of money, there is a tendency to value the IP in the spin-off on a historic cost basis. The effect is that the value of the company is artificially inflated in order to try and raise seed capital. Second, if equity is given away there may be a tendency to provide too much equity too early in order to raise money, which will result in diluting equity too early. In either case the effect of overvaluing the IP and/or diluting equity too early will reduce the attractiveness of the spin-off to potential VC investors. As a result, if these conditions hold, the implication of providing public seed capital may be merely to shift the equity gap to later in the process. We need to know much more about how any form of market intervention affects the behaviours of market participants if we are to be better able to design more effective public policy in the future.

References

Agarwal, R. and Bayus, B.L. (2002), 'The market evolution and sales takeoff of product innovations', *Management Science*, **48** (8), 1024–41.

Amason, A.C. and Sapienza H.J. (1997), 'The effects of top management team size and interaction norms on cognitive and affective conflict', *Journal of Management*, **23** (4), 495–516.

Ambassade de France à Berlin (2006), *La politique des biotechnologies en Allemagne*, Service pour la science et la technologie, Berlin, September.

Ambassade de France en République Fédérale d'Allemagne (2000), *Les programmes fédéraux de soutien à l'innovation technologique en Allemagne*. Note du Service pour la Science et la Technologie, September.

Amit, R. and Schoemaker, P. (1993), 'Strategic assets and organizational rent', *Strategic Management Journal*, **14** (1), 33–46.

Argyes, N. and Liebeskind, J. (1998), 'Privatizing the intellectual commons: universities and the organization of biotechnology', *Journal of Economic Behavior and Organization*, **35**, 427–54.

Association of University Technology Managers (AUTM) (2004), *AUTM US Licensing Survey: FY 2003*, Northbrook, IL: AUTM.

Association of University Technology Managers (AUTM) (2005), *AUTM US Licensing Survey: FY 2004*, Northbrook, IL: AUTM.

Audretsch, D. and Beckman, I. (2005), 'Entrepreneurship policies in Germany', presentation at the Ecole Nationale Supérieure des Mines de Paris, 9 December.

Autio, E. and Lumme, A. (1998), 'Does the innovator role affect the perceived potential for growth? Analysis of four types of new, technology-based firms', *Technology Analysis & Strategic Management*, **10**, 41–54.

Autio, E. and Yli-Renko, H. (1998), 'New technology based firms in small open economies – an analysis based on the Finnish experience', *Research Policy*, **26**, 973–87.

Baker, J. (1999), 'Creating knowledge creating wealth: realising the economic potential of public sector research establishments', a report by John Baker to the Minister for Science and the Financial Secretary to the Treasury, London: HMSO.

Bank of England (1996), *The Financing of Technology-based Firms*, October, London: Bank of England.

Bank of England (2003), *Finance for Small Firms – a Ninth Report*, April, London: Bank of England.

Barney, J.B. (1991), 'Firm resources and sustained competitive advantage', *Journal of Management*, **17**, 99–120.

Barney, J., Wright, M. and Ketchen, D. (2001), 'The resource based view: ten years after 1991', *Journal of Management*, **27** (6), 625–42.

Becker, R.M. and Hellmann, T.F. (2003), 'The genesis of venture capital: lessons from the German experience', March, CESifo, Working Paper Series No. 883.

Bhide, A. (1992), Bootstrap finance: the art of start-ups, *Harvard Business Review*, November–December, 109–17.

Black, B. and Gilson, S. (1998), 'Venture capital and the structure of capital markets: banks versus stock markets', *Journal of Financial Economics*, **47**, 243–77.

Bmb+f (2000), *EXIST, University-based Start-ups, Networks for Innovative Company Start-ups*, Bonn: Federal Ministry for Education and Research.

Boeker, W. (1989), 'Strategic change: the effect of founding and history', *Academy of Management Journal*, **32** (3), 489–515.

Borch, O.J., Huse, M. and Senneseth, K. (1999), 'Resource configurations, competitive strategies, and corporate entrepreneurship: an empirical examination of small firms', *Entrepreneurship Theory and Practice*, **24**, 49–70.

Bower, D. (2003), 'Business model fashion and the academic spinout firm', *R&D Management*, **33** (2), 97–105.

Branscomb, L.M. and Auerswald, P.E. (2001), *Taking Technical Risks: How Innovators, Executives, and Investors Manage High-Tech Risks*, Cambridge, MA: MIT Press.

British Venture Capital Association (BVCA) (2004), *Report on Investment Activity 2003*, London: BVCA.

Bruneel, J., Clarysse, B. and Yli-Renko, H. (2006), 'How key partners shape the extent of internationalisation of young, technology-based firms', University of Ghent Working Paper.

Brush, C.G., Greene, P.G and Hart, M.M. (2001), 'From initial idea to unique advantage: the entrepreneurial challenge of constructing a resource base', *Academy of Management Executive*, **15** (1), 64–81.

Brush, C.G., Greene, P.G., Hart, M.M. and Edelman, L.F. (1997), 'Resource configurations over the life cycle of ventures', in P.D. Reynolds, W.D. Bygrave, N.M. Carter, P. Davidson, W.B. Gartner, C. Mason and P.P. McDougall (eds), *Frontiers of Entrepreneurship Research, Proceedings of the Babson Conference 1997*, Wellesley, MA: Babson College.

Burgelman, R.A. (1983), 'A process model of internal corporate venturing in the diversified major firm', *Administrative Science Quarterly*, **28**, 223–44.

Callan, B. (2001), 'Generating spin-offs: Evidence from across the OECD', *STI Review*, special issue on 'Fostering high-tech spin-offs: a public strategy for innovation', **26**, 13–55, Paris: OECD.

Caracostas, P. and Muldur, U. (1998), *Society, the Endless frontier. A European Vision of Research and Innovation Policies for the 21st Century*, EN 17655, Luxembourg: Office for Official Publications of the European Communities.

Carayannis, E.G., Rogers, E.M., Kurihara, K. and Allbritton, M.M. (1998), 'High technology spin-offs from government R&D laboratories and research institutes', *Technovation*, **18** (1), 1–10.

Chandler, G., Honig, B. and Wiklund, J. (2005), 'Antecedents, moderators, and performance consequences of membership change in new venture teams', *Journal of Business Venturing*, **20** (5), 705–25.

Chesbrough, H. and Rosenbloom, R.S. (2002), 'The role of business model in capturing value from innovation', *Industrial and Corporate Change*, **11** (3), 529–44.

Chiesa, V. and Piccaluga, A. (2000), 'Exploitation and diffusion of public research: the general framework and the case of academic spin-off companies', *R&D Management*, **30**, 329–40.

Christensen, C.M. (1997), *The Innovator's Dilemma: When New Technologies Cause Great Firms to Fail*, Boston, MA: Harvard Business School Press.

Clarysse, B. (2004), *Eendagsvlieg of Pionier: welke ondernemer redt onze economie?*, Antwerp: Garank.

Clarysse, B. and Bruneel, J. (forthcoming), 'Nurturing and growing innovative start-ups: the roles of policy as an integrator', *R&D Management*.

Clarysse, B. and Moray, N. (2004), 'A process study of entrepreneurial team formation: the case of research-based spin-offs', *Journal of Business Venturing*, **19**, 55–79.

Clarysse, B., Heirman, A. and Degroof, J. (2000), 'Influence of the environment on the starting configuration of research based spin-offs in Europe', *STI Review*, 83–108, Paris: OECD.

Clarysse, B., Moray, N., Wright, M., Lockett, A. and Mustar, P. (2005b), 'Direct indicators for the commercialisation of research and technology: policy implications', University of Ghent Working Paper.

Clarysse, B., Wright, M., Lockett, A., van de Velde, E. and Vohora, A. (2005b), 'Spinning out new ventures: a typology of incubation strategies from European research institutions', *Journal of Business Venturing*, **20** (2), 183–216.

Clarysse, B., Wright, M. and Lockett, A. (2006a), 'Academic spin-offs, formal technology transfer and capital raising', Working Paper, Nottingham University Business School.

Clarysse, B., Wright, M., Knockaert, M. and Lockett, A. (2006b), 'Academic spin-offs', formal technology transfer and capital raising, CMBOR/UNIEI, Working Paper.

Cohen, W. and Levinthal, D. (1990), 'Absorptive capacity: a new perspective on learning and innovation', *Administrative Science Quarterly*, **35**, 128–52.

Colyvas, J., Crow, M., Gelijns, A., Mazzoleni, R., Nelson, R., Rosenberg, N. and Sampat, B.N. (2002), 'How do university inventions get into practice', *Management Science*, **48** (1), 61–72.

Commission of the European Communities (CEC) (2004), *SME Observatory*, Paris: CEC.

Confederation of British Industry (1997), *Tech Stars: Breaking the Growth Barriers for Technology-based SMEs*, London: CBI.

Cooper, A.C. and Bruno, A.V. (1977), 'Success among high-technology firms', *Business Horizons*, **20**, 16–22.

Cressy, R. (1996), 'Are business start-ups debt rationed?', *Economic Journal*, **1061**, 1253–70.

Dacin, T. (1997), 'Isomorphism in context: the power and prescriptions of institutional norms', *Academy of Management Journal*, **40** (1), 46–81.

Debackere, K. (2000), 'Academic R&D as a business: context, structure and processes', *R&D Management*, **30** (4), 323–9.

Degroof, J. (2002), 'The phenomenon spin-off', unpublished PhD dissertation, Sloan School of Management, MIT.

Delmar, F. and Sölvell, I. (2005), 'The development of growth-oriented high-tech firms in Sweden', research in progress, Stockholm School of Economics, Center for Entrepreneurship and Business Creation, May. Corresponding author address: ingela.solvell@hhs.se.

Department of Trade and Industry (DTI) (1998), *Our Competitive Future: Building the Knowledge Economy*, London: Stationery Office.

Department of Trade and Industry (DTI) (2000), *Science and Innovation: Excellence and Opportunity*, London: Stationery Office.

Di Gregorio, D. and Shane, S. (2003), 'Why do some universities generate more start-ups than others?', *Research Policy*, **32**, 209–27.

Direction de la technologie (2005), *Innovation et recherche technologique, État de la situation et bilan au 31 décembre 2004*, Paris: Ministère délégué à l'Enseignement supérieur et à la Recherche.

Direction de la technologie (2006), *Innovation et recherche technologique, État de la situation et bilan au 31 décembre 2005*, Paris: Ministère délégué à l'Enseignement supérieur et à la Recherche.

Druilhe, C. and Garnsey, E. (2004), 'Do academic spin-outs differ and does it matter?', *Journal of Technology Transfer*, **29** (3–4), 269–85.

Edwards, C. (1999), *Entrepreneurial Dynamism and the Success of US Hightech*, Joint Economic Committee Staff Report, Office of the Chairman, US Senator Connie Mack, Washington, DC: US Senate.

Ehrlich, S., DeNoble, A., Moore, T. and Weaver, R. (1994), 'After the cash arrives: a comparative study of venture capital and private investor involvement in entrepreneurial firms', *Journal of Business Venturing*, **9**, 67–82.

Eisenhardt, K., Kahwajy, J. and Bourgeois, L. (1997), 'How management teams can have a good fight', *Harvard Business Review*, **75** (4), July–August, 77–85.

Elfring, T. and Hulsink, W. (2003), 'Networks in entrepreneurship: the case of high-technology firms', *Small Business Economics*, **21**, 409–22.

Ensley, M.D. and Pearce, C.L. (2001), 'Shared cognition in top management teams: implications for new venture performance', *Journal of Organizational Behavior*, **22**, 145–60.

Ensley, M.D., Carland, J.C. and Carland, J.W. (1998), 'The effects of entrepreneurial team skill heterogeneity and functional diversity on new venture performance', *Journal of Business and Entrepreneurship*, **10** (1), 1–11.

Ensley, M.D., Pearson, A.W. and Amanson A.C. (2002), 'Understanding the dynamics of new venture top management teams: cohesion, conflict, and new venture performance', *Journal of Business Venturing*, **17**, 365–86.

Etzkowitz, H. (1983), 'Entrepreneurial scientists and entrepreneurial universities in American academic science', *Minerva*, **21** (2–3), 198–233.

European Commission (EC) (2000a), *Progress Report on the Risk Capital Action Plan*, Brussels and Luxembourg: European Commission.

European Commission (EC) (2000b), *Innovation in a Knowledge Driven Economy*, Brussels and Luxembourg: European Commission.

European Commission (EC) (2004), *Observatory of European SMEs 2003, No 8*, Luxembourg: European Commission.

European Report on Science and Technology Indicators (1994), EUR 15897 EN, Luxembourg: European Commission Publications.

European Report on Science and Technology Indicators (1997), EUR 17639 EN, Luxembourg: European Commission Publications.

European Venture Capital Association (EVCA), 2004, *Annual Report on Investment*, Zaventem: European Venture Capital Association.

European Venture Capital Association (EVCA)/Thompson Venture Economics (2004), 'Pan-European survey of performance', available at http://www. evca.com, accessed 24 September 2006.

Fiet, J. (1995), 'Reliance upon informants in the venture capital industry', *Journal of Business Venturing*, **10**, 195–223.

Fontes, M. (2001), 'Biotechnology entrepreneurs and technology transfer in an intermediate economy, *Technological Forecasting and Social Change*, **62** (1), 59–74.

Fontes, M. (2005), 'The process of transformation of scientific and technological knowledge into economic value conducted by biotechnology spin-offs', *Technovation*, **25**, 339–47.

Forbes, D., Borchert, P., Zellmer-Bruhn, M. and Sapienza, H. (2006), 'Entrepreneurial team formation: an exploration of new member addition', *Entrepreneurship Theory and Practice*, **30**, 225–48.

Francis, D.H. and Sandberg, W.R. (2000), 'Friendship within entrepreneurial teams and its association with team and venture performance', *Entrepreneurship: Theory and Practice*, **25**, 5–25.

Franklin, A., Wright, M. and Lockett, A. (2001), 'Academic and surrogate entrepreneurs in university spin-outs', *Journal of Technology Transfer*, **26**, 127–41.

Gartner, W.B., Shaver, K.G., Gatewood, E. and Katz, J.A. (1994), 'Finding the entrepreneur in entrepreneurship', *Entrepreneurship Theory and Practice*, **18** (3), 5–10.

Georghiou, L. (2001), 'The United Kingdom national system of research, technology and innovation', in P. Larédo and P. Mustar (eds), *Research and Innovation Policies in the New Global Economy: An International Comparative Analysis*, Cheltenham, UK: Edward Elgar, pp. 252–96.

Global Entrepreneurship Monitor (GEM) (2001), *2000 UK Executive Report*, London: London Business School, available at http://www.gemconsortium.org/download/1159180845578/GEM2000UK.pdf.

Global Entrepreneurship Monitor (GEM) (2004), *Financing Report*, by Bygrave, W.D. and Hunt, S.A., London and Babson Park, MA: London Business School and Babson College, available at http://www.gemconsortium.org/document.asp?id=365.

Global Entrepreneurship Monitor (GEM) (2005), *Excutive Report*, by Minniti, M. with Bygrave, W.D. and Autio, E., London and Babson Park, MA: London Business School and Babson College, available at http://www.gemconsortium.org/document.asp?id=448.

Golder, P.N. and Tellis, G.J. (1996), 'First to market, first to fail? Real causes of enduring market leadership', *Sloan Management Review*, Winter, 65–75.

Goldfarb, B. and Henrekson, M. (2003), 'Bottom-up versus top-down policies towards the commercialization of university intellectual property', *Research Policy*, **32**, 639–58.

Hambrick, D.C. and Mason, P.A. (1984), 'Upper echelons: the organization as a reflection of its top managers', *Academy of Management Review*, **9** (2), 193–207.

Heirman, A. and Clarysse, B. (2004), 'How and why do research-based start-ups differ at founding? A resource-based configurational perspective', *Journal of Technology Transfer*, **29**, 247–68.

Heirman, A. and Clarysse, B. (2006), 'Do intangible assets and pre-founding R&D matter for innovation speed in start-ups?', *Journal of Product Innovation Management*, forthcoming.

Hindle, K. and Yencken, J. (2004), 'Public research commercialisation, entrepreneurship and new technology based firms: an integrated model', *Technovation*, **24**, 793–803.

HM Treasury (2004), *Science and Innovation Investment Framework 2004–2014*, London: HMTreasury/DTI/Department for Education and Skills.

HM Treasury and Department of Trade and Industry (DTI) (1998), *Innovating for the Future: Investing in R&D*, London: Stationery Office.

Jacob, M., Lundqvist, M. and Hellsmark, H. (2003), 'Entrepreneurial transformations in the Swedish university system: the case of Chalmers University of Technology', *Research Policy*, **32** (9), 1555–68.

Jensen, R. and Thursby, M. (2001), 'Proofs and prototypes for sale: the licensing of university inventions', *American Economic Review*, **91** (1), 240–59.

Jones-Evans, D. (1995), 'A typology of technology-based entrepreneurs: a model based on previous occupational background', *International Journal of Entrepreneurial Behaviour & Research*, **1**, 26–47.

Kamm, J.B., Schuman, J.C., Seeger, J.A. and Nurick, A.J. (1990), 'Entrepreneurial teams in new venture creation: a research agenda', *Entrepreneurship Theory and Practice*, **14** (4), 7–17.

Karnebeek, A. (2001), *Spin-offs and the University of Twente – Sixteen Years of Experience in Incubating Start-ups*, Enschede: University of Twente Press.

Keasey, K. and Watson, R. (1992), *Investment and Financing Decisions and the Performance of Small Firms*. London: National Westminster Bank.

La Porta, R., Lopez-de Silanes, F., Shleifer, A. and Vishny, R. (1998), 'Law and finance', *Journal of Political Economy*, **106** (6), 1113–55.

Lambert, R. (2003), *Lambert Review of Business–University Collaboration*, London: HMSO.

Landstrom, H. (1993), 'Informal risk capital in Sweden and some international comparisons', *Journal of Business Venturing*, **8**, 525–40.

Lee, C., Lee, K. and Pennings, J.M. (2001), 'Internal capabilities, external networks, and performance: a study of technology-based ventures', *Strategic Management Journal*, **22**, 615–40.

Leonard-Barton, D. (1992), 'Core capabilities and core rigidities: a paradox in managing new product development', *Strategic Management Journal*, **13**, 111–25.

Lichtenstein, B. and Brush, C. (2001), 'How do "resource bundles" develop and change in new ventures? A dynamic model and longitudinal exploration', *Entrepreneurship Theory and Practice*, **25**, 37–58.

Lockett, A. and Wright, M. (2005), 'Resources, capabilities, risk capital and the creation of university spin-out companies', *Research Policy*, **34**, 1043–57.

Lockett, A., Murray, G. and Wright, M. (2002), 'Do UK venture capitalists still have a bias against investment in new technology firms?', *Research Policy*, **31**, 1009–30.

Lockett, A., Vohora, A. and Wright, M. (2003a), 'Incubators without walls', *International Journal of Entrepreneurship and Innovation*, November, 245–56.

Lockett A., Wright, M. and Franklin, S. (2003b), 'Technology transfer and universities' spin-out strategies', *Small Business Economics*, **20** (2), 185–203.

Lundqvist, J.M. and Hellsmark, M. (2003), 'Entrepreneurial transformations in the Swedish university system: the case of Chalmers University of Technology', *Research Policy*, **32**, 1555–68.

MacMillan, I.C., Zemann, L. and Subbanarasimha, P.N. (1987), 'Criteria distinguishing successful from unsuccessful ventures in the venture screening process', *Journal of Business Venturing*, **2**, 123–37.

Mangematin, V., Lemarié, S., Boissin, J.P., Catherine, D., Corolleur, F., Coronini, D. and Trommette, M. (2002), 'Development of SMEs and heterogeneity of trajectories: the case of biotechnology in France', *Research Policy*, **32**, 621–38.

Mason, C. and Harrison, R. (2004), 'Does investing in technology-based firms involve higher risk? An exploratory study of the performance of technology and non-technology investments by business angels', *Venture Capital*, **6** (4), 313–32.

McNally, K. (1997), *Corporate Venture Capital: Bridging the Equity Gap in the Small Business Sector*, London: Routledge.

Meyer, M. (2003), 'Academic entrepreneurs or entrepreneurial academics? Research-based ventures and public support mechanisms, *R&D Management*, **33** (2), 107–15.

Ministère délégué à l'enseignement supérieur et à la recherche.

Ministry of Research website (2000), *Action incubators*, February, available at http://www.recherche.gouv.fr.

Minshall, T.H.W. and Wicksteed, W. (2005), 'University spin-out companies: starting to fill the evidence gap', a report for the Gatsby Charitable Foundation.

Moore, B. (1994), 'Financial constraints to the growth and development of small, high-technology firms', in A. Hughes and D.J. Storey (eds), *Finance for Smaller Firms,* London: Routledge.

Moore, G.A. (1991), *Marketing and Selling High-Tech Products to Mainstream Customers: Crossing the Chasm,* NewYork: HarperBusiness.

Moray, N. and Clarysse, B. (2003), 'How do institutional logics shape the spin off process? An in depth analysis of a research institute', University of Ghent Working Paper.

Moray, N. and Clarysse, B. (2005), 'Institutional changes and resource endowments to science-based entrepreneurial firms', *Research Policy,* **34** (7), 1010–27.

Morgan, R.P., Kruytbosch, C. and Kannankutty, N. (2001), 'Patenting and invention activity of U.S. scientists and engineers in the academic sector: comparisons with industry', *Journal of Technology Transfer,* **26** (1–2), 173–83.

Mosey, S., Lockett, A. and Westhead, P. (2006), 'The importance of bridging networks for university technology transfer: a case study of the Medici Fellowship Scheme', *Technology Analysis and Strategic Management,* **18** (1), 71–91.

Mowery, D.C. (2001), 'The United States national innovation system after the cold war', in P. Larédo and P. Mustar (eds), *Research and Innovation Policies in the New Global Economy. An International Comparative Analysis,* Cheltenham, UK: Edward Elgar, pp. 15–46.

Mowery, D.C., Nelson, R.R., Sampat, B.N. and Ziedonis, A.A. (2001), 'The growth of patenting and licensing by U.S. universities: an assessment of the effects of the Bayh–Dole Act of 1980', *Research Policy,* **30**, 99–119.

Murray, G. and Lott, J. (1995), 'Have venture capitalists a bias against investment in new technology firms?', *Research Policy,* **24**, 283–99.

Mustar, P. (1988), *Science & Innovation,* Paris: CPE International, Economica.

Mustar, P. (1994), *Science & Innovation 1995,* Paris: Economica.

Mustar, P. (1997), 'Spin-off enterprises: how French academies create hi-tech companies: the condition for success or failure', *Science and Public Policy,* **24** (1), 37–43.

Mustar, P. (2002), 'Public support for the spin-off companies from higher education and research institutions', conference, STRATA, Brussels, 22–23 April.

Mustar, P. and Larédo, P. (2002), 'Innovation and research policy in France (1980–2000) on the disappearance of the Colbertist state', *Research Policy,* **31**, 55–72.

Mustar, P., Renault, M., Colombo, M., Piva, E., Fontes, M., Lockett, A.,

Wright, M., Clarysse, B. and Moray, N. (2006), 'Conceptualising the heterogeneity of research-based spin-offs: a multi-dimensional taxonomy', *Research Policy*, **35** (2), 289–308.

Muzyka, D., Birley, S. and Leleux, B. (1996), 'Trade-offs in the investment decisions of European venture capitalists', *Journal of Business Venturing*, **11** (4), 273–88.

Nerkar, A. and Shane, S. (2003), 'When do start-ups that exploit patented academic knowledge survive?', *International Journal of Industrial Organization*, **21**, 1391–410.

Nicolaou, N. and Birley, S. (2003a), 'Academic networks in a trichotomous categorisation of university spinouts', *Journal of Business Venturing*, **18** (3), 333–59.

Nicolaou, N. and Birley, S. (2003b), 'Social networks in organizational emergence: the university spin-out phenomenon', *Management Science*, **49** (12), 1702–25.

Office for Science and Technology (OST) (2003), *Les chiffres clés de la science et de la technologie*, Paris: Economica.

Office for Science and Technology (OST) (2004), *Les chiffres clés de la science et de la technologie*, Paris: Economica.

Office for Science and Technology (OST) (2006), *Les chiffres clés de la science et de la technologie*, Paris: Economica.

O'shea, R.P., Allen, T.J., Chevalier, A. and Roche, F. (2005), 'Entrepreneurial, orientation, technology transfer and spin-off performance of US universities', *Research Policy*, **34** (7), 994–1009.

Owen-Smith, J. and Powell, W.W. (2001), 'To patent or not: faculty decisions and institutional success at technology transfer', *Journal of Technology Transfer*, **26**, 99–114.

Penrose, E.T., (1959), *The Theory of Growth of the Firm*, Oxford: Blackwell.

Phan, P., Siegel, D. and Wright, M. (2005), 'Science parks and incubators: observations, synthesis and future research', *Journal of Business Venturing*, **20** (2), 165–82.

Pirnay, F., Surlemont, B. and Nlemvo, F. (2003), 'Towards a typoloy of university spin-offs', *Small Business Economics*, **21**, 355–69.

PriceWaterhouse/Coopers/British Venture Capital Association, (PWC/BVCA) (2004), *Performance of Venture Capital Investments*, London: BVCA.

Proton (2005), *Proton Europe Annual Survey: Financial Year 2004*, European Commission, available at http://www.protoneurope.org/news/2006/art2006/artjanmar06/zasty2004/attachment_download/file.

Quinn, R.E. (1988), *Beyond Rational Management*, San Francisco, CA: Jossey-Bass.

Radosevich, R. (1995), 'A model for entrepreneurial spin-offs from public technology sources', *International Journal of Technology Management*, **10**, 879–93.

Renault, C.S. (2006), 'Academic capitalism and university incentives for faculty entrepreneurship', *Journal of Technology Transfer*, **31** (2), 227–39.

Reynolds, P.D., Bygrave, W.D. and Autio, E. (2003), *GEM 2003 Global Report*, Kansas, MO: Kauffman Foundation.

Roberts, E.B. (1991), *High Tech Entrepreneurs: Lessons from MIT and Beyond*, New York: Oxford University Press.

Roberts, E.B. and Malone, D.E. (1996), 'Policies and structures for spinning out new companies from research and development organizations', *R&D Management*, **26** (1), 17–48.

Ruhnka, J., Feldman, H. and Dean, T. (1992), 'The living dead phenomenon in venture capital investment', *Journal of Business Venturing*, **7**, 137–55.

Saxenian, A. (1994a), *Regional Advantage: Culture and Competition in Silicon Valley and Route 128*, Cambridge, MA: Harvard University Press.

Saxenian, A. (1994b), 'The origins and dynamics of production networks in Silicon Valley', *Research Policy*, **20** (5), 423–38.

Scherr, F.C., Sugrue, T.F. and Ward, J.B. (1993), 'Financing the small firm start-up: determinants of debt use', *Journal of Small Business Finance*, **3** (1), 17–36.

Scholten, V., Omta, O. and Elfring, T. (2001), 'The significance of parenthood: the social capital of the parent organization and the entrepreneurial outcome', Rent XV Conference, 22–23 November, Finland.

Segal, Quince and Wicksteed Limited (SQW) (2005), *Interim Evaluation of Knowledge Transfer Programmes Funded by the Office of Science and Technology through the Science Budget*, Cambridge: SQW.

Shane, S. (2001), 'Selling university technology: patterns from MIT', *Management Science,* **48** (1), 122–38.

Shane, S. and Stuart, T. (2002), 'Organizational endowments and the performance of university start-ups', *Management Science*, **48** (1), 154–70.

Shane, S.A. (2004), *Academic Entrepreneurship: University Spinoffs and Wealth Creation*, Cheltenham, UK: Edward Elgar.

Siegel, D.S., Waldman, D. and Link, A. (2003a), 'Assessing the impact of organizational practices on the relative productivity of university technology transfer offices: an exploratory study', *Research Policy*, **32**, 27–48.

Siegel, D.S., Waldman, D., Atwater, L. and Link, A. (2003c), 'Commercial knowledge transfers from universities to firms: improving the effectiveness of university–industry collaboration', *Journal of High Technology Management Research*, **14**, 111–33.

Siegel, D., Westhead, P. and Wright, M. (2003b), 'Assessing the impact of science parks on the research productivity of firms: exploratory evidence from the UK', *International Journal of Industrial Organization*, **21** (9), 1357–69.

Smilor, R., Gibson, D. and Dietrich, G. (1990), 'University spin-off firms: technology start-ups from UT-Austin', *Journal of Business Venturing*, **5** (1), 63–76.

Stankiewicz, R. (1994), 'University firms: spin-off companies from universities', *Science and Public Policy*, **21** (2), 99–107.

Steffensen, M., Rogers E.M. and Speakman K. (2000), 'Spin-offs from research centers at a research university', *Journal of Business Venturing*, **15**, 93–111.

Suchman, M.C. (1994), 'On advice of counsel: law firms and venture capital funds as information intermediaries in the structuration of Silicon Valley', unpublished PhD dissertation, Department of Sociology, Stanford University.

Teece, D.J. (1987), 'Capturing value from technological innovation: integration, strategic partnering and licensing decisions', in B. Guile and H. Brooks (eds), *Technology and Global Industry*, Washington, DC: National Academy Press, pp. 65–95.

Tellis, G.J., Stremersch, S. and Yin, E. (2003), 'The international takeoff of new products: the role of economics, culture and country innovativeness', *Marketing Science.* **22** (2), 188–208.

Thornburn, L. (2001), 'Institutional structures and arrangements at Australian public sector laboratories', *STI Review*, OECD, July, 121–41.

Thursby, J. and Thursby, M. (2002), 'Who is selling the ivory tower? Sources of growth in university licensing', *Management Science*, **48**, 90–104.

Tiler, C., Metcalfe, S. and Connell, D. (1993), 'Business expansion through entrepreneurship: the influence of internal and external barriers to growth', *International Journal of Technology Management*, special publication on small firms and innovation, 15–52.

Ucbasaran, D., Lockett, A., Wright, M. and Westhead, P. (2003a), 'Entrepreneurial founder teams: factors associated with members' entry and exit', *Entrepreneurship Theory and Practice*, **28** (2), 107–28.

Ucbasaran, D., Wright, M., Westhead, P. and Busenitz, L. (2001), Entrepreneurial learning and opportunity recognition: habitual versus novice entrepreneurs', Working Paper, Nottingham University Business School.

Ucbasaran, D., Wright, M., Westhead, P. and Busenitz, L. (2003b), 'The impact of entrepreneurial experience on opportunity identification and exploitation: habitual and novice entrepreneurs', in J. Katz, and D.

Shepherd, (eds), *Advances in Entrepreneurship, Firm Emergence and Growth, Volume 6: Cognition and Decision-Making in the Entrepreneurial Context*, Greenwich, CT: JAI Press, pp. 231–63.

Universities' Companies Association (UNICO) (2005), 'Survey of UK university commercialisation shows a doubling of licensing activity in 2004', press release, 22 November.

Upstill, G. and Symington, D. (2002), 'Technology transfer and the creation of companies: the CSIRO experience', *R&D Management*, **32** (3), 233–9.

Van Looy, B., Ranga, M., Callaert, J., Debackere, K. and Zimmerman, E. (2004), 'Combining entrepreneurial and scientific performance in academia: towards a compound and reciprocal Matthew-effect?', *Research Policy*, **33**, 425–41.

Van Muijen, J.J., Koopman, P., De Witte, K., De Cock, G., Susanj, Z., Lemoine, C., Bourantas, D., Papalexandris, N., Branyicski, I., Spaltro, E., Jesuino, J., Gonzalves Das Neves, J., Pitariu, H., Konrad, E., Pieró, J., González-Romá, V. and Turnipseed, D. (1999), 'Organizational culture: the focus questionnaire', *European Journal of Work and Organizational Psychology*, **8** (4), 551–68.

Vanaelst, I., Clarysse, B., Wright, M., Lockett, A., Moray, N. and S'Jegers, R. (2006), 'Entrepreneurial team development in academic spin-outs: an examination of team heterogeneity', *Entrepreneurship Theory and Practice*, **30**, 249–72.

Vohora, A., Wright, M. and Lockett, A. (2004), 'Critical junctures in the growth in university high-tech spinout companies', *Research Policy*, **33**, 147–75.

Von Burg, U. and Kenney, M. (2000), 'Venture capital and the birth of the local area network industry', *Research Policy*, **29**, 1135–55.

Watson, R. and Wilson, N. (2002), 'Small and medium size enterprise financing: a note on some of the empirical implications of a pecking order', *Journal of Business Finance & Accounting*, **29** (3 and 4), 557–78.

Westhead, P. and Storey, D. (1997), 'Financial constraints on the growth of high technology small firms in the UK', *Applied Financial Economics*, **7**, 197–201.

Williams, E. (2005), 'Too few university spin-out companies', Warwick Ventures, Warwick University.

Wilson, H. (1979), *Committee to review the functioning of financial institutions: Evidence on the Financing of Industry and Trade*, London: HMSO.

Worms, G. (2005), 'Recommandations pour favoriser le développement des entreprises innovantes', *Rapport du groupe de travail de l'opération FutuRIS*, Paris: ANRT.

Wright, M. and Robbie, K. (1999), *Venture Capital into the Next Millennium*, London: British Venture Capital Association.

Wright, M., Birley, S. and Mosey, S. (2004a), 'Entrepreneurship and university technology transfer', *Journal of Technology Transfer*, **29** (3/4), 235–46.

Wright, M., Pruthi, S. and Lockett, A. (2005), 'International venture capital research: from cross-country comparisons to crossing borders', *International Journal of Management Reviews*, **7**, 135–66.

Wright, M., Sapienza, H. and Busenitz, L. (2003), *Venture Capital Vol. I*, Cheltenham, UK: Edward Elgar.

Wright, M., Vohora, A. and Lockett, A. (2004b), 'The formation of high tech university spinout companies: the role of joint ventures and venture capital investors', *Journal of Technology Transfer*, **29** (3/4), 287–310.

Wright, M., Binks, M., Vohora, A. and Lockett, A. (2003), *UK University Commercialisation Survey Financial Year 2002*, Nottingham: NUBS.

Wright, M., Clarysse, B., Lockett, A. and Binks, M. (2006b), 'University spin-out companies and venture capital', *Research Policy*, **35** (4), 481–501.

Wright, M., Clarysse, B., Lockett, A. and Knockaert, M. (2006a), 'University–industry linkages: evidence from mid-range universities in Europe', paper presented at Academy of Management Conference, Atlanta, 14 August.

Wright, M., Lockett, A., Mosey, S. and Piva, E. (2006c), 'Academic entrepreneurship and the challenges for business schools', CMBOR Occasional Paper.

Wtterwulghe, R. (1998), *La P.M.E. Une entreprise humaine*, Brussels: De Boeck Universite.

Zahra, S. and George, G. (2002), 'Absorptive capacity: a review, reconceptualization and extension', *Academy of Management Review*, **27**, 185–203.

Zahra, S. and Wicklund, J. (2000), 'Top management team characteristics and resource recombinations among new ventures', paper presented at the Stategic Management Society Annual Meeting, Vancouver, 15–18 October.

Zeitlyn, M. and Horne, J. (2002), *Business Interface Training Provision Review* (BITS Review), report produced for the DTI, UK.

Zott, C. and Amit, R. (2005), 'Business model', in M. Hitt and D. Ireland (eds), *The Blackwell Encyclopaedia of Management: Vol III Entrepreneurship*, Oxford: Blackwell Publishing, pp. 20–24.

Index